Just The Facts 101
Textbook Key Facts

The Psychology of Positive Thinking

by Cram101

Textbook NOT Included

Table of Contents

Title Page

Copyright

Foundations of Psychology

History of Psychology

Educational Psychology

Biopsychology

Developmental Psychology

Cognitive Psychology

Abnormal Psychology

Social Psychology

Applied Psychology

People

Index: Answers

Just The Facts101

Exam Prep for

The Psychology of Positive Thinking

Just The Facts101 Exam Prep is your link from
the textbook and lecture to your exams.

**Just The Facts101 Exam Preps are unauthorized and comprehensive reviews
of your textbooks.**

All material provided by CTI Publications (c) 2019

Textbook publishers and textbook authors do not participate in or contribute to these reviews.

Just The Facts101 Exam Prep

Copyright © 2019 by CTI Publications. All rights reserved.

eAIN 459074

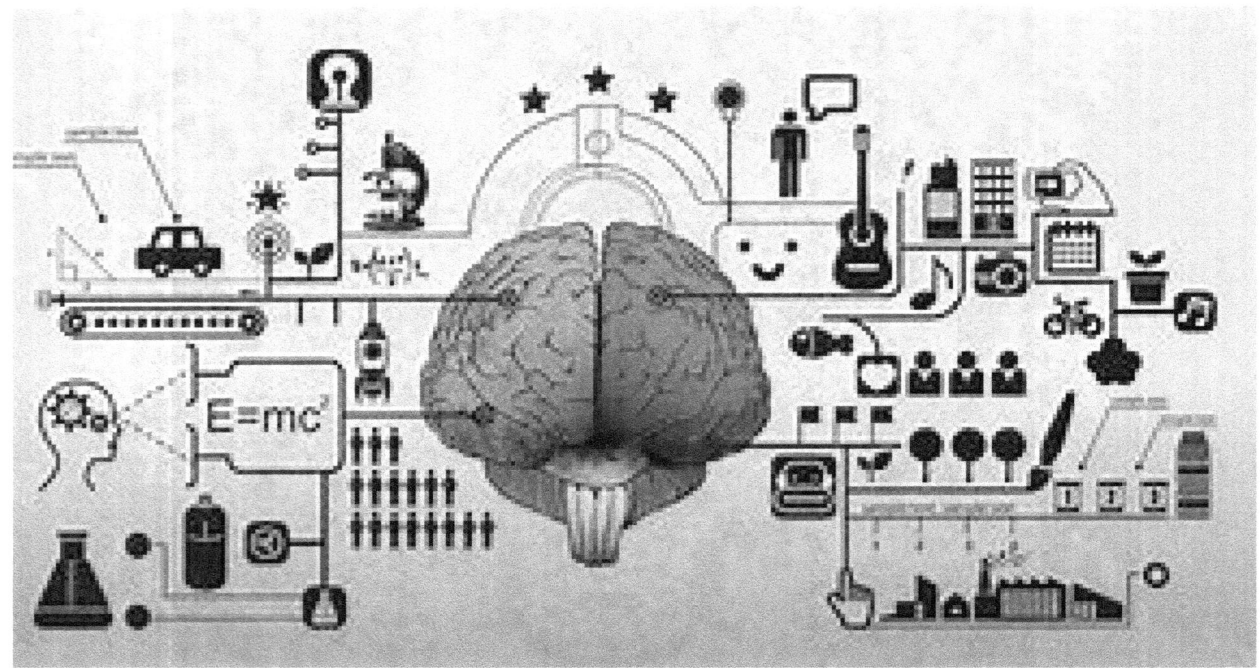

Foundations of Psychology

Psychology is the study of behavior and mind, embracing all aspects of human experience. It is an academic discipline and an applied science which seeks to understand individuals and groups by establishing general principles and researching specific cases.

:: Cognitive science ::

_____ is "the mental action or process of acquiring knowledge and understanding through thought, experience, and the senses". It encompasses many aspects of intellectual functions and processes such as attention, the formation of knowledge, memory and working memory, judgment and evaluation, reasoning and "computation", problem solving and decision making, comprehension and production of language. Cognitive processes use existing knowledge and generate new knowledge.

Exam Probability: **Low**

1. *Answer choices:*

(see index for correct answer)

- a. Dissociation
- b. Mental model
- c. Situated cognition
- d. Cognition

Guidance: level 1

:: Clinical psychology ::

_____ is an existential/experiential form of psychotherapy that emphasizes personal responsibility, and that focuses upon the individual's experience in the present moment, the therapist–client relationship, the environmental and social contexts of a person's life, and the self-regulating adjustments people make as a result of their overall situation.

Exam Probability: **High**

2. *Answer choices:*

(see index for correct answer)

- a. Supportive psychotherapy
- b. Rorschach test

- c. Mindfulness
- d. Transference focused psychotherapy

Guidance: level 1

:: Communication ::

_____ is the act of conveying meanings from one entity or group to another through the use of mutually understood signs, symbols, and semiotic rules.

Exam Probability: **Medium**

3. *Answer choices:*
(see index for correct answer)

- a. Internal communications
- b. Virtual world framework
- c. Communication
- d. Allen curve

Guidance: level 1

:: Sexual abuse ::

_____, also referred to as molestation, is usually undesired sexual behavior by one person upon another. It is often perpetrated using force or by taking advantage of another. When force is immediate, of short duration, or infrequent, it is called sexual assault. The offender is referred to as a _____r or molester. The term also covers any behavior by an adult or older adolescent towards a child to stimulate any of the involved sexually. The use of a child, or other individuals younger than the age of consent, for sexual stimulation is referred to as child _____ or statutory rape.

Exam Probability: **Medium**

4. *Answer choices:*

(see index for correct answer)

- a. Sexual Attitude Reassessment
- b. Aloisiuskolleg
- c. Sexual abuse
- d. National Sexual Violence Resource Center

Guidance: level 1

:: Human pregnancy ::

_____ includes the development of the embryo and of the fetus during a viviparous animal's gestation. _____ starts with fertilization, in the germinal stage of embryonic development, and continues in fetal development until birth.

Exam Probability: **Medium**

5. *Answer choices:*

(see index for correct answer)

- a. Period of viability
- b. Pregnancy over age 50
- c. Prenatal development
- d. Spiegelberg criteria

Guidance: level 1

:: Cognitive science ::

_____ is the process of acquiring new, or modifying existing, knowledge, behaviors, skills, values, or preferences. The ability to learn is possessed by humans, animals, and some machines; there is also evidence for some kind of _____ in some plants. Some _____ is immediate, induced by a single event , but much skill and knowledge accumulates from repeated experiences. The changes induced by _____ often last a lifetime, and it is hard to distinguish learned material that seems to be "lost" from that which cannot be retrieved.

Exam Probability: **Low**

6. *Answer choices:*

(see index for correct answer)

- a. Crosslinguistic influence
- b. Situated cognition
- c. Learning
- d. Macrocognition

Guidance: level 1

:: Behavioural sciences ::

_____ is an integration of science, theory, and clinical knowledge for the purpose of understanding, preventing, and relieving psychologically-based distress or dysfunction and to promote subjective well-being and personal development. Central to its practice are psychological assessment, clinical formulation, and psychotherapy, although clinical psychologists also engage in research, teaching, consultation, forensic testimony, and program development and administration. In many countries, _____ is a regulated mental health profession.

Exam Probability: **Medium**

7. *Answer choices:*

(see index for correct answer)

- a. Level of analysis
- b. Personnel selection
- c. Response Prompting Procedures
- d. Clinical psychology

Guidance: level 1

:: Cognition ::

_____ is a psychological process related to an abstract or physical object, such as a person, situation, or message whereby one is able to think about it and use concepts to deal adequately with that object. _____ is a relation between the knower and an object of _____ . _____ implies abilities and dispositions with respect to an object of knowledge that are sufficient to support intelligent behaviour.

Exam Probability: **High**

8. *Answer choices:*
(see index for correct answer)

- a. Understanding
- b. The Emotion Machine
- c. Mental chronometry
- d. Rapid serial visual presentation

Guidance: level 1

:: Social psychology ::

_____ is a process of social, psychological, and cultural change that stems from the balancing of two cultures while adapting to the prevailing culture of the society. Individuals of a differing culture try to incorporate themselves into the new more prevalent culture by participating in aspects of the more prevalent culture, such as their traditions, but still hold onto their original cultural values and traditions. The effects of _____ can be seen at multiple levels in both the devotee of the prevailing culture and those who are assimilating into the culture.

Exam Probability: **High**

9. *Answer choices:*

(see index for correct answer)

- a. Rapport congruency
- b. Ambiguity tolerance
- c. Artificial demand
- d. Seriality

Guidance: level 1

:: Personality tests ::

In psychology, a _____ is a personality test designed to let a person respond to ambiguous stimuli, presumably revealing hidden emotions and internal conflicts projected by the person into the test. This is sometimes contrasted with a so-called "objective test" / "self-report test", which adopt a "structured" approach as responses are analyzed according to a presumed universal standard , and are limited to the content of the test. The responses to _____ s are content analyzed for meaning rather than being based on presuppositions about meaning, as is the case with objective tests. _____ s have their origins in psychoanalysis, which argues that humans have conscious and unconscious attitudes and motivations that are beyond or hidden from conscious awareness.

Exam Probability: **High**

10. *Answer choices:*

(see index for correct answer)

- a. ProScan Survey
- b. Oxford Capacity Analysis
- c. Projective test
- d. Personality and Preference Inventory

Guidance: level 1

:: Causes of death ::

_____ or brain injury is the destruction or degeneration of brain cells. Brain injuries occur due to a wide range of internal and external factors. In general, _____ refers to significant, undiscriminating trauma-induced damage, while neurotoxicity typically refers to selective, chemically induced neuron damage.

Exam Probability: **Medium**

11. *Answer choices:*

(see index for correct answer)

- a. Death by natural causes
- b. Electrocution
- c. Dry drowning
- d. Brain damage

Guidance: level 1

:: Memory ::

In communications and information processing, code is a system of rules to convert information—such as a letter, word, sound, image, or gesture—into another form or representation, sometimes shortened or secret, for communication through a communication channel or storage in a storage medium. An early example is the invention of language, which enabled a person, through speech, to communicate what they saw, heard, felt, or thought to others. But speech limits the range of communication to the distance a voice can carry, and limits the audience to those present when the speech is uttered. The invention of writing, which converted spoken language into visual symbols, extended the range of communication across space and time.

Exam Probability: **Medium**

12. *Answer choices:*

(see index for correct answer)

- a. Encoding
- b. Procedural memory
- c. Redintegration
- d. Multiple trace theory

Guidance: level 1

:: Reasoning ::

_____ s are steps in reasoning, moving from premises to logical consequences; etymologically, the word infer means to "carry forward". _____ is theoretically traditionally divided into deduction and induction, a distinction that in Europe dates at least to Aristotle. Deduction is _____ deriving logical conclusions from premises known or assumed to be true, with the laws of valid _____ being studied in logic. Induction is _____ from particular premises to a universal conclusion. A third type of _____ is sometimes distinguished, notably by Charles Sanders Peirce, distinguishing abduction from induction, where abduction is _____ to the best explanation.

Exam Probability: **Medium**

13. *Answer choices:*

(see index for correct answer)

- a. Text inferencing
- b. Doxastic logic
- c. Logical reasoning
- d. Inference

Guidance: level 1

:: Human communication ::

_____ is a system that consists of the development, acquisition, maintenance and use of complex systems of communication, particularly the human ability to do so; and a _____ is any specific example of such a system.

Exam Probability: **Low**

14. *Answer choices:*

(see index for correct answer)

- a. Cultural dimensions
- b. Care perspective
- c. U and non-U English
- d. Chew the fat

Guidance: level 1

:: Intelligence by type ::

An intelligence quotient is a total score derived from several standardized tests designed to assess human intelligence. The abbreviation "IQ" was coined by the psychologist William Stern for the German term Intelligenzquotient, his term for a scoring method for _____ s at University of Breslau he advocated in a 1912 book. Historically, IQ is a score obtained by dividing a person's mental age score, obtained by administering an _____ , by the person's chronological age, both expressed in terms of years and months. The resulting fraction is multiplied by 100 to obtain the IQ score.

Exam Probability: **High**

15. *Answer choices:*

(see index for correct answer)

- a. Spatial intelligence
- b. Theory of multiple intelligences
- c. Emotional intelligence
- d. Intelligence Test

Guidance: level 1

:: Ethology ::

_____ or innate behavior is the inherent inclination of a living organism towards a particular complex behavior. The simplest example of an _____ ive behavior is a fixed action pattern , in which a very short to medium length sequence of actions, without variation, are carried out in response to a corresponding clearly defined stimulus.

Exam Probability: **Low**

16. *Answer choices:*
(see index for correct answer)

- a. Avoidance response
- b. Instinct
- c. Species-typical behavior
- d. Anthrozoology

Guidance: level 1

:: Stress ::

_____ is a wide spectrum of techniques and psychotherapies aimed at controlling a person's level of stress, especially chronic stress, usually for the purpose of and for the motive of improving everyday functioning. In this context, the term 'stress' refers only to a stress with significant negative consequences, or distress in the terminology advocated by Hans Selye, rather than what he calls eustress, a stress whose consequences are helpful or otherwise.

Exam Probability: **High**

17. *Answer choices:*

(see index for correct answer)

- a. Psychotic break
- b. Stress management
- c. Life Events and Difficulties Schedule
- d. Breaking point

Guidance: level 1

:: Neuroanatomy ::

A _____ is an enclosed, cable-like bundle of _____ fibres called axons, in the peripheral nervous system. A _____ provides a common pathway for the electrochemical _____ impulses called action potentials that are transmitted along each of the axons to peripheral organs or, in the case of sensory _____ s, from the periphery back to the central nervous system. Each axon within the _____ is an extension of an individual neuron, along with other supportive cells such as Schwann cells that coat the axons in myelin.

Exam Probability: **Low**

18. *Answer choices:*

(see index for correct answer)

- a. Neuropil
- b. Nerve
- c. Raphe nuclei
- d. Group B nerve fiber

Guidance: level 1

:: Mental health ::

_____ is defined as the level of psychological well-being or an absence of mental illness. It is the state of someone who is "functioning at a satisfactory level of emotional and behavioural adjustment". From the perspectives of positive psychology or of holism, _____ may include an individual's ability to enjoy life, and to create a balance between life activities and efforts to achieve psychological resilience. According to the World Health Organization, _____ includes "subjective well-being, perceived self-efficacy, autonomy, competence, inter-generational dependence, and self-actualization of one's intellectual and emotional potential, among others." The WHO further states that the well-being of an individual is encompassed in the realization of their abilities, coping with normal stresses of life, productive work and contribution to their community. Cultural differences, subjective assessments, and competing professional theories all affect how one defines "_____".

Exam Probability: **High**

19. *Answer choices:*

(see index for correct answer)

- a. Befriender
- b. Care programme approach
- c. Emotional well-being
- d. Mental health

Guidance: level 1

:: Psychological schools ::

_____ is a psychological perspective that rose to prominence in the mid-20th century in answer to the limitations of Sigmund Freud's psychoanalytic theory and B. F. Skinner's behaviorism. With its roots running from Socrates through the Renaissance, this approach emphasizes individuals' inherent drive towards self-actualization, the process of realizing and expressing one's own capabilities and creativity.

Exam Probability: **Low**

20. *Answer choices:*

(see index for correct answer)

- a. Isomorphism
- b. Ecological psychology
- c. Institute for International and Cross-Cultural Psychology
- d. Archetypal psychology

Guidance: level 1

:: Mind ::

The _____ is a set of cognitive faculties including consciousness, imagination, perception, thinking, judgement, language and memory. It is usually defined as the faculty of an entity's thoughts and consciousness. It holds the power of imagination, recognition, and appreciation, and is responsible for processing feelings and emotions, resulting in attitudes and actions.

Exam Probability: **High**

21. *Answer choices:*

(see index for correct answer)

- a. Neuroanatomy of intimacy
- b. Cittabhumi
- c. Mind
- d. Mental operations

Guidance: level 1

:: Neuroimaging ::

_____ or brain imaging is the use of various techniques to either directly or indirectly image the structure, function, or pharmacology of the nervous system. It is a relatively new discipline within medicine, neuroscience, and psychology. Physicians who specialize in the performance and interpretation of _____ in the clinical setting are neuroradiologists.

Exam Probability: **High**

22. *Answer choices:*

(see index for correct answer)

- a. Intracortical encephalogram signal analysis
- b. FMRIB Software Library

- c. Neuroimaging
- d. Positron emission tomography

Guidance: level 1

:: Scientific method ::

In the social sciences and life sciences, a _____ is a research method involving an up-close, in-depth, and detailed examination of a subject of study, as well as its related contextual conditions.

Exam Probability: **Low**

23. *Answer choices:*

(see index for correct answer)

- a. History of scientific method
- b. Blind taste test
- c. Deductive-nomological model
- d. Adversarial review

Guidance: level 1

:: Communication disorders ::

_____ is an inability to comprehend or formulate language because of damage to specific brain regions. This damage is typically caused by a cerebral vascular accident, or head trauma; however, these are not the only possible causes. To be diagnosed with _____, a person's speech or language must be significantly impaired in one of the four communication modalities following acquired brain injury or have significant decline over a short time period. The four communication modalities are auditory comprehension, verbal expression, reading and writing, and functional communication.

Exam Probability: **Medium**

24. *Answer choices:*
(see index for correct answer)

- a. Language disorder
- b. Nuffield Speech and Language Unit
- c. National Stuttering Association
- d. Aphasia

Guidance: level 1

:: Neuroanatomy ::

An _____ , or nerve fiber, is a long, slender projection of a nerve cell, or neuron, in vertebrates, that typically conducts electrical impulses known as action potentials away from the nerve cell body. The function of the _____ is to transmit information to different neurons, muscles, and glands. In certain sensory neurons , such as those for touch and warmth, the _____ s are called afferent nerve fibers and the electrical impulse travels along these from the periphery to the cell body, and from the cell body to the spinal cord along another branch of the same _____ . _____ dysfunction has caused many inherited and acquired neurological disorders which can affect both the peripheral and central neurons. Nerve fibers are classed into three types – group A nerve fibers, group B nerve fibers, and group C nerve fibers. Groups A and B are myelinated, and group C are unmyelinated. These groups include both sensory fibers and motor fibers. Another classification groups only the sensory fibers as Type I, Type II, Type III, and Type IV.

Exam Probability: **Medium**

25. *Answer choices:*

(see index for correct answer)

- a. Axon
- b. Cerebellopontine angle
- c. Genitourinary nerve
- d. Taenia thalami

Guidance: level 1

:: Behaviorism ::

A _____ is a routine of behavior that is repeated regularly and tends to occur subconsciously.

Exam Probability: **High**

26. *Answer choices:*

(see index for correct answer)

- a. Taste aversion
- b. Single-subject design
- c. Behavior management
- d. Assessment of Basic Language and Learning Skills

Guidance: level 1

:: Human female reproductive system ::

A _____ is a eukaryotic cell formed by a fertilization event between two gametes. The _____ 's genome is a combination of the DNA in each gamete, and contains all of the genetic information necessary to form a new individual. In multicellular organisms, the _____ is the earliest developmental stage. In single-celled organisms, the _____ can divide asexually by mitosis to produce identical offspring.

Exam Probability: **Low**

27. *Answer choices:*

(see index for correct answer)

- a. Zygote
- b. fallopian
- c. Perineal sponge
- d. Human female reproductive system

Guidance: level 1

:: Behaviorism ::

_____ is, in contrast to analog observation, a research tool in which a subject is observed in its natural habitat without any manipulation by the observer. During _____, researchers take great care to avoid interfering with the behavior they are observing by using unobtrusive methods. _____ involves two main differences that set it apart from other forms of data gathering. In the context of a _____, the environment is in no way being manipulated by the observer nor was it created by the observer.

Exam Probability: **Medium**

28. *Answer choices:*

(see index for correct answer)

- a. Reward system
- b. Fear conditioning
- c. Curriculum-based measurement
- d. Functional analytic psychotherapy

Guidance: level 1

:: Knowledge ::

_____ is a familiarity, awareness, or understanding of someone or something, such as facts, information, descriptions, or skills, which is acquired through experience or education by perceiving, discovering, or learning.

Exam Probability: **Medium**

29. *Answer choices:*

(see index for correct answer)

- a. Lambert Review
- b. Knowledge
- c. Knowledge ark
- d. Faith literate

Guidance: level 1

:: Developmental psychology ::

_____ entails the biological, psychological and emotional changes that occur in human beings between birth and the conclusion of adolescence, as the individual progresses from dependency to increasing autonomy. It is a continuous process with a predictable sequence, yet having a unique course for every child. It does not progress at the same rate and each stage is affected by the preceding developmental experiences. Because these developmental changes may be strongly influenced by genetic factors and events during prenatal life, genetics and prenatal development are usually included as part of the study of _____ . Related terms include developmental psychology, referring to development throughout the lifespan, and pediatrics, the branch of medicine relating to the care of children. Developmental change may occur as a result of genetically-controlled processes known as maturation, or as a result of environmental factors and learning, but most commonly involves an interaction between the two. It may also occur as a result of human nature and our ability to learn from our environment.

Exam Probability: **High**

30. *Answer choices:*

(see index for correct answer)

- a. Child development
- b. Imaginary audience
- c. Career consolidation
- d. Bioecological model

Guidance: level 1

:: Group processes ::

_____ is the act of matching attitudes, beliefs, and behaviors to group norms or politics. Norms are implicit, specific rules, shared by a group of individuals, that guide their interactions with others. People often choose to conform to society rather than to pursue personal desires because it is often easier to follow the path others have made already, rather than creating a new one. This tendency to conform occurs in small groups and/or society as a whole, and may result from subtle unconscious influences, or direct and overt social pressure. _____ can occur in the presence of others, or when an individual is alone. For example, people tend to follow social norms when eating or watching television, even when alone.

Exam Probability: **Low**

31. *Answer choices:*

(see index for correct answer)

- a. Conformity
- b. Groupshift
- c. Pseudoconsensus
- d. Group psychotherapy

Guidance: level 1

:: Cerebrum ::

The _____ is one of the four major lobes of the cerebral cortex in the brain of mammals. The _____ is positioned above the temporal lobe and behind the frontal lobe and central sulcus.

Exam Probability: **Low**

32. *Answer choices:*

(see index for correct answer)

- a. Medial longitudinal fissure
- b. Gustatory area
- c. Middle cerebellar peduncle
- d. Parietal lobe

Guidance: level 1

:: Psychiatry ::

A _____ is a physician who specializes in psychiatry, the branch of medicine devoted to the diagnosis, prevention, study, and treatment of mental disorders. _____ s are medical doctors, unlike psychologists, and must evaluate patients to determine whether their symptoms are the result of a physical illness, a combination of physical and mental ailments, or strictly psychiatric. A _____ usually works as the clinical leader of the multi-disciplinary team, which may comprise psychologists, social workers, occupational therapists and nursing staff. _____ s have broad training in a bio-psycho-social approach to assessment and management of mental illness.

Exam Probability: **Low**

33. *Answer choices:*

(see index for correct answer)

- a. Psychopathology
- b. Autokabalesis
- c. Diagnostic and Statistical Manual of Mental Disorders
- d. Stilted speech

Guidance: level 1

:: Psychoactive drugs ::

A _____ , psychopharmaceutical, or psychotropic drug is a chemical substance that changes brain function and results in alterations in perception, mood, consciousness, cognition, or behavior. These substances may be used medically; recreationally; to purposefully improve performance or alter one`s consciousness; as entheogens; for ritual, spiritual, or shamanic purposes; or for research. Some categories of _____ s, which have therapeutic value, are prescribed by physicians and other healthcare practitioners. Examples include anesthetics, analgesics, anticonvulsant and antiparkinsonian drugs as well as medications used to treat neuropsychiatric disorders, such as antidepressants, anxiolytics, antipsychotics, and stimulant medications. Some psychoactive substances may be used in the detoxification and rehabilitation programs for persons dependent on or addicted to other _____ s.

Exam Probability: **Low**

34. *Answer choices:*

(see index for correct answer)

- a. Truth serum
- b. Psychotropic

- c. Strictamine
- d. Psychoactive drug

Guidance: level 1

:: Personality tests ::

_____, developed by Leslie Morey, is a self-report 344-item personality test that assesses a respondent's personality and psychopathology. Each item is a statement about the respondent that the respondent rates with a 4-point scale. It is used in various contexts, including psychotherapy, crisis/evaluation, forensic, personnel selection, pain/medical, and child custody assessment. The test construction strategy for the PAI was primarily deductive and rational. It shows good convergent validity with other personality tests, such as the Minnesota Multiphasic Personality Inventory and the Revised NEO Personality Inventory.

Exam Probability: **High**

35. *Answer choices:*
(see index for correct answer)

- a. Morrisby Profile
- b. Bernreuter Personality Inventory
- c. Personality Assessment Inventory
- d. Facet

Guidance: level 1

:: Therapy ::

The therapeutic relationship refers to the relationship between a healthcare professional and a client. It is the means by which a therapist and a client hope to engage with each other, and effect beneficial change in the client.

Exam Probability: **High**

36. *Answer choices:*

(see index for correct answer)

- a. Therapeutic alliance
- b. Working alliance
- c. Reality testing

Guidance: level 1

:: Cognitive disorders ::

_____ is a broad category of brain diseases that cause a long-term and often gradual decrease in the ability to think and remember that is great enough to affect a person's daily functioning. Other common symptoms include emotional problems, difficulties with language, and a decrease in motivation. A person's consciousness is usually not affected. A _____ diagnosis requires a change from a person's usual mental functioning and a greater decline than one would expect due to aging. These diseases also have a significant effect on a person's caregivers.

Exam Probability: **High**

37. *Answer choices:*

(see index for correct answer)

- a. Delirium
- b. Dementia
- c. Postoperative cognitive dysfunction
- d. Semantic dementia

Guidance: level 1

:: Perception ::

In neuroscience and psychophysics, an _____ was originally defined as the lowest level of a stimulus – light, sound, touch, etc. – that an organism could detect. Under the influence of signal detection theory, _____ has been redefined as the level at which a stimulus will be detected a specified percentage of the time. The _____ can be influenced by several different factors, such as the subject's motivations and expectations, cognitive processes, and whether the subject is adapted to the stimulus. The _____ can be compared to the difference threshold, which is the measure of how different two stimuli must be for the subject to notice that they are not the same.

Exam Probability: **High**

38. *Answer choices:*

(see index for correct answer)

- a. Falling
- b. Absolute threshold
- c. Sonochromatism
- d. Naivety

Guidance: level 1

:: Motivation ::

_____ is an individual's belief in their innate ability to achieve goals. Albert Bandura defines it as a personal judgment of "how well one can execute courses of action required to deal with prospective situations". Expectations of _____ determine whether an individual will be able to exhibit coping behavior and how long effort will be sustained in the face of obstacles. Individuals who have high _____ will exert sufficient effort that, if well executed, leads to successful outcomes, whereas those with low _____ are likely to cease effort early and fail. Psychologists have studied _____ from several perspectives, noting various paths in the development of _____ ; the dynamics of _____ , and lack thereof, in many different settings; interactions between _____ and self-concept; and habits of attribution that contribute to, or detract from, _____ . Kathy Kolbe adds, "Belief in innate abilities means valuing one's particular set of cognitive strengths. It also involves determination and perseverance to overcome obstacles that would interfere with utilizing those innate abilities to achieve goals."

Exam Probability: **High**

39. *Answer choices:*

(see index for correct answer)

- a. Self-efficacy
- b. The Winning Edge
- c. Promotion
- d. Cooling Out

Guidance: level 1

:: Friendship ::

_____ is a relationship of mutual affection between people. _____ is a stronger form of interpersonal bond than an association. _____ has been studied in academic fields such as communication, sociology, social psychology, anthropology, and philosophy. Various academic theories of _____ have been proposed, including social exchange theory, equity theory, relational dialectics, and attachment styles.

Exam Probability: **Medium**

40. *Answer choices:*

(see index for correct answer)

- a. Friendship
- b. Bromance
- c. Owen and Mzee
- d. Female bonding

Guidance: level 1

:: Mood disorders ::

_____ , also known as mood affective disorders, is a group of conditions where a disturbance in the person's mood is the main underlying feature. The classification is in the Diagnostic and Statistical Manual of Mental Disorders and International Classification of Diseases .

Exam Probability: **Medium**

41. *Answer choices:*

(see index for correct answer)

- a. S100A10
- b. Inositol monophosphatase
- c. Mood disorder
- d. Postpartum depression

Guidance: level 1

:: Fertility ::

_____ , or o _____ , is the primary female sex hormone. It is responsible for the development and regulation of the female reproductive system and secondary sex characteristics. There are three major endogenous _____ s in females that have _____ ic hormonal activity: estrone, estradiol, and estriol. The estrane steroid estradiol is the most potent and prevalent of these.

Exam Probability: **High**

42. *Answer choices:*

(see index for correct answer)

- a. Human sexual response cycle
- b. Spermatozoon
- c. Estrogen
- d. Fecundity

Guidance: level 1

:: Neurotic, stress-related and somatoform disorders ::

_____ is an anxiety disorder characterized by symptoms of anxiety in situations where the person perceives their environment to be unsafe with no easy way to escape. These situations can include open spaces, public transit, shopping centers, or simply being outside their home. Being in these situations may result in a panic attack. The symptoms occur nearly every time the situation is encountered and last for more than six months. Those affected will go to great lengths to avoid these situations. In severe cases people may become completely unable to leave their homes.

Exam Probability: **High**

43. *Answer choices:*

(see index for correct answer)

- a. Agoraphobia
- b. Acrophobia
- c. Psychasthenia
- d. Remote Location Stress Reaction

Guidance: level 1

:: Devices to alter consciousness ::

_____ is the process of gaining greater awareness of many physiological functions primarily using instruments that provide information on the activity of those same systems, with a goal of being able to manipulate them at will. Some of the processes that can be controlled include brainwaves, muscle tone, skin conductance, heart rate and pain perception. In _____ , you are connected to electrical sensors that help you receive information about your body.

Exam Probability: **Low**

44. *Answer choices:*
(see index for correct answer)

- a. Sonic weapon
- b. Hemi-Sync
- c. The Lightning Process
- d. Biofeedback

Guidance: level 1

:: Central nervous system ::

The _____ is the part of the nervous system consisting of the brain and spinal cord. The CNS is so named because it integrates the received information and coordinates and influences the activity of all parts of the bodies of bilaterally symmetric animals—that is, all multicellular animals except sponges and radially symmetric animals such as jellyfish—and it contains the majority of the nervous system. Many consider the retina and the optic nerve, as well as the olfactory nerves and olfactory epithelium as parts of the CNS, synapsing directly on brain tissue without intermediate ganglia. As such, the olfactory epithelium is the only central nervous tissue in direct contact with the environment, which opens up for therapeutic treatments. The CNS is contained within the dorsal body cavity, with the brain housed in the cranial cavity and the spinal cord in the spinal canal. In vertebrates, the brain is protected by the skull, while the spinal cord is protected by the vertebrae. The brain and spinal cord are both enclosed in the meninges. Within the CNS, the interneuronal space is filled with a large amount of supporting non-nervous cells called neuroglial cells.

Exam Probability: **Low**

45. *Answer choices:*

(see index for correct answer)

- a. Central nervous system depression
- b. Cerebrospinal fibers
- c. Gray matter
- d. Central nervous system

Guidance: level 1

:: Collaboration ::

Systems theory is the interdisciplinary study of systems. A system is a cohesive conglomeration of interrelated and interdependent parts that is either natural or man-made. Every system is delineated by its spatial and temporal boundaries, surrounded and influenced by its environment, described by its structure and purpose or nature and expressed in its functioning. In terms of its effects, a system can be more than the sum of its parts if it expresses synergy or emergent behavior. Changing one part of the system usually affects other parts and the whole system, with predictable patterns of behavior. For systems that are self-learning and self-adapting, the positive growth and adaptation depend upon how well the system is adjusted with its environment. Some systems function mainly to support other systems by aiding in the maintenance of the other system to prevent failure. The goal of systems theory is systematically discovering a system's dynamics, constraints, conditions and elucidating principles that can be discerned and applied to systems at every level of nesting, and in every field for achieving optimized equifinality.

Exam Probability: **Low**

46. *Answer choices:*

(see index for correct answer)

- a. Social collaboration
- b. Interdependence
- c. Stone Soup
- d. Collaborative product development

Guidance: level 1

:: Behaviorism ::

_____ is a learning process through which the strength of a behavior is modified by reinforcement or punishment. It is also a procedure that is used to bring about such learning.

Exam Probability: **High**

47. *Answer choices:*

(see index for correct answer)

- a. Acceptance and commitment therapy
- b. Operant conditioning
- c. Habit
- d. Functional analysis

Guidance: level 1

:: Autonomic nervous system ::

The _____ , formerly the vegetative nervous system, is a division of the peripheral nervous system that supplies smooth muscle and glands, and thus influences the function of internal organs. The _____ is a control system that acts largely unconsciously and regulates bodily functions such as the heart rate, digestion, respiratory rate, pupillary response, urination, and sexual arousal. This system is the primary mechanism in control of the fight-or-flight response.

Exam Probability: **Medium**

48. *Answer choices:*

(see index for correct answer)

- a. Non-noradrenergic, non-cholinergic transmitter
- b. Autonomic nervous system
- c. Autonomic ganglion
- d. San Francisco Syncope Rule

Guidance: level 1

:: Twelve-step programs ::

_____ is an international fellowship of men and women who have had a drinking problem. Their stated purpose is to enable "members to stay sober and help other alcoholics achieve sobriety." It is nonprofessional, self-supporting, and apolitical. The only requirement for membership is a desire to stop drinking. The AA program is set forth in the Twelve Steps and discussed at AA group meetings.

Exam Probability: **Medium**

49. *Answer choices:*

(see index for correct answer)

- a. Pagans in Recovery
- b. Sex Addicts Anonymous

- c. Alcoholics Anonymous
- d. Horizon Services

Guidance: level 1

:: Family ::

In the context of human society, a _____ is a group of people related either by consanguinity, affinity, or co-residence or some combination of these. Members of the immediate _____ may include spouses, parents, brothers, sisters, sons, and daughters. Members of the extended _____ may include grandparents, aunts, uncles, cousins, nephews, nieces, and siblings-in-law. Sometimes these are also considered members of the immediate _____, depending on an individual's specific relationship with them.

Exam Probability: **High**

50. *Answer choices:*

(see index for correct answer)

- a. Casa Mesita
- b. Family
- c. Association of Family Case Workers
- d. Families OverComing Under Stress

Guidance: level 1

:: Neuroanatomy ::

The _____ , also known as the cerebral mantle, is the outer layer of neural tissue of the cerebrum of the brain, in humans and other mammals. It is separated into two cortices, by the longitudinal fissure that divides the cerebrum into the left and right cerebral hemispheres. The two hemispheres are joined beneath the cortex by the corpus callosum. The _____ is the largest site of neural integration in the central nervous system. It plays a key role in memory, attention, perception, awareness, thought, language, and consciousness.

Exam Probability: **High**

51. *Answer choices:*
(see index for correct answer)

- a. Sacral spinal nerve 1
- b. Primary olfactory cortex
- c. Nucleus
- d. Rhinal cortex

Guidance: level 1

:: Emotion ::

A _____ is one or more motions or positions of the muscles beneath the skin of the face. According to one set of controversial theories, these movements convey the emotional state of an individual to observers. _____s are a form of nonverbal communication. They are a primary means of conveying social information between humans, but they also occur in most other mammals and some other animal species.

Exam Probability: **High**

52. *Answer choices:*

(see index for correct answer)

- a. Limbic resonance
- b. Two-factor theory of emotion
- c. Empathic accuracy
- d. Facial expression

Guidance: level 1

:: Cognitive neuroscience ::

Functional magnetic resonance imaging or _____ measures brain activity by detecting changes associated with blood flow. This technique relies on the fact that cerebral blood flow and neuronal activation are coupled. When an area of the brain is in use, blood flow to that region also increases.

Exam Probability: **Low**

53. Answer choices:

(see index for correct answer)

- a. Default mode network
- b. Structural information theory
- c. Bayesian approaches to brain function
- d. Neurognosis

Guidance: level 1

:: Behavioural sciences ::

_____ is the scientific study of how people's thoughts, feelings and behaviors are influenced by the actual, imagined or implied presence of others. In this definition, scientific refers to the empirical investigation using the scientific method. The terms thoughts, feelings and behavior refer to psychological variables that can be measured in humans. The statement that others' presence may be imagined or implied suggests that humans are malleable to social influences even when alone, such as when watching television looking at reality shows, music videos and movies they can be influenced to follow the behaviour in the visual setting or following internalized cultural norms. Social psychologists typically explain human behavior as a result of the interaction of mental states and social situations.

Exam Probability: **Low**

54. Answer choices:

(see index for correct answer)

- a. Association for Behavior Analysis International
- b. Virginia Durr Moment
- c. Correlates of crime
- d. Social psychology

Guidance: level 1

:: Perception ::

_____ is an ability of animals to perceive differences between light composed of different wavelengths independently of light intensity. The perception is a part of the larger vision system and is mediated by a complex process between neurons that begins with differential stimulation of different types of photoreceptors by light entering the eye. Those photoreceptors then emit outputs that are then propagated through many layers of neurons and then ultimately to the brain. _____ is found in many animals and is mediated by similar underlying mechanisms with common types of biological molecules and a complex history of evolution in different animal taxa. In primates, _____ may have evolved to under selective pressure for a variety of visual tasks including the foraging for nutritious young leaves, ripe fruit and flowers as well as detecting predator camouflage and emotional states in other primates.

Exam Probability: **Medium**

55. *Answer choices:*

(see index for correct answer)

- a. Positive illusions
- b. Set

- c. Chubb illusion
- d. Jamais vu

Guidance: level 1

:: Cognitive science ::

_____ is the means to see, hear, or become aware of something or someone through our fundamental senses. The term _____ derives from the Latin word perceptio, and is the organization, identification, and interpretation of sensory information in order to represent and understand the presented information, or the environment.

Exam Probability: **Medium**

56. *Answer choices:*
(see index for correct answer)

- a. Approximate number system
- b. Perception
- c. Bongard problem
- d. Informatics

Guidance: level 1

:: Cognitive science ::

_____ is the scientific study of language. It involves analysing language form, language meaning, and language in context. The earliest activities in the documentation and description of language have been attributed to the 6th-century-BC Indian grammarian Paini who wrote a formal description of the Sanskrit language in his Aadhyayi.

Exam Probability: **Medium**

57. *Answer choices:*

(see index for correct answer)

- a. Mental rotation
- b. Augmented learning
- c. Body schema
- d. Linguistics

Guidance: level 1

:: Knowledge sharing ::

_____ is the process of facilitating learning, or the acquisition of knowledge, skills, values, beliefs, and habits. _____ al methods include storytelling, discussion, teaching, training, and directed research. _____ frequently takes place under the guidance of educators and also learners may also educate themselves. _____ can take place in formal or informal settings and any experience that has a formative effect on the way one thinks, feels, or acts may be considered _____ al. The methodology of teaching is called pedagogy.

Exam Probability: **Low**

58. *Answer choices:*

(see index for correct answer)

- a. American Association of Pharmaceutical Scientists
- b. Knowledge sharing
- c. Free Knowledge Institute
- d. Education

Guidance: level 1

:: Discrimination ::

In human social behavior, _____ is treatment or consideration of, or making a distinction towards, a person based on the group, class, or category to which the person is perceived to belong. These include age, colour, criminal record, height, disability, ethnicity, family status, gender identity, generation, genetic characteristics, marital status, nationality, race, religion, sex, and sexual orientation. _____ consists of treatment of an individual or group, based on their actual or perceived membership in a certain group or social category, "in a way that is worse than the way people are usually treated". It involves the group's initial reaction or interaction going on to influence the individual's actual behavior towards the group leader or the group, restricting members of one group from opportunities or privileges that are available to another group, leading to the exclusion of the individual or entities based on illogical or irrational decision making.

Exam Probability: **High**

59. *Answer choices:*

(see index for correct answer)

- a. Microinequity
- b. Discrimination
- c. Sectarian discrimination
- d. Burning of books and burying of scholars

Guidance: level 1

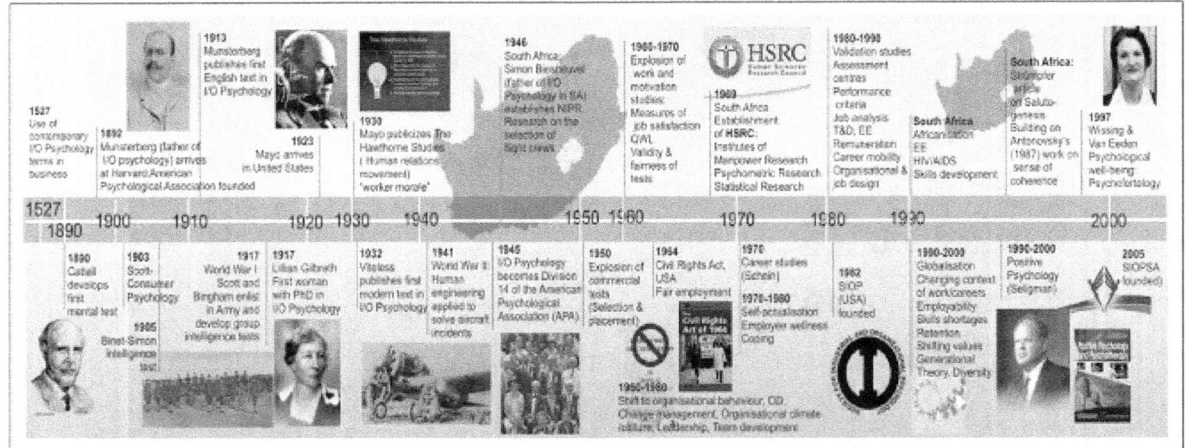

History of Psychology

Psychology was a branch of the domain of philosophy until the 1870s, when it developed as an independent scientific discipline in Germany and the United States. Psychology as a self-conscious field of experimental study began in 1879, in Leipzig Germany, when Wilhelm Wundt founded the first laboratory dedicated exclusively to psychological research in Germany. Wundt was also the first person to refer to himself as a psychologist. Other important early contributors to the field include Hermann Ebbinghaus (a pioneer in the study of memory), William James (the American father of pragmatism), and Ivan Pavlov (who developed the procedures associated with classical conditioning).

:: Consciousness ::

_____ is the ability to directly know and perceive, to feel, or to be cognizant of events. More broadly, it is the state of being conscious of something. Another definition describes it as a state wherein a subject is aware of some information when that information is directly available to bring to bear in the direction of a wide range of behavioral processes. The concept is often synonymous to consciousness and is also understood as being consciousness itself.

Exam Probability: **High**

1. *Answer choices:*

(see index for correct answer)

- a. Awareness
- b. Secondary consciousness
- c. Consciousness Industry
- d. Chaitanya

Guidance: level 1

:: Perception ::

In physiology, psychology, or psychophysics, a _____ or a liminal point is a threshold of a physiological or psychological response. It is the boundary of perception. On one side of a _____ a stimulus is perceivable, on the other side it is not.

Exam Probability: **High**

2. *Answer choices:*

(see index for correct answer)

- a. Sensory neuroscience
- b. Perceptual paradox
- c. Critical realism

- d. Sensation

Guidance: level 1

:: Philosophy of life ::

In philosophy, _____ means the existence of a thing. Anything that exists has _____ . Ontology is the branch of philosophy that studies _____ . _____ is a concept encompassing objective and subjective features of reality and existence. Anything that partakes in _____ is also called a "_____", though often this usage is limited to entities that have subjectivity . The notion of "_____" has, inevitably, been elusive and controversial in the history of philosophy, beginning in Western philosophy with attempts among the pre-Socratics to deploy it intelligibly. The first effort to recognize and define the concept came from Parmenides, who famously said of it that "what is-is". Common words such as "is", "are", and "am" refer directly or indirectly to _____ .

Exam Probability: **Medium**

3. *Answer choices:*

(see index for correct answer)

- a. Femininism
- b. Philosophy of futility
- c. Meaning of life
- d. Alternative lifestyle

Guidance: level 1

:: Theories of mind ::

In sociology, _____ is a theoretical perspective that derives social processes from human interaction. It is the study of how individuals shape society and are shaped by society through meaning that arises in interactions. Interactionist theory has grown in the latter half of the twentieth century and has become one of the dominant sociological perspectives in the world today. George Herbert Mead, as an advocate of pragmatism and the subjectivity of social reality, is considered a leader in the development of _____ . Herbert Blumer expanded on Mead's work and coined the term "symbolic _____ ".

Exam Probability: **High**

4. *Answer choices:*
(see index for correct answer)

- a. Hylopathism
- b. Psychological nominalism
- c. Panpsychism
- d. Instrumentalism

Guidance: level 1

:: Psychology ::

A _____ is the formulation of general concepts from specific instances by abstracting common properties. _____ s posit the existence of a domain or set of elements, as well as one or more common characteristics shared by those elements. As such, they are the essential basis of all valid deductive inferences. The process of verification is necessary to determine whether a _____ holds true for any given situation.

Exam Probability: **Low**

5. *Answer choices:*
(see index for correct answer)

- a. Faculty psychology
- b. Exemplar theory
- c. Trans-species psychology
- d. Generalization

Guidance: level 1

:: Personality ::

_____ is defined as the characteristic set of behaviors, cognitions, and emotional patterns that evolve from biological and environmental factors. While there is no generally agreed upon definition of _____ , most theories focus on motivation and psychological interactions with one's environment. Trait-based _____ theories, such as those defined by Raymond Cattell define _____ as the traits that predict a person's behavior. On the other hand, more behaviorally based approaches define _____ through learning and habits. Nevertheless, most theories view _____ as relatively stable.

Exam Probability: **Low**

6. *Answer choices:*

(see index for correct answer)

- a. Agreeableness
- b. The Astrology of Personality
- c. Cognitive complexity
- d. Optimism

Guidance: level 1

:: Memory biases ::

In psychology, the _____ states that people remember uncompleted or interrupted tasks better than completed tasks. In Gestalt psychology, the _____ has been used to demonstrate the general presence of Gestalt phenomena: not just appearing as perceptual effects, but also present in cognition.

Exam Probability: **High**

7. *Answer choices:*

(see index for correct answer)

- a. Google effect
- b. Misinformation effect
- c. Cue-dependent forgetting
- d. Zeigarnik effect

Guidance: level 1

:: Causality ::

An _____ is a set of statements usually constructed to describe a set of facts which clarifies the causes, context, and consequences of those facts. This description of the facts et cetera may establish rules or laws, and may clarify the existing rules or laws in relation to any objects, or phenomena examined. The components of an _____ can be implicit, and interwoven with one another.

Exam Probability: **Low**

8. *Answer choices:*

(see index for correct answer)

- a. Explanation
- b. Fatalism

- c. Potentiality and actuality
- d. Chronology protection conjecture

Guidance: level 1

:: Scientific method ::

In philosophy of science, _____ is a model of scientific inquiry that emphasizes the need for alternative hypotheses, rather than a single hypothesis to avoid confirmation bias.

Exam Probability: **Medium**

9. *Answer choices:*

(see index for correct answer)

- a. Violation paradigm
- b. Strong inference
- c. Open notebook science
- d. Observational study

Guidance: level 1

:: Defence mechanisms ::

_____, in ordinary English usage, is asserting that a statement or allegation is not true. The same word, and also abnegation, is used for a psychological defense mechanism postulated by psychoanalyst Sigmund Freud, in which a person is faced with a fact that is too uncomfortable to accept and rejects it instead, insisting that it is not true despite what may be overwhelming evidence. An individual that exhibits such behavior is described as a _____ ist or true believer. _____ also could mean denying the happening of an event or the reliability of information, which can lead to a feeling of aloofness and to the ignoring of possibly beneficial information.

Exam Probability: **High**

10. *Answer choices:*

(see index for correct answer)

- a. Undoing
- b. Minimisation
- c. Humour
- d. Denial

Guidance: level 1

:: Self ::

_____ is a central philosophical concept, related to consciousness, agency, personhood, reality, and truth, which has been variously defined by sources. Three common definitions include that _____ is the quality or condition of.

Exam Probability: **Low**

11. *Answer choices:*

(see index for correct answer)

- a. Self-schema
- b. Nigredo
- c. Destructiveness
- d. Generalized other

Guidance: level 1

:: Theories of mind ::

_____ is a position on the mind–body problem which holds that physical and biochemical events within the human body are causal with respect to mental events. According to this view, subjective mental events are completely dependent for their existence on corresponding physical and biochemical events within the human body and themselves have no causal efficacy on physical events. The appearance that subjective mental states influence physical events is merely an illusion. For instance, fear seems to make the heart beat faster, but according to _____ the biochemical secretions of the brain and nervous system —not the experience of fear—is what raises the heartbeat. Because mental events are a kind of overflow that cannot cause anything physical, yet have non-physical properties, _____ is viewed as a form of property dualism.

Exam Probability: **Low**

12. Answer choices:

(see index for correct answer)

- a. Symbiomism
- b. Epiphenomenalism
- c. Instrumentalism
- d. Type physicalism

Guidance: level 1

:: Design of experiments ::

An _____ , also known as an independent ethics committee , ethical review board , or research ethics board , is a type of committee that applies research ethics by reviewing the methods proposed for research to ensure that they are ethical. Such boards are formally designated to approve , monitor, and review biomedical and behavioral research involving humans. They often conduct some form of risk-benefit analysis in an attempt to determine whether or not research should be conducted. The purpose of the IRB is to assure that appropriate steps are taken to protect the rights and welfare of humans participating as subjects in a research study. Along with developed countries, many developing countries have established national, regional or local _____ s in order to safeguard ethical conduct of research concerning both national and international norms, regulations or codes.

Exam Probability: **High**

13. Answer choices:

(see index for correct answer)

- a. Block design
- b. Surrogate model
- c. Drug design
- d. Orthogonal array testing

Guidance: level 1

:: Philosophy of mind ::

_____ is a philosophical concept and is defined by the Stanford Encyclopedia of Philosophy as "the power of minds to be about, to represent, or to stand for, things, properties and states of affairs". The once obsolete term dates from medieval scholastic philosophy, but in more recent times it has been resurrected by Franz Brentano and adopted by Edmund Husserl. The earliest theory of _____ is associated with St. Anselm`s ontological argument for the existence of God, and with his tenets distinguishing between objects that exist in the understanding and objects that exist in reality.

Exam Probability: **Medium**

14. *Answer choices:*
(see index for correct answer)

- a. Intentionality
- b. Reincarnation
- c. Concept and object
- d. Intellect

Guidance: level 1

:: Information science ::

In the study of history as an academic discipline, a _____ is an artifact, document, diary, manuscript, autobiography, recording, or any other source of information that was created at the time under study. It serves as an original source of information about the topic. Similar definitions can be used in library science, and other areas of scholarship, although different fields have somewhat different definitions. In journalism, a _____ can be a person with direct knowledge of a situation, or a document written by such a person.

Exam Probability: **High**

15. *Answer choices:*

(see index for correct answer)

- a. Library and Information Science Abstracts
- b. Information flow
- c. Primary source
- d. Geoinformatics

Guidance: level 1

:: Data analysis ::

In statistics, an _____ is a data point that differs significantly from other observations. An _____ may be due to variability in the measurement or it may indicate experimental error; the latter are sometimes excluded from the data set. An _____ can cause serious problems in statistical analyses.

Exam Probability: **High**

16. *Answer choices:*

(see index for correct answer)

- a. TinkerPlots
- b. Outlier
- c. LISREL
- d. Item tree analysis

Guidance: level 1

:: Cognitive psychology ::

_____ is an anticipated goal-oriented movement. The concept arises in many areas of study, including cognitive psychology, operant conditioning, philosophy, neurology, and criminology among others, and it has various meanings depending on the context in which it is used. For example, operant psychology uses the term to refer to the actions that are modifiable by their consequences. A more cognitive account may refer to _____ as involving the identification of a desired outcome together with the action necessary to achieve that outcome. _____ is often associated with consciousness and will. For example, Psychologist Charles Nuckolls holds that we control our voluntary behavior, and that it is not known how we come to plan what actions will be executed. Many psychologists, notably Tolman, apply the concept of _____ to both animal and human behavior, raising the issue of animal consciousness and its role in _____.

Exam Probability: **Medium**

17. *Answer choices:*

(see index for correct answer)

- a. Voluntary action
- b. Cognitive resource theory
- c. Association value
- d. International Association for the Cognitive Science of Religion

Guidance: level 1

:: Behavior ::

_____ or behaviour is the range of actions and mannerisms made by individuals, organisms, systems, or artificial entities in conjunction with themselves or their environment, which includes the other systems or organisms around as well as the physical environment. It is the computed response of the system or organism to various stimuli or inputs, whether internal or external, conscious or subconscious, overt or covert, and voluntary or involuntary.

Exam Probability: **Medium**

18. *Answer choices:*

(see index for correct answer)

- a. Licking
- b. Behavior
- c. Swarm behaviour
- d. Jeitinho

Guidance: level 1

:: Human behavior ::

In psychology, _____ is a lack of restraint manifested in disregard of social conventions, impulsivity, and poor risk assessment. _____ affects motor, instinctual, emotional, cognitive, and perceptual aspects with signs and symptoms similar to the diagnostic criteria for mania. Hypersexuality, hyperphagia, and aggressive outbursts are indicative of disinhibited instinctual drives.

Exam Probability: **Low**

19. *Answer choices:*

(see index for correct answer)

- a. Behavioral modernity
- b. Disinhibition
- c. Irrationality
- d. Evasion

Guidance: level 1

:: Mind ::

The _____ is a set of cognitive faculties including consciousness, imagination, perception, thinking, judgement, language and memory. It is usually defined as the faculty of an entity's thoughts and consciousness. It holds the power of imagination, recognition, and appreciation, and is responsible for processing feelings and emotions, resulting in attitudes and actions.

Exam Probability: **Low**

20. *Answer choices:*

(see index for correct answer)

- a. Mind
- b. Neuroanatomy of intimacy

- c. Personal experience
- d. Consciousness after death

Guidance: level 1

:: Mental and behavioural disorders ::

A _____, also called a mental illness or psychiatric disorder, is a behavioral or mental pattern that causes significant distress or impairment of personal functioning. Such features may be persistent, relapsing and remitting, or occur as a single episode. Many disorders have been described, with signs and symptoms that vary widely between specific disorders. Such disorders may be diagnosed by a mental health professional.

Exam Probability: **Medium**

21. *Answer choices:*

(see index for correct answer)

- a. Catatonia
- b. Mental disorder
- c. Grisi siknis
- d. Jumping Frenchmen of Maine

Guidance: level 1

:: Philosophy of life ::

_____ is a concept introduced by German philosopher Martin Heidegger to describe humans' individual existences as "being thrown" into the world.

Exam Probability: **Low**

22. *Answer choices:*

(see index for correct answer)

- a. Meaning and Purpose
- b. Death anxiety
- c. Thrownness
- d. Egotism

Guidance: level 1

:: History of psychology ::

_____ is the idea that mental processes operate by the association of one mental state with its successor states. It holds that all mental processes are made up of discrete psychological elements and their combinations, which are believed to be made up of sensations or simple feelings. In philosophy, this idea is viewed as the outcome of empiricism and sensationism. The concept encompasses a psychological theory as well as comprehensive philosophical foundation, and scientific methodology.

Exam Probability: **Low**

23. Answer choices:

(see index for correct answer)

- a. Functional psychology
- b. Oneirocritica
- c. Extraordinary Popular Delusions and the Madness of Crowds
- d. Genetic Studies of Genius

Guidance: level 1

:: Individualism ::

_____ is the philosophical study that begins with the human subject—not merely the thinking subject, but the acting, feeling, living human individual. It is associated mainly with certain 19th and 20th-century European philosophers who, despite profound doctrinal differences, shared the belief in that beginning of philosophical thinking.

Exam Probability: **Medium**

24. Answer choices:

(see index for correct answer)

- a. Individualism Index
- b. Perspectives on capitalism
- c. Anticonformism
- d. Objectivism

Guidance: level 1

:: Sleep ::

_____ is a naturally recurring state of mind and body, characterized by altered consciousness, relatively inhibited sensory activity, inhibition of nearly all voluntary muscles, and reduced interactions with surroundings. It is distinguished from wakefulness by a decreased ability to react to stimuli, but more reactive than coma or disorders of consciousness, _____ displaying very different and active brain patterns.

Exam Probability: **Low**

25. *Answer choices:*
(see index for correct answer)

- a. Polyphasic sleep
- b. Nocturnal emission
- c. Polysomnographic technologist
- d. Bundling

Guidance: level 1

:: Analysis of variance ::

In statistics, a confounder is a variable that influences both the dependent variable and independent variable, causing a spurious association. _____ is a causal concept, and as such, cannot be described in terms of correlations or associations.

Exam Probability: **Low**

26. *Answer choices:*

(see index for correct answer)

- a. False positive rate
- b. ANOVA on ranks
- c. Fixed effects model
- d. Principle of marginality

Guidance: level 1

:: Scientific method ::

The _____ is an empirical method of acquiring knowledge that has characterized the development of science since at least the 17th century. It involves careful observation, applying rigorous skepticism about what is observed, given that cognitive assumptions can distort how one interprets the observation. It involves formulating hypotheses, via induction, based on such observations; experimental and measurement-based testing of deductions drawn from the hypotheses; and refinement of the hypotheses based on the experimental findings. These are principles of the _____ , as distinguished from a definitive series of steps applicable to all scientific enterprises.

Exam Probability: **Medium**

27. *Answer choices:*

(see index for correct answer)

- a. Science of team science
- b. Scientific formalism
- c. Consilience
- d. Translational science

Guidance: level 1

:: Self ::

The _____ is an individual person as the object of his or her own reflective consciousness. This reference is necessarily subjective, thus _____ is a reference by a subject to the same subject. The sense of having a _____ —or _____ -hood—should, however, not be confused with subjectivity it _____ . Ostensibly, there is a directness outward from the subject that refers inward, back to its ` _____ ` . Examples of psychiatric conditions where such `sameness` is broken include depersonalization, which sometimes occur in schizophrenia: the _____ appears different to the subject.

Exam Probability: **Medium**

28. *Answer choices:*

(see index for correct answer)

- a. Self-discrepancy theory
- b. Self
- c. True self and false self
- d. Procrastination

Guidance: level 1

:: Pseudoscience ::

_____, also known as zone therapy, is an alternative medicine involving application of pressure to the feet and hands with specific thumb, finger, and hand techniques without the use of oil or lotion. It is based on a pseudoscientific system of zones and reflex areas that purportedly reflect an image of the body on the feet and hands, with the premise that such work effects a physical change to the body.

Exam Probability: **Low**

29. *Answer choices:*

(see index for correct answer)

- a. Reflexology
- b. Medical astrology
- c. Blood type diet
- d. Tobacco smoke enema

Guidance: level 1

:: Psycholinguistics ::

_____ or psychology of language is the study of the interrelation between linguistic factors and psychological aspects.

Exam Probability: **Medium**

30. *Answer choices:*
(see index for correct answer)

- a. Lexicalization
- b. Max Planck Institute for Psycholinguistics
- c. Psycholinguistics
- d. Conversational model

Guidance: level 1

:: Humour ::

Humour , also spelt as _____ , is the tendency of experiences to provoke laughter and provide amusement. The term derives from the _____ al medicine of the ancient Greeks, which taught that the balance of fluids in the human body, known as humours , controlled human health and emotion.

Exam Probability: **Medium**

31. *Answer choices:*

(see index for correct answer)

- a. How It Should Have Ended
- b. Trash-talk
- c. Nonsense word
- d. Humor

Guidance: level 1

:: Philosophy of sexuality ::

_____ is a person's overall sexual drive or desire for sexual activity. _____ is influenced by biological, psychological and social factors. Biologically, the sex hormones and associated neurotransmitters that act upon the nucleus accumbens regulate _____ in humans. Social factors, such as work and family, and internal psychological factors, such as personality and stress, can affect _____ . _____ can also be affected by medical conditions, medications, lifestyle and relationship issues, and age. A person who has extremely frequent or a suddenly increased sex drive may be experiencing hypersexuality, while the opposite condition is hyposexuality.

Exam Probability: **Low**

32. *Answer choices:*

(see index for correct answer)

- a. Sarah Kofman

- b. Philosophy of sex
- c. Sexual ethics
- d. Monique Wittig

Guidance: level 1

:: Motivation ::

A _____ is an idea of the future or desired result that a person or a group of people envisions, plans and commits to achieve. People endeavor to reach _____ s within a finite time by setting deadlines.

Exam Probability: **High**

33. *Answer choices:*

(see index for correct answer)

- a. Burnout
- b. Will to live
- c. Keep Calm and Carry On
- d. Goal

Guidance: level 1

:: Hypothesis testing ::

In statistical hypothesis testing, a result has _____ when it is very unlikely to have occurred given the null hypothesis. More precisely, a study's defined significance level, denoted a, is the probability of the study rejecting the null hypothesis, given that the null hypothesis were true; and the p-value of a result, p, is the probability of obtaining a result at least as extreme, given that the null hypothesis were true. The result is statistically significant, by the standards of the study, when p < a. The significance level for a study is chosen before data collection, and typically set to 5% or much lower, depending on the field of study.

Exam Probability: **Medium**

34. *Answer choices:*

(see index for correct answer)

- a. Statistical significance
- b. P-value
- c. Optimality criterion
- d. False discovery rate

Guidance: level 1

:: Validity (statistics) ::

In psychometrics, _____ refers to the extent to which a measure represents all facets of a given construct. For example, a depression scale may lack _____ if it only assesses the affective dimension of depression but fails to take into account the behavioral dimension. An element of subjectivity exists in relation to determining _____ , which requires a degree of agreement about what a particular personality trait such as extraversion represents. A disagreement about a personality trait will prevent the gain of a high _____ .

Exam Probability: **Medium**

35. *Answer choices:*

(see index for correct answer)

- a. Verification and validation
- b. Convergent validity
- c. Content validity
- d. Test validity

Guidance: level 1

:: Evaluation ::

_____ solving consists of using generic or ad hoc methods in an orderly manner to find solutions to _____ s. Some of the _____ -solving techniques developed and used in philosophy, artificial intelligence, computer science, engineering, mathematics, or medicine are related to mental _____ -solving techniques studied in psychology.

Exam Probability: **Low**

36. *Answer choices:*

(see index for correct answer)

- a. Evaluation
- b. Outcome mapping
- c. Continuous assessment
- d. Problem

Guidance: level 1

:: History of psychology ::

_____ is a book by Sigmund Freud, the founder of psychoanalysis. It was written in 1929 and first published in German in 1930 as Das Unbehagen in der Kultur . Exploring what Freud sees as the important clash between the desire for individuality and the expectations of society, the book is considered one of Freud's most important and widely read works, and one of the most influential and studied books in the field of modern psychology.

Exam Probability: **High**

37. *Answer choices:*

(see index for correct answer)

- a. Structuralism
- b. Principles of Psychology

- c. Tabula rasa
- d. Civilization and Its Discontents

Guidance: level 1

:: Psychological schools ::

_____ is "the scientific study of what makes life most worth living", or "the scientific study of positive human functioning and flourishing on multiple levels that include the biological, personal, relational, institutional, cultural, and global dimensions of life". _____ is concerned with eudaimonia, "the good life", reflection about what holds the greatest value in life – the factors that contribute the most to a well-lived and fulfilling life.

Exam Probability: **Low**

38. *Answer choices:*

(see index for correct answer)

- a. Rational behavior therapy
- b. Classical Adlerian psychotherapy
- c. Postmodern psychology
- d. Cognitive therapy

Guidance: level 1

:: Philosophers of mind ::

_____ was a philosopher during the Classical period in Ancient Greece, the founder of the Lyceum and the Peripatetic school of philosophy and Aristotelian tradition. Along with his teacher Plato, he is considered the "Father of Western Philosophy". His writings cover many subjects – including physics, biology, zoology, metaphysics, logic, ethics, aesthetics, poetry, theatre, music, rhetoric, psychology, linguistics, economics, politics and government. _____ provided a complex synthesis of the various philosophies existing prior to him, and it was above all from his teachings that the West inherited its intellectual lexicon, as well as problems and methods of inquiry. As a result, his philosophy has exerted a unique influence on almost every form of knowledge in the West and it continues to be a subject of contemporary philosophical discussion.

Exam Probability: **Low**

39. *Answer choices:*

(see index for correct answer)

- a. Eugene Halliday
- b. Aristotle
- c. Ayn Rand
- d. Peter Lipton

Guidance: level 1

:: Giftedness ::

A _____ is a person who displays exceptional intellectual ability, creative productivity, universality in genres or originality, typically to a degree that is associated with the achievement of new advances in a domain of knowledge. Despite the presence of scholars in many subjects throughout history, many _____ es have shown high achievements in only a single kind of activity.

Exam Probability: **Low**

40. *Answer choices:*

(see index for correct answer)

- a. Ronald K. Hoeflin
- b. Sarah Chang
- c. Boris Sidis
- d. Ronan Farrow

Guidance: level 1

:: Research ::

Within natural science, disciplines that are basic science, also called pure science, develop basic information to predict and perhaps explain and understand phenomena in the natural world. Applied science is the use of scientific processes and knowledge as the means to achieve a particular practical or useful result. This includes a broad range of applied science related fields from engineering, business, medicine to early childhood education.

Exam Probability: **High**

41. *Answer choices:*

(see index for correct answer)

- a. Applied research
- b. Clinical and Translational Science Award
- c. Blue skies research
- d. New investigator

Guidance: level 1

:: Psychiatry ::

The _____ , published by the American Psychiatric Association , offers a common language and standard criteria for the classification of mental disorders. It is used, or relied upon, by clinicians, researchers, psychiatric drug regulation agencies, health insurance companies, pharmaceutical companies, the legal system, and policy makers together with alternatives such as the ICD-10 Classification of Mental and Behavioural Disorders, produced by the WHO.

Exam Probability: **High**

42. *Answer choices:*

(see index for correct answer)

- a. A Stranger in The Family: Culture, Families, and Therapy
- b. Stilted speech

- c. Therapygenetics
- d. Clinical neuroscience

Guidance: level 1

:: Psychotherapy ::

_____ was developed by neurologist and psychiatrist Viktor Frankl, on a concept based on the premise that the primary motivational force of an individual is to find a meaning in life. It is considered the "Third Viennese School of Psychotherapy" along with Freud's psychoanalysis and Adler's individual psychology.

Exam Probability: **Medium**

43. *Answer choices:*
(see index for correct answer)

- a. Psychiatric somatotherapy
- b. Reality therapy
- c. Internal Family Systems Model
- d. Logotherapy

Guidance: level 1

:: Information science ::

_____ is the resolution of uncertainty; it is that which answers the question of "what an entity is" and thus defines both its essence and nature of its characteristics. _____ relates to both data and knowledge, as data is meaningful _____ representing values attributed to parameters, and knowledge signifies understanding of a concept. _____ is uncoupled from an observer, which is an entity that can access _____ and thus discern what it specifies; _____ exists beyond an event horizon for example. In the case of knowledge, the _____ itself requires a cognitive observer to be obtained.

Exam Probability: **High**

44. *Answer choices:*

(see index for correct answer)

- a. The Social Life of Information
- b. Suzanne Briet
- c. Robert Freeman Asleson
- d. BRS/Search

Guidance: level 1

:: Philosophy of life ::

_____ is the view that every entity has a set of attributes that are necessary to its identity and function. In early Western thought Plato's idealism held that all things have such an "essence"—an "idea" or "form". In Categories, Aristotle similarly proposed that all objects have a substance that, as George Lakoff put it "make the thing what it is, and without which it would be not that kind of thing". The contrary view—non-_____—denies the need to posit such an "essence`".

Exam Probability: **Medium**

45. *Answer choices:*

(see index for correct answer)

- a. Atheist existentialism
- b. Egotism
- c. The Myth of Male Power
- d. Essentialism

Guidance: level 1

:: Self ::

An _____ is that which exists as a distinct entity. _____ity is the state or quality of being an _____ ; particularly of being a person separate from other people and possessing their own needs or goals, rights and responsibilities. The exact definition of an _____ is important in the fields of biology, law, and philosophy.

Exam Probability: **Low**

46. *Answer choices:*

(see index for correct answer)

- a. Person
- b. Metaphysical solipsism
- c. Self-determination theory
- d. Individual

Guidance: level 1

:: Design of experiments ::

_____ or random placement is an experimental technique for assigning human participants or animal subjects to different groups in an experiment using randomization, such as by a chance procedure or a random number generator. This ensures that each participant or subject has an equal chance of being placed in any group. _____ of participants helps to ensure that any differences between and within the groups are not systematic at the outset of the experiment. Thus, any differences between groups recorded at the end of the experiment can be more confidently attributed to the experimental procedures or treatment.

Exam Probability: **Low**

47. *Answer choices:*

(see index for correct answer)

- a. Random assignment
- b. Adversarial collaboration
- c. Combinatorial design
- d. Ignorability

Guidance: level 1

:: Research methods ::

_____ is a type of research which involves seeking out and extracting evidence from archival records. These records may be held either in collecting institutions, such as libraries and museums, or in the custody of the organization that originally generated or accumulated them, or in that of a successor body. _____ can be contrasted with secondary research, which involves identifying and consulting secondary sources relating to the topic of enquiry; and with other types of primary research and empirical investigation such as fieldwork and experiment.

Exam Probability: **Medium**

48. *Answer choices:*

(see index for correct answer)

- a. New Zealand Attitudes and Values Study
- b. Unobtrusive research
- c. Computer-assisted web interviewing
- d. Experience sampling method

Guidance: level 1

:: Conceptions of self ::

_____ is an intellectual stance that emphasizes the importance of human persons. Various conceptualizations have been explored, so _____ exists in many different versions, and this makes it somewhat difficult to define as a philosophical and theological movement. The term "_____" has been used in print first by F. D. E. Schleiermacher in the last year of the 18th. century. The idea can be traced back to earlier thinkers in various parts of the world

Exam Probability: **Low**

49. *Answer choices:*

(see index for correct answer)

- a. Internarrative identity
- b. New Man
- c. Looking-glass self
- d. Personalism

Guidance: level 1

:: Behaviorism ::

_____ is a branch of mathematical analysis, the core of which is formed by the study of vector spaces endowed with some kind of limit-related structure and the linear functions defined on these spaces and respecting these structures in a suitable sense. The historical roots of _____ lie in the study of spaces of functions and the formulation of properties of transformations of functions such as the Fourier transform as transformations defining continuous, unitary etc. operators between function spaces. This point of view turned out to be particularly useful for the study of differential and integral equations.

Exam Probability: **Low**

50. *Answer choices:*

(see index for correct answer)

- a. Token economy
- b. Social competence
- c. behavior therapy
- d. Functional analysis

Guidance: level 1

:: Psychodynamics ::

_____ is defined as redirection of a psychotherapist's feelings toward a client – or, more generally, as a therapist's emotional entanglement with a client.

Exam Probability: **Medium**

51. *Answer choices:*

(see index for correct answer)

- a. Countertransference
- b. Resistance
- c. Transference
- d. Apollo archetype

Guidance: level 1

:: Psychotherapy ::

_____ is a form of training with the goal of making people more aware of their own goals as well as their prejudices, and more sensitive to others and to the dynamics of group interaction.

Exam Probability: **Medium**

52. *Answer choices:*

(see index for correct answer)

- a. Contemplative psychotherapy
- b. Personal relationship skills
- c. Thanatotherapy
- d. Writing therapy

Guidance: level 1

:: Validity (statistics) ::

_____ is a type of evidence that can be gathered to defend the use of a test for predicting other outcomes. It is a parameter used in sociology, psychology, and other psychometric or behavioral sciences. _____ is demonstrated when a test correlates well with a measure that has previously been validated. The two measures may be for the same construct, but more often used for different, but presumably related, constructs.

Exam Probability: **High**

53. *Answer choices:*
(see index for correct answer)

- a. Concurrent validity
- b. Nomological validity
- c. Test validity
- d. Face validity

Guidance: level 1

:: History of psychology ::

The _____ , also known as the greater male _____ , states that males display greater variability in traits than females do. It has often been discussed in relation to cognitive ability, where it has been observed that human males are more likely than females to have either very high or very low intelligence. The sex-difference in the variability of intelligence has been discussed since at least Charles Darwin. Sex-differences in variability are present in many abilities and traits — including physical, psychological and genetic ones. It is not only found in humans but in other sexually dimorphic species as well.

Exam Probability: **Medium**

54. *Answer choices:*

(see index for correct answer)

- a. Stanford prison experiment
- b. Milgram experiment
- c. Variability hypothesis
- d. Virtual Laboratory

Guidance: level 1

:: Validity (statistics) ::

_____ is the validity of applying the conclusions of a scientific study outside the context of that study. In other words, it is the extent to which the results of a study can be generalized to and across other situations, people, stimuli, and times. In contrast, internal validity is the validity of conclusions drawn within the context of a particular study. Because general conclusions are almost always a goal in research, _____ is an important property of any study. Mathematical analysis of _____ concerns a determination of whether generalization across heterogeneous populations is feasible, and devising statistical and computational methods that produce valid generalizations.

Exam Probability: **Medium**

55. *Answer choices:*

(see index for correct answer)

- a. External validity
- b. Verification and validation
- c. Nomological network
- d. Test validity

Guidance: level 1

:: Psychological schools ::

_____ is the psychological method or science founded by the Viennese psychiatrist Alfred Adler. The English edition of Adler's work on the subject is a collection of papers and lectures given mainly in 1912–1914, and covers the whole range of human psychology in a single survey, intended to mirror the indivisible unity of the personality.

Exam Probability: **High**

56. *Answer choices:*

(see index for correct answer)

- a. Individual psychology
- b. Organismic theory
- c. Cognitive therapy
- d. Classical Adlerian psychotherapy

Guidance: level 1

:: Psychology organizations ::

The _____ is the primary organization representing psychologists throughout Canada. It was organized in 1939 and incorporated under the Canada Corporations Act, Part II, in May 1950.

Exam Probability: **Low**

57. *Answer choices:*

(see index for correct answer)

- a. Canadian Psychological Association
- b. Norwegian Society of Psychological Science
- c. National Association for Self-Esteem
- d. Association for Women in Psychology

Guidance: level 1

:: Cognitive psychology ::

_____ quantitatively investigates the relationship between physical stimuli and the sensations and perceptions they produce. _____ has been described as "the scientific study of the relation between stimulus and sensation" or, more completely, as "the analysis of perceptual processes by studying the effect on a subject's experience or behaviour of systematically varying the properties of a stimulus along one or more physical dimensions".

Exam Probability: **Low**

58. *Answer choices:*

(see index for correct answer)

- a. Cognition and Brain Sciences Unit
- b. Reconstructive memory
- c. Psychophysics
- d. Theory of indispensable attributes

Guidance: level 1

:: Epistemology ::

_____ is a philosophical and ethical stance that emphasizes the value and agency of human beings, individually and collectively, and generally prefers critical thinking and evidence over acceptance of dogma or superstition. The meaning of the term _____ has fluctuated according to the successive intellectual movements which have identified with it. The term was coined by theologian Friedrich Niethammer at the beginning of the 19th century to refer to a system of education based on the study of classical literature. Generally, however, _____ refers to a perspective that affirms some notion of human freedom and progress. It views humans as solely responsible for the promotion and development of individuals and emphasizes a concern for man in relation to the world.

Exam Probability: **Low**

59. *Answer choices:*

(see index for correct answer)

- a. Egocentric predicament
- b. Preface paradox
- c. Gettier problem
- d. Humanism

Guidance: level 1

Educational Psychology

Educational psychology is the branch of psychology concerned with the scientific study of human learning. The study of learning processes, from both cognitive and behavioral perspectives, allows researchers to understand individual differences in intelligence, cognitive development, affect, motivation, self-regulation, and self-concept, as well as their role in learning. The field of educational psychology relies heavily on quantitative methods, including testing and measurement, to enhance educational activities related to instructional design, classroom management, and assessment, which serve to facilitate learning processes in various educational settings across the lifespan.

:: Educational psychology ::

Educational technology is "the study and ethical practice of facilitating learning and improving performance by creating, using, and managing appropriate technological processes and resources".

Exam Probability: **High**

1. *Answer choices:*

(see index for correct answer)

- a. Reading disability
- b. Knowledge divide
- c. Creative Pedagogy
- d. E-learning

Guidance: level 1

:: Human–computer interaction ::

_____ consists of tailoring a service or a product to accommodate specific individuals, sometimes tied to groups or segments of individuals. A wide variety of organizations use _____ to improve customer satisfaction, digital sales conversion, marketing results, branding, and improved website metrics as well as for advertising. _____ is a key element in social media and recommender systems.

Exam Probability: **Medium**

2. *Answer choices:*

(see index for correct answer)

- a. Digital Writing and Research Lab
- b. Remote Touch

- c. Personalization
- d. Office Assistant

Guidance: level 1

:: bad_topic ::

In statistics, a _____ is a list, table or graph that displays the frequency of various outcomes in a sample. Each entry in the table contains the frequency or count of the occurrences of values within a particular group or interval, and in this way, the table summarizes the distribution of values in the sample.

Exam Probability: **Medium**

3. *Answer choices:*

(see index for correct answer)

- a. Frequency distribution
- b. Oral language
- c. Visual impairment
- d. Percentile rank

Guidance: level 1

:: Logical fallacies ::

An _____ is a formal fallacy in the interpretation of statistical data that occurs when inferences about the nature of individuals are deduced from inferences about the group to which those individuals belong. _____ sometimes refers to the fallacy of division, which is not a statistical issue. The four common statistical ecological fallacies are: confusion between ecological correlations and individual correlations, confusion between group average and total average, Simpson's paradox, and confusion between higher average and higher likelihood.

Exam Probability: **High**

4. *Answer choices:*

(see index for correct answer)

- a. Proving too much
- b. Masked man fallacy
- c. Idola tribus
- d. Ecological fallacy

Guidance: level 1

:: Social status ::

_____ is an economic and sociological combined total measure of a person's work experience and of an individual's or family's economic and social position in relation to others, based on household income, earners' education, and occupation are examined, as well as combined income, whereas for an individual's SES only their own attributes are assessed. However, SES is more commonly used to depict an economic difference in society as a whole.

Exam Probability: **Low**

5. *Answer choices:*

(see index for correct answer)

- a. Socioeconomic Status
- b. Exploitation
- c. Social exchange

Guidance: level 1

:: Problem solving ::

_____ is a fundamental method of problem solving. It is characterised by repeated, varied attempts which are continued until success, or until the agent stops trying.

Exam Probability: **High**

6. *Answer choices:*

(see index for correct answer)

- a. Trial and error
- b. Dilemma
- c. Systems thinking
- d. Puzzle

Guidance: level 1

:: Abstraction ::

A _____ is a mark, sign or word that indicates, signifies, or is understood as representing an idea, object, or relationship. _____ s allow people to go beyond what is known or seen by creating linkages between otherwise very different concepts and experiences. All communication is achieved through the use of _____ s. _____ s take the form of words, sounds, gestures, ideas or visual images and are used to convey other ideas and beliefs. For example, a red octagon may be a _____ for "STOP". On a map, a blue line might represent a river. Numerals are _____ s for numbers. Alphabetic letters may be _____ s for sounds. Personal names are _____ s representing individuals. A red rose may _____ ize love and compassion. The variable `x`, in a mathematical equation, may _____ ize the position of a particle in space.

Exam Probability: **Medium**

7. *Answer choices:*

(see index for correct answer)

- a. Symbol
- b. Abstractionism
- c. Simplicity
- d. Metamechanics

Guidance: level 1

:: Dyslexia ::

_____ is a term that is used to refer to the brain's ability to use and interpret visual information from the world around us. The process of converting light energy into a meaningful image is a complex process that is facilitated by numerous brain structures and higher level cognitive processes. On an anatomical level, light energy first enters the eye through the cornea, where the light is bent. After passing through the cornea, light passes through the pupil and then lens of the eye, where it is bent to a greater degree and focused upon the retina. The retina is where a group of light-sensing cells, called photoreceptors are located. There are two types of photoreceptors: rods and cones. Rods are sensitive to dim light and cones are better able to transduce bright light. Photoreceptors connect to bipolar cells, which induce action potentials in retinal ganglion cells. These retinal ganglion cells form a bundle at the optic disc, which is a part of the optic nerve. The two optic nerves from each eye meet at the optic chiasm, where nerve fibers from each nasal retina cross which results in the right half of each eye's visual field being represented in the left hemisphere and the left half of each eye's visual fields being represented in the right hemisphere. The optic tract then diverges into two visual pathways, the geniculostriate pathway and the tectopulvinar pathway, which send visual information to the visual cortex of the occipital lobe for higher level processing .

Exam Probability: **Low**

8. *Answer choices:*

(see index for correct answer)

- a. Dybuster
- b. Dyscalculia
- c. Strephosymbolia
- d. Visual processing

Guidance: level 1

:: Validity (statistics) ::

In psychometrics, criterion or concrete validity is the extent to which a measure is related to an outcome. _____ is often divided into concurrent and predictive validity. Concurrent validity refers to a comparison between the measure in question and an outcome assessed at the same time. In Standards for Educational & Psychological Tests, it states, "concurrent validity reflects only the status quo at a particular time." Predictive validity, on the other hand, compares the measure in question with an outcome assessed at a later time. Although concurrent and predictive validity are similar, it is cautioned to keep the terms and findings separated. "Concurrent validity should not be used as a substitute for predictive validity without an appropriate supporting rationale."

Exam Probability: **Low**

9. *Answer choices:*

(see index for correct answer)

- a. Criterion validity
- b. Nomological network
- c. Construct validity
- d. Verification and validation

Guidance: level 1

:: Neuropsychological assessment ::

_____ is the faculty of the brain by which information is encoded, stored, and retrieved when needed.

Exam Probability: **Medium**

10. *Answer choices:*
(see index for correct answer)

- a. Natural language
- b. Adaptive memory
- c. Memory
- d. Problem solving

Guidance: level 1

:: Educational psychology ::

_____ is the ability to reflect on one's actions so as to engage in a process of continuous learning. According to one definition it involves "paying critical attention to the practical values and theories which inform everyday actions, by examining practice reflectively and reflexively. This leads to developmental insight". A key rationale for _____ is that experience alone does not necessarily lead to learning; deliberate reflection on experience is essential.

Exam Probability: **Medium**

11. *Answer choices:*

(see index for correct answer)

- a. Instructor-led training
- b. Rapid automatized naming
- c. Triarchic theory of intelligence
- d. Cultural learning

Guidance: level 1

:: Behavior ::

_____ , used in psychology, education, and communication, holds that portions of an individual's knowledge acquisition can be directly related to observing others within the context of social interactions, experiences, and outside media influences. This theory was advanced by Albert Bandura as an extension of his social learning theory. The theory states that when people observe a model performing a behavior and the consequences of that behavior, they remember the sequence of events and use this information to guide subsequent behaviors. Observing a model can also prompt the viewer to engage in behavior they already learned. In other words, people do not learn new behaviors solely by trying them and either succeeding or failing, but rather, the survival of humanity is dependent upon the replication of the actions of others. Depending on whether people are rewarded or punished for their behavior and the outcome of the behavior, the observer may choose to replicate behavior modeled. Media provides models for a vast array of people in many different environmental settings.

Exam Probability: **Low**

12. *Answer choices:*

(see index for correct answer)

- a. Crying
- b. Statary
- c. Challenging behaviour
- d. Jeitinho

Guidance: level 1

:: Educational psychology research methods ::

In statistics, an _____ is a quantitative measure of the magnitude of a phenomenon. Examples of _____ s are the correlation between two variables, the regression coefficient in a regression, the mean difference, or even the risk with which something happens, such as how many people survive after a heart attack for every one person that does not survive. For most types of _____ , a larger absolute value always indicates a stronger effect, with the main exception being if the _____ is an odds ratio. _____ s complement statistical hypothesis testing, and play an important role in power analyses, sample size planning, and in meta-analyses. They are the first item in the MAGIC criteria for evaluating the strength of a statistical claim.Especially in meta-analysis, where the purpose is to combine multiple _____ s, the standard error of the _____ is of critical importance. The S.E. of the _____ is used to weigh _____ s when combining studies, so that large studies are considered more important than small studies in the analysis. The S.E. of the _____ is calculated differently for each type of _____ , but generally only requires knowing the study's sample size , or the number of observations in each group .

Exam Probability: **High**

13. *Answer choices:*

(see index for correct answer)

- a. Likert scale
- b. Grounded theory
- c. Reliability
- d. Effect size

Guidance: level 1

:: Educational psychology ::

_____ is a mental disorder of the neurodevelopmental type. It is characterized by difficulty paying attention, excessive activity, and behavior without regards to consequences which is not appropriate for a person's age. There are also often problems with regulation of emotions. The symptoms appear before a person is twelve years old, are present for more than six months, and cause problems in at least two settings . In children, problems paying attention may result in poor school performance. Additionally there is an association with other mental disorders and substance misuse. Although it causes impairment, particularly in modern society, many people with ADHD can have sustained attention for tasks they find interesting or rewarding .

Exam Probability: **High**

14. *Answer choices:*

(see index for correct answer)

- a. Latent learning
- b. Meta-analysis
- c. Activity theory
- d. Attention deficit hyperactivity disorder

Guidance: level 1

:: Stage theories ::

Erikson's stages of _____ , as articulated in the second half of the 20th century by Erik Erikson in collaboration with Joan Erikson, is a comprehensive psychoanalytic theory that identifies a series of eight stages that a healthy developing individual should pass through from infancy to late adulthood.

Exam Probability: **High**

15. *Answer choices:*
(see index for correct answer)

- a. Psychosocial development
- b. stages of change
- c. Erikson's stages of psychosocial development
- d. Loevinger's stages of ego development

Guidance: level 1

:: Knowledge engineering ::

In information science a _____ is an abstract simplified view of some selected part of the world, containing the objects, concepts, and other entities that are presumed of interest for some particular purpose and the relationships between them. An explicit specification of a _____ is an ontology, and it may occur that a _____ can be realized by several distinct ontologies. An ontological commitment in describing ontological comparisons is taken to refer to that subset of elements of an ontology shared with all the others. "An ontology is language-dependent", its objects and interrelations described within the language it uses, while a _____ is always the same, more general, its concepts existing "independently of the language used to describe it". The relation between these terms is shown in the figure to the right.

Exam Probability: **Low**

16. *Answer choices:*

(see index for correct answer)

- a. POSC Caesar
- b. Conceptualization
- c. Knowledge engineer
- d. International Journal of Software Engineering and Knowledge Engineering

Guidance: level 1

:: Motivation ::

_____ is an individual's subjective evaluation of their own worth. _____ encompasses beliefs about oneself as well as emotional states, such as triumph, despair, pride, and shame. Smith and Mackie defined it by saying "The self-concept is what we think about the self; _____ , is the positive or negative evaluations of the self, as in how we feel about it."

Exam Probability: **Medium**

17. *Answer choices:*

(see index for correct answer)

- a. Double Demotivation
- b. Employee motivation
- c. Self-esteem
- d. Keep Calm and Carry On

Guidance: level 1

:: Educational psychology ::

_____ has been defined in many ways, including: the capacity for logic, understanding, self-awareness, learning, emotional knowledge, reasoning, planning, creativity, critical thinking, and problem solving. More generally, it can be described as the ability to perceive or infer information, and to retain it as knowledge to be applied towards adaptive behaviors within an environment or context.

Exam Probability: **Low**

18. *Answer choices:*

(see index for correct answer)

- a. Intelligence
- b. Pedagogy
- c. Instructional scaffolding
- d. Opportunistic collaboration

Guidance: level 1

:: Neurological disorders in children ::

The diagnostic category _____ s , as opposed to specific developmental disorders , is a group of five disorders characterized by delays in the development of multiple basic functions including socialization and communication. The _____ s are: All autism spectrum disorders and Rett syndrome.

Exam Probability: **High**

19. *Answer choices:*

(see index for correct answer)

- a. Canavan disease
- b. Idiopathic childhood occipital epilepsy of Gastaut
- c. Panayiotopoulos syndrome
- d. Krabbe disease

Guidance: level 1

:: Research methods ::

An _____ is a conversation where questions are asked and answers are given. In common parlance, the word "_____" refers to a one-on-one conversation between an _____ er and an _____ ee. The _____ er asks questions to which the _____ ee responds, usually so information may be transferred from _____ ee to _____ er. Sometimes, information can be transferred in both directions. It is a communication, unlike a speech, which produces a one-way flow of information.

Exam Probability: **Medium**

20. *Answer choices:*

(see index for correct answer)

- a. Non-response bias
- b. Mystery shopping
- c. Interview
- d. Longitudinal study

Guidance: level 1

:: Brain ::

The _____ is an organ that serves as the center of the nervous system in all vertebrate and most invertebrate animals. The _____ is located in the head, usually close to the sensory organs for senses such as vision. The _____ is the most complex organ in a vertebrate's body. In a human, the cerebral cortex contains approximately 14–16 billion neurons, and the estimated number of neurons in the cerebellum is 55–70 billion. Each neuron is connected by synapses to several thousand other neurons. These neurons communicate with one another by means of long protoplasmic fibers called axons, which carry trains of signal pulses called action potentials to distant parts of the _____ or body targeting specific recipient cells.

Exam Probability: **High**

21. *Answer choices:*

(see index for correct answer)

- a. Tegmentum
- b. Brachium of inferior colliculus
- c. Orbitofrontal cortex
- d. Wilder Brain Collection

Guidance: level 1

:: Metalogic ::

_____ is a fundamental concept in logic, which describes the relationship between statements that hold true when one statement logically follows from one or more statements. A valid logical argument is one in which the conclusion is entailed by the premises, because the conclusion is the consequence of the premises. The philosophical analysis of _____ involves the questions: In what sense does a conclusion follow from its premises and What does it mean for a conclusion to be a consequence of premises All of philosophical logic is meant to provide accounts of the nature of _____ and the nature of logical truth.

Exam Probability: **High**

22. *Answer choices:*

(see index for correct answer)

- a. Proof theory
- b. Well-formed formula
- c. Metalogic
- d. Metacommunication

Guidance: level 1

:: Cognitive architecture ::

Transition Region and Coronal Explorer was a NASA heliophysics and solar observatory designed to investigate the connections between fine-scale magnetic fields and the associated plasma structures on the Sun by providing high resolution images and observation of the solar photosphere, the transition region, and the corona. A main focus of the _____ instrument is the fine structure of coronal loops low in the solar atmosphere. _____ is the fourth spacecraft in the Small Explorer program, launched on April 2, 1998, and obtained its last science image in 2010.

Exam Probability: **Medium**

23. *Answer choices:*

(see index for correct answer)

- a. LIDA
- b. Parallel terraced scan
- c. ACT-R
- d. TRACE

Guidance: level 1

:: Educational psychology ::

An _____ is a component of a competence to do a certain kind of work at a certain level. Outstanding _____ can be considered "talent". An _____ may be physical or mental. _____ is inborn potential to do certain kinds of work whether developed or undeveloped. Ability is developed knowledge, understanding, learned or acquired abilities or attitude. The innate nature of _____ is in contrast to skills and achievement, which represent knowledge or ability that is gained through learning.

Exam Probability: **High**

24. *Answer choices:*
(see index for correct answer)

- a. Distributed scaffolding
- b. Aptitude
- c. Norm-referenced test
- d. Project-based learning

Guidance: level 1

:: Educational psychology ::

_____, learning disorder or learning difficulty is a condition in the brain that causes difficulties comprehending or processing information and can be caused by several different factors. Given the "difficulty learning in a typical manner", this does not exclude the ability to learn in a different manner. Therefore, some people can be more accurately described as having a "learning difference", thus avoiding any misconception of being disabled with a lack of ability to learn and possible negative stereotyping. In the United Kingdom, the term "_____" generally refers to an intellectual disability, while difficulties such as dyslexia and dyspraxia are usually referred to as "learning difficulties".

Exam Probability: **High**

25. *Answer choices:*

(see index for correct answer)

- a. Thesis circle
- b. Standards for Educational and Psychological Testing
- c. Collaborative learning
- d. Learning disability

Guidance: level 1

:: Educational psychology ::

In education, _____ is an approach to academic intervention used in the United States to provide early, systematic, and appropriately intensive assistance to children who are at risk for or already underperforming as compared to appropriate grade- or age-level standards. RTI seeks to promote academic success through universal screening, early intervention, frequent progress monitoring, and increasingly intensive research-based instruction or interventions for children who continue to have difficulty. RTI is a multileveled approach for aiding students that is adjusted and modified as needed if they are failing.

Exam Probability: **Low**

26. *Answer choices:*
(see index for correct answer)

- a. Response to intervention
- b. Instructional design
- c. Active learning
- d. Dyslexia

Guidance: level 1

:: Sampling techniques ::

In statistics, _____ is a method of sampling from a population which can be partitioned into subpopulations.

Exam Probability: **Medium**

27. Answer choices:

(see index for correct answer)

- a. Stratified sampling
- b. Quota sampling
- c. Distance sampling
- d. Nonprobability sampling

Guidance: level 1

:: Research methods ::

_____, field studies, or fieldwork is the collection of raw data outside a laboratory, library, or workplace setting. The approaches and methods used in _____ vary across disciplines. For example, biologists who conduct _____ may simply observe animals interacting with their environments, whereas social scientists conducting _____ may interview or observe people in their natural environments to learn their languages, folklore, and social structures.

Exam Probability: **High**

28. Answer choices:

(see index for correct answer)

- a. Field research
- b. Implementation research
- c. Unobtrusive research

- d. Online research community

Guidance: level 1

:: Behavior ::

_____ refers to behavior that enables a person to get along in his or her environment with greatest success and least conflict with others. This is a term used in the areas of psychology and special education. _____ relates to every day skills or tasks that the average person is able to complete, similar to the term life skills.

Exam Probability: **Low**

29. *Answer choices:*
(see index for correct answer)

- a. Adaptive behavior
- b. Model of hierarchical complexity
- c. Horse behavior
- d. Crying

Guidance: level 1

:: Dispositional beliefs ::

_____ es can be learned implicitly within cultural contexts. People may develop _____ es toward or against an individual, an ethnic group, a sexual or gender identity, a nation, a religion, a social class, a political party, theoretical paradigms and ideologies within academic domains, or a species. _____ ed means one-sided, lacking a neutral viewpoint, or not having an open mind. _____ can come in many forms and is related to prejudice and intuition.

Exam Probability: **Low**

30. *Answer choices:*
(see index for correct answer)

- a. Graphocentrism
- b. Exclusivism
- c. Denialism
- d. Bias

Guidance: level 1

:: Death customs ::

A _____ is an inert substance or treatment which is not designed to have a therapeutic value. Common _____ s include inert tablets, inert injections, sham surgery, and other procedures.

Exam Probability: **Medium**

31. *Answer choices:*

(see index for correct answer)

- a. Archimime
- b. Space burial
- c. Military rites
- d. Placebo

Guidance: level 1

:: Statistical terminology ::

In mathematical modeling, statistical modeling and experimental sciences, the values of _____ s depend on the values of in _____ s. The _____ s represent the output or outcome whose variation is being studied. The in _____ s, also known in a statistical context as regressors, represent inputs or causes, that is, potential reasons for variation. In an experiment, any variable that the experimenter manipulates can be called an in _____ . Models and experiments test the effects that the in _____ s have on the _____ s. Sometimes, even if their influence is not of direct interest, in _____ s may be included for other reasons, such as to account for their potential confounding effect.

Exam Probability: **Medium**

32. *Answer choices:*

(see index for correct answer)

- a. Independent variable

- b. Floor effect
- c. Dependent variable
- d. marginal distribution

Guidance: level 1

:: Social information processing ::

_____ is a multilingual online encyclopedia with exclusively free content and no ads , based on open collaboration through a model of content editing using web-based applications such as web browsers, called wiki. It is the largest and most popular general reference work on the World Wide Web, and is one of the most popular websites by Alexa rank as of April 2019. It is owned and supported by the Wikimedia Foundation, a non-profit organization that operates on money it receives from donors to remain ad-free.

Exam Probability: **Medium**

33. *Answer choices:*

(see index for correct answer)

- a. Wikipedia
- b. StixCamp
- c. Online community
- d. Enterprise bookmarking

Guidance: level 1

:: Self ::

_____ is a macro theory of human motivation and personality that concerns people's inherent growth tendencies and innate psychological needs. It is concerned with the motivation behind choices people make without external influence and interference. SDT focuses on the degree to which an individual's behavior is self-motivated and self-determined.

Exam Probability: **Medium**

34. *Answer choices:*

(see index for correct answer)

- a. Self-disclosure
- b. Subjective character of experience
- c. Self-determination theory
- d. Self-perception theory

Guidance: level 1

:: Speech and language pathology ::

_____ is an umbrella term that encompasses the communication methods used to supplement or replace speech or writing for those with impairments in the production or comprehension of spoken or written language. AAC is used by those with a wide range of speech and language impairments, including congenital impairments such as cerebral palsy, intellectual impairment and autism, and acquired conditions such as amyotrophic lateral sclerosis and Parkinson's disease. AAC can be a permanent addition to a person's communication or a temporary aid.

Exam Probability: **Medium**

35. *Answer choices:*

(see index for correct answer)

- a. National Center for Voice and Speech
- b. Speech and language disability
- c. Telepractice
- d. American Institute for Stuttering

Guidance: level 1

:: Cognitive science ::

_____, a theory of cognition, was hypothesized by Allan Paivio of the University of Western Ontario in 1971. In developing this theory, Paivio used the idea that the formation of mental images aids in learning. According to Paivio, there are two ways a person could expand on learned material: verbal associations and visual imagery. _____ postulates that both visual and verbal information is used to represent information. Visual and verbal information are processed differently and along distinct channels in the human mind, creating separate representations for information processed in each channel. The mental codes corresponding to these representations are used to organize incoming information that can be acted upon, stored, and retrieved for subsequent use. Both visual and verbal codes can be used when recalling information. For example, say a person has stored the stimulus concept "dog" as both the word `dog` and as the image of a dog. When asked to recall the stimulus, the person can retrieve either the word or the image individually, or both simultaneously. If the word is recalled, the image of the dog is not lost and can still be retrieved at a later point in time. The ability to code a stimulus two different ways increases the chance of remembering that item compared to if the stimulus was only coded one way.

Exam Probability: **Low**

36. *Answer choices:*

(see index for correct answer)

- a. Cognitive specialization
- b. Biolinguistics
- c. Dual-coding theory
- d. Psychotechnology

Guidance: level 1

:: Communication disorders ::

Hearing loss, also known as hearing impairment, is a partial or total inability to hear. A deaf person has little to no hearing. Hearing loss may occur in one or both ears. In children, hearing problems can affect the ability to learn spoken language and in adults it can create difficulties with social interaction and at work. In some people, particularly older people, hearing loss can result in loneliness. Hearing loss can be temporary or permanent.

Exam Probability: **Medium**

37. *Answer choices:*
(see index for correct answer)

- a. Multisystem developmental disorder
- b. Audiometry
- c. National Stuttering Association
- d. Deafness

Guidance: level 1

:: Educational psychology ::

One's _____ is a collection of beliefs about oneself. Generally, _____ embodies the answer to "Who am I".

Exam Probability: **Medium**

38. Answer choices:

(see index for correct answer)

- a. Autodidacticism
- b. Self-concept
- c. Standards for Educational and Psychological Testing
- d. Storyline method

Guidance: level 1

:: Heuristics ::

The _____ is used when making judgments about the probability of an event under uncertainty. It is one of a group of heuristics proposed by psychologists Amos Tversky and Daniel Kahneman in the early 1970s. Heuristics are described as "judgmental shortcuts that generally get us where we need to go – and quickly – but at the cost of occasionally sending us off course." Heuristics are useful because they use effort-reduction and simplification in decision-making.

Exam Probability: **Medium**

39. Answer choices:

(see index for correct answer)

- a. Scientific enterprise
- b. Meta-optimization
- c. Representativeness heuristic

- d. Contagion heuristic

Guidance: level 1

:: Learning ::

One suggested reason for the primacy effect is that the initial items presented are most effectively stored in dormant memory because of the greater amount of processing devoted to them. The primacy effect is reduced when items are presented quickly and is enhanced when presented slowly. Longer presentation lists have been found to reduce the primacy effect.

Exam Probability: **Low**

40. *Answer choices:*
(see index for correct answer)

- a. Serial position effect
- b. Information ladder
- c. Time-Place learning
- d. Learning enterprises

Guidance: level 1

:: Special education ::

The _____, also called the IEP, is a document that is developed for each public school child who needs special education. The IEP is created through a team effort, reviewed periodically. In the United States, this program is known as an _____, and similarly in Canada it is referred to as an Individualized Education Plan or a Special Education Plan. In the United Kingdom, an equivalent document is called an Individual Education System. In Saudi Arabia, the document is known as an Individual Education Program.

Exam Probability: **Medium**

41. *Answer choices:*

(see index for correct answer)

- a. Conductive education
- b. National Instructional Materials Accessibility Standard
- c. Individualized Education Program
- d. Peer-mediated instruction

Guidance: level 1

:: Anxiety ::

_____ is a combination of physiological over-arousal, tension and somatic symptoms, along with worry, dread, fear of failure, and catastrophizing, that occur before or during test situations. It is a physiological condition in which people experience extreme stress, anxiety, and discomfort during and/or before taking a test. This anxiety creates significant barriers to learning and performance. Research suggests that high levels of emotional distress have a direct correlation to reduced academic performance and higher overall student drop-out rates. _____ can have broader consequences, negatively affecting a student's social, emotional and behavioural development, as well as their feelings about themselves and school.

Exam Probability: **Low**

42. *Answer choices:*

(see index for correct answer)

- a. schizotypal
- b. Test anxiety
- c. The Worry Trap
- d. Somatic anxiety

Guidance: level 1

:: Regression analysis ::

In statistical modeling, _____ is a set of statistical processes for estimating the relationships among variables. It includes many techniques for modeling and analyzing several variables, when the focus is on the relationship between a dependent variable and one or more independent variables . More specifically, _____ helps one understand how the typical value of the dependent variable changes when any one of the independent variables is varied, while the other independent variables are held fixed.

Exam Probability: **Low**

43. *Answer choices:*
(see index for correct answer)

- a. Regression analysis
- b. Bayesian multivariate linear regression
- c. Coefficient of determination
- d. Hat matrix

Guidance: level 1

:: Philosophy of life ::

_____ or moral philosophy is a branch of philosophy that involves systematizing, defending, and recommending concepts of right and wrong conduct. The field of _____ , along with aesthetics, concerns matters of value, and thus comprises the branch of philosophy called axiology.

Exam Probability: **Low**

44. Answer choices:

(see index for correct answer)

- a. Being
- b. Atheist existentialism
- c. Ethics
- d. Intellectualism

Guidance: level 1

:: Language acquisition ::

_____ is a process starting early in human life. Infants start without knowing a language, yet by 10 months, babies can distinguish speech sounds and engage in babbling. Some research has shown that the earliest learning begins in utero when the fetus starts to recognize the sounds and speech patterns of its mother's voice and differentiate them from other sounds after birth.

Exam Probability: **Low**

45. Answer choices:

(see index for correct answer)

- a. Non-native pronunciations of English
- b. Semanticity
- c. Language development
- d. Human Speechome Project

Guidance: level 1

:: Educational psychology ::

_____ is a technique of inquiry-based learning and is considered a constructivist based approach to education. It is also referred to as problem-based learning, experiential learning and 21st century learning. It is supported by the work of learning theorists and psychologists Jean Piaget, Jerome Bruner, and Seymour Papert.

Exam Probability: **Medium**

46. *Answer choices:*

(see index for correct answer)

- a. Discovery learning
- b. Legitimate peripheral participation
- c. Pedagogy
- d. Evolutionary educational psychology

Guidance: level 1

:: Educational psychology research methods ::

_____ is a systematic methodology in the social sciences involving the construction of theories through methodical gathering and analysis of data. _____ is a research methodology which operates inductively, in contrast to the hypothetico-deductive approach. A study using _____ is likely to begin with a question, or even just with the collection of qualitative data. As researchers review the data collected, repeated ideas, concepts or elements become apparent, and are tagged with codes, which have been extracted from the data. As more data is collected, and re-reviewed, codes can be grouped into concepts, and then into categories. These categories may become the basis for new theory. Thus, _____ is quite different from the traditional model of research, where the researcher chooses an existing theoretical framework, and only then collects data to show how the theory does or does not apply to the phenomenon under study.

Exam Probability: **Low**

47. *Answer choices:*

(see index for correct answer)

- a. Visual analogue scale
- b. Reliability
- c. Likert scale
- d. Grounded theory

Guidance: level 1

:: Survey methodology ::

A _____ is the procedure of systematically acquiring and recording information about the members of a given population. The term is used mostly in connection with national population and housing _____ es; other common _____ es include agriculture, business, and traffic _____ es. The United Nations defines the essential features of population and housing _____ es as "individual enumeration, universality within a defined territory, simultaneity and defined periodicity", and recommends that population _____ es be taken at least every 10 years. United Nations recommendations also cover _____ topics to be collected, official definitions, classifications and other useful information to co-ordinate international practice.

Exam Probability: **Medium**

48. *Answer choices:*

(see index for correct answer)

- a. Allegiance
- b. Political forecasting
- c. Computer-assisted survey information collection
- d. Census

Guidance: level 1

:: Human behavior ::

_____ is the reason for people's actions, willingness and goals. _____ is derived from the word motive in the English language which is defined as a need that requires satisfaction. These needs could also be wants or desires that are acquired through influence of culture, society, lifestyle, etc. or generally innate. _____ is one's direction to behaviour, or what causes a person to want to repeat a behaviour, a set of force that acts behind the motives. An individual's _____ may be inspired by others or events or it may come from within the individual. _____ has been considered as one of the most important reasons that inspires a person to move forward in life. _____ results from the interaction of both conscious and unconscious factors. Mastering _____ to allow sustained and deliberate practice is central to high levels of achievement e.g. in the worlds of elite sport, medicine or music.

Exam Probability: **Low**

49. *Answer choices:*

(see index for correct answer)

- a. Infomania
- b. Critical-Creative Thinking and Behavioral Research Laboratory
- c. Ritualization
- d. Human Behavior and Evolution Society

Guidance: level 1

:: Bilingual education ::

_____ involves teaching academic content in two languages, in a native and secondary language with varying amounts of each language used in accordance with the program model. _____ refers to the utilization of two languages as means of instruction for students and considered part of or the entire school curriculum.

Exam Probability: **High**

50. *Answer choices:*

(see index for correct answer)

- a. Bilingual education
- b. National Association for Bilingual Education
- c. Intercultural bilingual education
- d. Content and language integrated learning

Guidance: level 1

:: Signal transduction ::

A _____ is any member of a class of signaling molecules produced by glands in multicellular organisms that are transported by the circulatory system to target distant organs to regulate physiology and behavior. _____ s have diverse chemical structures, mainly of three classes: eicosanoids, steroids, and amino acid/protein derivatives . The glands that secrete _____ s comprise the endocrine signaling system. The term _____ is sometimes extended to include chemicals produced by cells that affect the same cell or nearby cells .

Exam Probability: **Low**

51. *Answer choices:*

(see index for correct answer)

- a. Inositol trisphosphate
- b. Hormone
- c. Tryptophan-rich sensory protein
- d. STAT1

Guidance: level 1

:: Error ::

In statistics, _____ is incurred when the statistical characteristics of a population are estimated from a subset, or sample, of that population. Since the sample does not include all members of the population, statistics on the sample, such as means and quartiles, generally differ from the characteristics of the entire population, which are known as parameters. For example, if one measures the height of a thousand individuals from a country of one million, the average height of the thousand is typically not the same as the average height of all one million people in the country. Since sampling is typically done to determine the characteristics of a whole population, the difference between the sample and population values is considered an error. Exact measurement of _____ is generally not feasible since the true population values are unknown.

Exam Probability: **Medium**

52. *Answer choices:*

(see index for correct answer)

- a. Sampling error
- b. Dead letter mail
- c. Error card
- d. Blooper

Guidance: level 1

:: Teaching ::

_____ and assessment, also known as differentiated learning or, in education, simply, differentiation, is a framework or philosophy for effective teaching that involves providing all students within their diverse classroom community of learners a range of different avenues for understanding new information in terms of: acquiring content; processing, constructing, or making sense of ideas; and developing teaching materials and assessment measures so that all students within a classroom can learn effectively, regardless of differences in ability. Students vary in culture, socioeconomic status, language, gender, motivation, ability/disability, personal interests and more, and teachers must be aware of these varieties as they plan curriculum. By considering varied learning needs, teachers can develop personalized instruction so that all children in the classroom can learn effectively. Differentiated classrooms have also been described as ones that respond to student variety in readiness levels, interests and learning profiles. It is a classroom that includes all students and can be successful. To do this, a teacher sets different expectations for task completion for students based upon their individual needs.

Exam Probability: **Medium**

53. Answer choices:

(see index for correct answer)

- a. Tutorial system
- b. Alternative teacher certification
- c. Teaching as a Subversive Activity
- d. Instructional simulation

Guidance: level 1

:: Educational psychology ::

_____ is the process whereby concepts and relationships between them change over the course of an individual person's lifetime or over the course of history. Research in four different fields – cognitive psychology, cognitive developmental psychology, science education, and history and philosophy of science - has sought to understand this process. Indeed, the convergence of these four fields, in their effort to understand how concepts change in content and organization, has led to the emergence of an interdisciplinary sub-field in its own right. This sub-field is referred to as " _____ " research.

Exam Probability: **Low**

54. Answer choices:

(see index for correct answer)

- a. Inquiry education
- b. Test

- c. Attention deficit hyperactivity disorder
- d. Learning by teaching

Guidance: level 1

:: Giftedness ::

_____ is a condition in which someone with significant mental disabilities demonstrates certain abilities far in excess of average. The skills at which savants excel are generally related to memory. This may include rapid calculation, artistic ability, map making, or musical ability. Usually just one special skill is present.

Exam Probability: **Medium**

55. *Answer choices:*

(see index for correct answer)

- a. Illui
- b. Marilyn vos Savant
- c. Eidetic memory
- d. Twice exceptional

Guidance: level 1

:: Fiction ::

_____, in a literary text, is an author's use of vivid and descriptive language to add depth to their work. It appeals to human senses to deepen the reader's understanding of the work. Powerful forms of _____ engage all of the senses.

Exam Probability: **Low**

56. *Answer choices:*

(see index for correct answer)

- a. Authoritarian literature
- b. Plot device
- c. Stream of unconsciousness
- d. Imagery

Guidance: level 1

:: Problem solving ::

_____ is a method of reasoning in which the premises are viewed as supplying some evidence for the truth of the conclusion; this is in contrast to deductive reasoning. While the conclusion of a deductive argument is certain, the truth of the conclusion of an inductive argument may be probable, based upon the evidence given.

Exam Probability: **Low**

57. Answer choices:

(see index for correct answer)

- a. How to Solve it by Computer
- b. Brainstorming
- c. Method of focal objects
- d. Inductive reasoning

Guidance: level 1

:: Applied learning ::

_____ is the measurement of "intellectual accomplishments that are worthwhile, significant, and meaningful," as contrasted to multiple choice standardized tests. _____ can be devised by the teacher, or in collaboration with the student by engaging student voice. When applying _____ to student learning and achievement, a teacher applies criteria related to "construction of knowledge, disciplined inquiry, and the value of achievement beyond the school."

Exam Probability: **Low**

58. Answer choices:

(see index for correct answer)

- a. Web-based Inquiry Science Environment
- b. Authentic assessment
- c. Technology education

- d. Firsthand learning

Guidance: level 1

:: Deductive reasoning ::

_____ is the process of using data analysis to deduce properties of an underlying probability distribution. Inferential statistical analysis infers properties of a population, for example by testing hypotheses and deriving estimates. It is assumed that the observed data set is sampled from a larger population.

Exam Probability: **High**

59. *Answer choices:*

(see index for correct answer)

- a. Statistical inference
- b. Good and necessary consequence
- c. A priori probability
- d. Natural deduction

Guidance: level 1

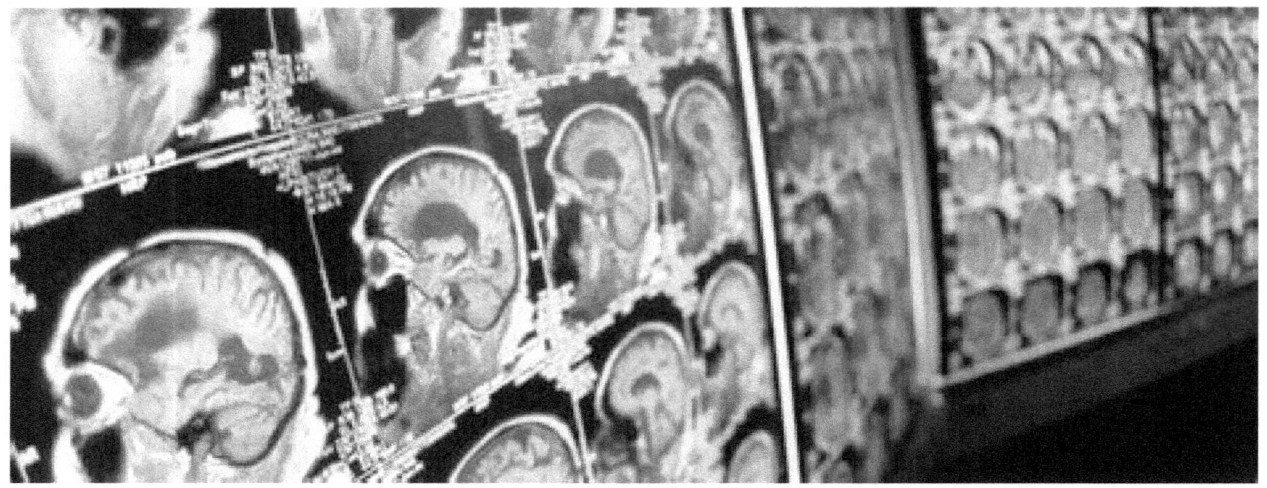

Biopsychology

Behavioral neuroscience, also known as biological psychology, biopsychology, or psychobiology is the application of the principles of biology to the study of physiological, genetic, and developmental mechanisms of behavior in humans and other animals.

The distinguishing characteristic of a behavioral neuroscience experiment is that either the independent variable of the experiment is biological, or some dependent variable is biological. In other words, the nervous system of the organism under study is permanently or temporarily altered, or some aspect of the nervous system is measured (usually to be related to a behavioral variable).

:: Agnosia ::

_____ is an impairment in recognition of visually presented objects. It is not due to a deficit in vision, language, memory, or intellect. While cortical blindness results from lesions to primary visual cortex, _____ is often due to damage to more anterior cortex such as the posterior occipital and/or temporal lobe in the brain.[2] There are two types of _____ : apperceptive agnosia and associative agnosia.

Exam Probability: **Low**

1. *Answer choices:*
(see index for correct answer)

- a. Autotopagnosia
- b. Integrative agnosia
- c. Amusia
- d. Visual agnosia

Guidance: level 1

:: Reflexes ::

A _____ , or _____ action, is an involuntary and nearly instantaneous movement in response to a stimulus. A _____ is made possible by neural pathways called _____ arcs which can act on an impulse before that impulse reaches the brain. The _____ is then an automatic response to a stimulus that does not receive or need conscious thought.

Exam Probability: **Low**

2. Answer choices:

(see index for correct answer)

- a. Reflex
- b. Bulbocavernosus reflex
- c. Palmomental reflex
- d. Placing reflexes

Guidance: level 1

:: Computational neuroscience ::

A _____ is a small membranous protrusion from a neuron's dendrite that typically receives input from a single axon at the synapse. _____ s serve as a storage site for synaptic strength and help transmit electrical signals to the neuron's cell body. Most spines have a bulbous head , and a thin neck that connects the head of the spine to the shaft of the dendrite. The dendrites of a single neuron can contain hundreds to thousands of spines. In addition to spines providing an anatomical substrate for memory storage and synaptic transmission, they may also serve to increase the number of possible contacts between neurons.

Exam Probability: **Medium**

3. Answer choices:

(see index for correct answer)

- a. Laurent Itti
- b. Dendritic spine

- c. Brain-reading
- d. Pulse computation

Guidance: level 1

:: Reflexes ::

_____ is the involuntary, forceful expulsion of the contents of one's stomach through the mouth and sometimes the nose.

Exam Probability: **High**

4. *Answer choices:*

(see index for correct answer)

- a. Enterogastric reflex
- b. Vomiting
- c. Reflex
- d. Arthrokinetic reflex

Guidance: level 1

:: Electroencephalography ::

_____, often referred to as deep sleep, consists of stage three of non-rapid eye movement sleep. Initially, SWS consisted of both Stage 3, which has 20-50 percent delta wave activity, and Stage 4, which has more than 50 percent delta wave activity. However, as of 2008, the American Academy of Sleep Medicine has discontinued the use of Stage four as a separate stage. Thus, the two stages are now combined as "Stage three" or N3. An epoch which consists of 20% or more slow-wave sleep is now considered to be stage three.

Exam Probability: **Medium**

5. *Answer choices:*

(see index for correct answer)

- a. Joseph Kubanek
- b. Lateralized readiness potential
- c. Somatosensory evoked potential
- d. EEGLAB

Guidance: level 1

:: Neuroanatomy ::

The _____ is the region of the cerebral cortex involved in the planning, control, and execution of voluntary movements. Classically the _____ is an area of the frontal lobe located in the posterior precentral gyrus immediately anterior to the central sulcus.

Exam Probability: **Medium**

6. *Answer choices:*

(see index for correct answer)

- a. Lamina pyramidalis interna
- b. Proisocortex
- c. Superior longitudinal fasciculus
- d. Amygdalohippocampal area

Guidance: level 1

:: Memory ::

The _____, also known as the paleomammalian cortex, is a set of brain structures located on both sides of the thalamus, immediately beneath the medial temporal lobe of the cerebrum primarily in the midbrain.

Exam Probability: **High**

7. *Answer choices:*

(see index for correct answer)

- a. Metamemory
- b. MegaMemory
- c. Limbic system
- d. Spatial memory

Guidance: level 1

:: Attention ::

_____ is the state of active attention by high sensory awareness such as being watchful and prompt to meet danger or emergency, or being quick to perceive and act. It is related to psychology as well as to physiology. A lack of _____ is a symptom of a number of conditions, including narcolepsy, attention deficit disorder, chronic fatigue syndrome, depression, Addison's disease, or sleep deprivation. Pronounced lack of _____ can be graded as an altered level of consciousness. The word is formed from "alert", which comes from the Italian "all`erta"

Exam Probability: **High**

8. *Answer choices:*
(see index for correct answer)

- a. Hyper attention
- b. Alertness
- c. Attentive user interface
- d. The Sensory Enhancement Theory of Object-Based Attention

Guidance: level 1

:: Sleep ::

A _____ is a natural, internal process that regulates the sleep-wake cycle and repeats roughly every 24 hours. It can refer to any biological process that displays an endogenous, entrainable oscillation of about 24 hours. These 24-hour rhythms are driven by a circadian clock, and they have been widely observed in plants, animals, fungi, and cyanobacteria.

Exam Probability: **Medium**

9. *Answer choices:*

(see index for correct answer)

- a. Circadian rhythm
- b. Start School Later movement
- c. Sleep diary
- d. Bedtime

Guidance: level 1

:: Ear ::

The _____ is a bed of sensory cells in the inner ear. It translates head movements into neural impulses for the brain to interpret. The _____ detects linear accelerations and head tilts in the vertical plane. When the head moves vertically, the sensory cells of the _____ are disturbed and the neurons connected to them begin transmitting impulses to the brain. These impulses travel along the vestibular portion of the eighth cranial nerve to the vestibular nuclei in the brainstem.

Exam Probability: **Medium**

10. *Answer choices:*

(see index for correct answer)

- a. Prominent ear
- b. Earwax
- c. Perilymphatic duct
- d. Saccule

Guidance: level 1

:: Human hormones ::

_____ is a peptide hormone produced by beta cells of the pancreatic islets; it is considered to be the main anabolic hormone of the body. It regulates the metabolism of carbohydrates, fats and protein by promoting the absorption of carbohydrates, especially glucose from the blood into liver, fat and skeletal muscle cells. In these tissues the absorbed glucose is converted into either glycogen via glycogenesis or fats via lipogenesis, or, in the case of the liver, into both. Glucose production and secretion by the liver is strongly inhibited by high concentrations of _____ in the blood. Circulating _____ also affects the synthesis of proteins in a wide variety of tissues. It is therefore an anabolic hormone, promoting the conversion of small molecules in the blood into large molecules inside the cells. Low _____ levels in the blood have the opposite effect by promoting widespread catabolism, especially of reserve body fat.

Exam Probability: **High**

11. Answer choices:

(see index for correct answer)

- a. FGF19
- b. Prolactin-releasing hormone
- c. Insulin
- d. Glucagon

Guidance: level 1

:: Phenomenology ::

_____ is the state or quality of awareness or of being aware of an external object or something within oneself. It has been defined variously in terms of sentience, awareness, qualia, subjectivity, the ability to experience or to feel, wakefulness, having a sense of selfhood or soul, the fact that there is something "that it is like" to "have" or "be" it, and the executive control system of the mind. Despite the difficulty in definition, many philosophers believe that there is a broadly shared underlying intuition about what _____ is. As Max Velmans and Susan Schneider wrote in The Blackwell Companion to _____ : "Anything that we are aware of at a given moment forms part of our _____ , making conscious experience at once the most familiar and most mysterious aspect of our lives."

Exam Probability: **High**

12. Answer choices:

(see index for correct answer)

- a. Visual space
- b. Fundamental ontology
- c. Consciousness
- d. Central European Institute of Philosophy

Guidance: level 1

:: Meninges ::

The meninges are the three membranes that envelop the brain and spinal cord. In mammals, the meninges are the dura mater, the arachnoid mater, and the pia mater. Cerebrospinal fluid is located in the _____ between the arachnoid mater and the pia mater. The primary function of the meninges is to protect the central nervous system.

Exam Probability: **High**

13. *Answer choices:*
(see index for correct answer)

- a. Subarachnoid space
- b. Interpeduncular cistern
- c. Arachnoid granulation
- d. Denticulate ligaments

Guidance: level 1

:: Sensory organs ::

The _____ s or semicircular ducts are three semicircular, interconnected tubes located in the innermost part of each ear, the inner ear. The three canals are the horizontal, superior and posterior _____ s.

Exam Probability: **Medium**

14. *Answer choices:*

(see index for correct answer)

- a. Rostral organ
- b. Semicircular canal
- c. Tympanal organ
- d. Pilifer

Guidance: level 1

:: Peripheral nervous system ::

The _____ is one of two components that make up the nervous system of bilateral animals, with the other part being the central nervous system . The PNS consists of the nerves and ganglia outside the brain and spinal cord. The main function of the PNS is to connect the CNS to the limbs and organs, essentially serving as a relay between the brain and spinal cord and the rest of the body. Unlike the CNS, the PNS is not protected by the vertebral column and skull, or by the blood–brain barrier, which leaves it exposed to toxins and mechanical injuries.

Exam Probability: **High**

15. *Answer choices:*

(see index for correct answer)

- a. Peripheral nervous system
- b. Dorsal root ganglion
- c. Spinocervical pathway
- d. Spinal nerve

Guidance: level 1

:: Cerebrum ::

The _____ , or corpus _____ is a nucleus in the subcortical basal ganglia of the forebrain. The _____ is a critical component of the motor and reward systems; receives glutamatergic and dopaminergic inputs from different sources; and serves as the primary input to the rest of the basal ganglia.

Exam Probability: **Low**

16. *Answer choices:*

(see index for correct answer)

- a. Striatum
- b. Central sulcus

- c. Color center
- d. Ventral posterolateral nucleus

Guidance: level 1

:: Ear ::

_____ is the fluid contained in the membranous labyrinth of the inner ear. The major cation in _____ is potassium, with the values of sodium and potassium concentration in the _____ being 0.91 mM and 154 mM, respectively. It is also called Scarpa's fluid, after Antonio Scarpa.

Exam Probability: **High**

17. *Answer choices:*

(see index for correct answer)

- a. Oblique muscle of auricle
- b. Incudomalleolar joint
- c. Earwax
- d. Ear instillation

Guidance: level 1

:: Neurons ::

An _____ is a broad class of neurons found in the human body. _____s create neural circuits, enabling communication between sensory or motor neurons and the central nervous system. They have been found to function in reflexes, neuronal oscillations, and neurogenesis in the adult mammalian brain.

Exam Probability: **Medium**

18. *Answer choices:*

(see index for correct answer)

- a. Martinotti cell
- b. Golgi II
- c. Interneuron
- d. Cone cell

Guidance: level 1

:: Cerebrum ::

The _____ is a round structure located at the base of the forebrain. The _____ and caudate nucleus together form the dorsal striatum. It is also one of the structures that comprise the basal ganglia. Through various pathways, the _____ is connected to the substantia nigra, the globus pallidus, the claustrum, and the thalamus, in addition to many regions of the cerebral cortex. A primary function of the _____ is to regulate movements at various stages and influence various types of learning. It employs GABA, acetylcholine, and enkephalin to perform its functions. The _____ also plays a role in degenerative neurological disorders, such as Parkinson's disease.

Exam Probability: **Medium**

19. *Answer choices:*

(see index for correct answer)

- a. Inferior longitudinal fasciculus
- b. Ventral nuclear group
- c. Central sulcus
- d. Putamen

Guidance: level 1

:: Cellular neuroscience ::

In biology, _____ is a change within a cell, during which the cell undergoes a shift in electric charge distribution, resulting in less negative charge inside the cell. _____ is essential to the function of many cells, communication between cells, and the overall physiology of an organism.

Exam Probability: **High**

20. *Answer choices:*

(see index for correct answer)

- a. Afterhyperpolarization
- b. Actin remodeling of neurons
- c. Acclimatisation
- d. Action potential

Guidance: level 1

:: Human physiology ::

_____ is part of the complex biological response of body tissues to harmful stimuli, such as pathogens, damaged cells, or irritants, and is a protective response involving immune cells, blood vessels, and molecular mediators. The function of _____ is to eliminate the initial cause of cell injury, clear out necrotic cells and tissues damaged from the original insult and the inflammatory process, and initiate tissue repair.

Exam Probability: **High**

21. *Answer choices:*

(see index for correct answer)

- a. Composition of the human body
- b. Inflammation

- c. Urine osmolality
- d. Human feces

Guidance: level 1

:: Drinking culture ::

_____ is the act of ingesting water or other liquids into the body through the mouth. Water is required for many physiological processes. Both excessive and inadequate water intake are associated with health problems.

Exam Probability: **High**

22. *Answer choices:*

(see index for correct answer)

- a. My Drunk Kitchen
- b. Drinking
- c. Keg stand
- d. Alcohol enema

Guidance: level 1

:: Anxiogenics ::

_____ is a selective GABAA antagonist administered via injection or intranasally. Therapeutically, it acts as both an antagonist and antidote to benzodiazepines, through competitive inhibition.

Exam Probability: **Medium**

23. *Answer choices:*

(see index for correct answer)

- a. Flumazenil
- b. ZK-93426
- c. Yohimbine
- d. FG-7142

Guidance: level 1

:: Meninges ::

The _____ is a plexus of cells that produces the cerebrospinal fluid in the ventricles of the brain. The _____ consists of modified ependymal cells.

Exam Probability: **High**

24. *Answer choices:*

(see index for correct answer)

- a. Leptomeninges
- b. Arachnoid trabeculae
- c. Cisterna magna
- d. Chiasmatic cistern

Guidance: level 1

:: Cellular neuroscience ::

In the nervous system, a _____ is a structure that permits a neuron to pass an electrical or chemical signal to another neuron or to the target effector cell.

Exam Probability: **High**

25. *Answer choices:*
(see index for correct answer)

- a. Sholl analysis
- b. Spike directivity
- c. Active zone
- d. Synapse

Guidance: level 1

:: Substance abuse ::

_____ encompasses a spectrum of unhealthy alcohol drinking behaviors, ranging from binge drinking to alcohol dependence.

Exam Probability: **Medium**

26. *Answer choices:*

(see index for correct answer)

- a. Alcohol abuse
- b. Polysubstance dependence
- c. Substance abuse prevention
- d. Inhalant

Guidance: level 1

:: Neurotoxins ::

_____ is a Gram-positive, rod-shaped, anaerobic, spore-forming, motile bacterium with the ability to produce the neurotoxin botulinum.

Exam Probability: **Medium**

27. *Answer choices:*

(see index for correct answer)

- a. Para-Chloroamphetamine

- b. Phoneutria nigriventer toxin-3
- c. Para-Bromoamphetamine
- d. Diisopropyl fluorophosphate

Guidance: level 1

:: Depressogenics ::

_____ is an undecapeptide member of the tachykinin neuropeptide family. It is a neuropeptide, acting as a neurotransmitter and as a neuromodulator. _____ and its closely related neurokinin A are produced from a polyprotein precursor after differential splicing of the preprotachykinin A gene. The deduced amino acid sequence of _____ is as follows.

Exam Probability: **Medium**

28. *Answer choices:*

(see index for correct answer)

- a. Dynorphin
- b. Goserelin
- c. Leuprorelin
- d. Substance P

Guidance: level 1

:: Entheogens ::

3,4-Methylenedioxymethamphetamine, commonly known as ecstasy, is a psychoactive drug primarily used as a recreational drug. The desired effects include altered sensations and increased energy, empathy, and pleasure. When taken by mouth, effects begin after 30–45 minutes and last 3–6 hours.

Exam Probability: **Medium**

29. *Answer choices:*
(see index for correct answer)

- a. MDMA
- b. Psilocybe kumaenorum
- c. Acacia salicina
- d. Psychotria viridis

Guidance: level 1

:: Neuropsychology ::

_____ is when, during waking up or falling asleep, a person is aware but unable to move or speak. During an episode, one may hallucinate, which often results in fear. Episodes generally last less than a couple of minutes. It may occur as a single episode or be recurrent.

Exam Probability: **High**

30. *Answer choices:*

(see index for correct answer)

- a. Mismatch negativity
- b. Sleep paralysis
- c. Language center
- d. Opponent-process theory

Guidance: level 1

:: Circadian rhythm ::

A _____ is any external or environmental cue that entrains or synchronizes an organism's biological rhythms to the Earth's 24-hour light/dark cycle and 12-month cycle.

Exam Probability: **High**

31. *Answer choices:*

(see index for correct answer)

- a. Giant retinal ganglion cells
- b. Zeitgeber
- c. Circaseptan
- d. Franz Halberg

Guidance: level 1

:: Cerebrum ::

The _____ is a relay center in the thalamus for the visual pathway. It receives a major sensory input from the retina. The LGN is the main central connection for the optic nerve to the occipital lobe, particularly the primary visual cortex. In humans, each LGN has six layers of neurons alternating with optic fibers.

Exam Probability: **Low**

32. *Answer choices:*

(see index for correct answer)

- a. Prefrontal cortex
- b. Collateral fissure
- c. Lateral geniculate nucleus
- d. Cortical homunculus

Guidance: level 1

:: Cerebrum ::

The _____ is a part of the brain situated in the medial aspect of the cerebral cortex. The _____ includes the entire cingulate gyrus, which lies immediately above the corpus callosum, and the continuation of this in the cingulate sulcus. The _____ is usually considered part of the limbic lobe.

Exam Probability: **Low**

33. *Answer choices:*

(see index for correct answer)

- a. Leukoaraiosis
- b. Medial longitudinal fissure
- c. Circumventricular organs
- d. Interpeduncular nucleus

Guidance: level 1

:: Cerebral palsy and other paralytic syndromes ::

_____ is a loss of muscle function for one or more muscles. _____ can be accompanied by a loss of feeling in the affected area if there is sensory damage as well as motor. In the United States, roughly 1 in 50 people have been diagnosed with some form of permanent or transient _____. The word comes from the Greek pas, "disabling of the nerves", itself from pa, "beside, by" and s, "making loose". A _____ accompanied by involuntary tremors is usually called "palsy".

Exam Probability: **High**

34. *Answer choices:*

(see index for correct answer)

- a. Tetraplegia
- b. Paraplegia
- c. Cauda equina syndrome
- d. Monoplegia

Guidance: level 1

:: Meninges ::

_____ is a thick membrane made of dense irregular connective tissue that surrounds the brain and spinal cord. It is the outermost of the three layers of membrane called the meninges that protect the central nervous system. The other two meningeal layers are the arachnoid mater and the pia mater. The dura surrounds the brain and the spinal cord and is responsible for keeping in the cerebrospinal fluid. It is derived from neural crest cells.

Exam Probability: **Medium**

35. *Answer choices:*

(see index for correct answer)

- a. Arachnoid trabeculae
- b. Trigeminal cave

- c. Dura mater
- d. Falx cerebri

Guidance: level 1

:: Entheogens ::

Hyoscine, also known as _____ , is a medication used to treat motion sickness and postoperative nausea and vomiting. It is also sometimes used before surgery to decrease saliva. When used by injection, effects begin after about 20 minutes and last for up to 8 hours. It may also be used by mouth and as a skin patch.

Exam Probability: **Medium**

36. *Answer choices:*

(see index for correct answer)

- a. Psilocybe baeocystis
- b. Kykeon
- c. Psilocybe hoogshagenii
- d. Psilocybe caeruleoannulata

Guidance: level 1

:: Meninges ::

_____, often referred to as simply the pia, is the delicate innermost layer of the meninges, the membranes surrounding the brain and spinal cord. _____ is medieval Latin meaning "tender mother". The other two meningeal membranes are the dura mater and the arachnoid mater. Both the pia and arachnoid mater are derivatives of the neural crest while the dura is derived from embryonic mesoderm. The _____ is a thin fibrous tissue that is permeable to water and small solutes. The _____ allows blood vessels to pass through and nourish the brain. The perivascular space between blood vessels and _____ is proposed to be part of a psuedolymphatic system for the brain. When the _____ becomes irritated and inflamed the result is meningitis.

Exam Probability: **Medium**

37. *Answer choices:*

(see index for correct answer)

- a. Trigeminal cave
- b. Meninges
- c. Pia mater
- d. Tentorium cerebelli

Guidance: level 1

:: Cognitive science ::

_____ is the process of thinking about the activities required to achieve a desired goal. It is the first and foremost activity to achieve desired results. It involves the creation and maintenance of a plan, such as psychological aspects that require conceptual skills. There are even a couple of tests to measure someone's capability of _____ well. As such, _____ is a fundamental property of intelligent behavior. An important further meaning, often just called " _____ " is the legal context of permitted building developments.

Exam Probability: **High**

38. *Answer choices:*

(see index for correct answer)

- a. Linguistics
- b. Planning
- c. Category utility
- d. Number form

Guidance: level 1

:: Vision ::

_____ , or indirect vision, is vision as it occurs outside the point of fixation, i.e. away from the center of gaze. The vast majority of the area in the visual field is included in the notion of _____ . "Far peripheral" vision refers to the area at the edges of the visual field, "mid-peripheral" vision refers to medium eccentricities, and "near-peripheral", sometimes referred to as "para-central" vision, exists adjacent to the center of gaze..

Exam Probability: **Medium**

39. *Answer choices:*

(see index for correct answer)

- a. Peripheral vision
- b. Colavita visual dominance effect
- c. Distorted vision
- d. Horopter

Guidance: level 1

:: Emotion ::

_____ is a mental state associated with the nervous system brought on by chemical changes variously associated with thoughts, feelings, behavioural responses, and a degree of pleasure or displeasure. There is currently no scientific consensus on a definition. _____ is often intertwined with mood, temperament, personality, disposition, and motivation.

Exam Probability: **Low**

40. *Answer choices:*

(see index for correct answer)

- a. Group emotion
- b. Emotion

- c. Stoic passions
- d. Voodoo death

Guidance: level 1

:: Memory processes ::

> Explicit memory is one of the two main types of long-term human memory. It is the conscious, intentional recollection of factual information, previous experiences, and concepts. Explicit memory can be divided into two categories: episodic memory, which stores specific personal experiences, and semantic memory, which stores factual information.

Exam Probability: **Medium**

41. *Answer choices:*

(see index for correct answer)

- a. Declarative memory
- b. Memory for the future
- c. Flashbulb memory
- d. Cued recall

Guidance: level 1

:: Neurophysiology ::

In neurobiology, _____ is the capacity of an excited neuron to reduce the activity of its neighbors. _____ disables the spreading of action potentials from excited neurons to neighboring neurons in the lateral direction. This creates a contrast in stimulation that allows increased sensory perception. It is also referred to as lateral antagonism and occurs primarily in visual processes, but also in tactile, auditory, and even olfactory processing. Cells that utilize _____ appear primarily in the cerebral cortex and thalamus and make up lateral inhibitory networks . Artificial _____ has been incorporated into artificial sensory systems, such as vision chips, hearing systems, and optical mice. An often under-appreciated point is that although _____ is visualised in a spatial sense, it is also thought to exist in what is known as "_____ across abstract dimensions." This refers to _____ between neurons that are not adjacent in a spatial sense, but in terms of modality of stimulus. This phenomenon is thought to aid in colour discrimination.

Exam Probability: **Low**

42. *Answer choices:*

(see index for correct answer)

- a. Transcranial alternating current stimulation
- b. Electrical synapse
- c. Lateral inhibition
- d. Neuromuscular junction

Guidance: level 1

:: Brain ::

The _____ is a prefrontal cortex region in the frontal lobes of the brain which is involved in the cognitive process of decision-making. In non-human primates it consists of the association cortex areas Brodmann area 11, 12 and 13; in humans it consists of Brodmann area 10, 11 and 47.

Exam Probability: **Medium**

43. *Answer choices:*
(see index for correct answer)

- a. Tegmentum
- b. Folium vermis
- c. Synaptic fatigue
- d. Orbitofrontal cortex

Guidance: level 1

:: Brainstem ::

The _____, also known as Reil's band or Reil's ribbon, is a large ascending bundle of heavily myelinated axons that decussate in the brainstem, specifically in the medulla oblongata. The _____ is formed by the crossings of the internal arcuate fibers. The internal arcuate fibers are composed of axons of nucleus gracilis and nucleus cuneatus. The axons of the nucleus gracilis and nucleus cuneatus in the _____ have cell bodies that lie contralaterally.

Exam Probability: **Medium**

44. Answer choices:

(see index for correct answer)

- a. Medial lemniscus
- b. Nucleus incertus
- c. Metencephalon
- d. Vasomotor center

Guidance: level 1

:: Cerebrum ::

The _____ is one of the four major lobes of the cerebral cortex in the brain of mammals. The _____ is the visual processing center of the mammalian brain containing most of the anatomical region of the visual cortex. The primary visual cortex is Brodmann area 17, commonly called V1 . Human V1 is located on the medial side of the _____ within the calcarine sulcus; the full extent of V1 often continues onto the posterior pole of the _____ . V1 is often also called striate cortex because it can be identified by a large stripe of myelin, the Stria of Gennari. Visually driven regions outside V1 are called extrastriate cortex. There are many extrastriate regions, and these are specialized for different visual tasks, such as visuospatial processing, color differentiation, and motion perception. The name derives from the overlying occipital bone, which is named from the Latin ob, behind, and caput, the head. Bilateral lesions of the _____ can lead to cortical blindness .

Exam Probability: **Medium**

45. Answer choices:

(see index for correct answer)

- a. Anterior nuclei of thalamus
- b. Medial superior temporal area
- c. Occipital lobe
- d. Subparietal sulcus

Guidance: level 1

:: Developmental neuroscience ::

A _____ is a large actin-supported extension of a developing or regenerating neurite seeking its synaptic target. Their existence was originally proposed by Spanish histologist Santiago Ramón y Cajal based upon stationary images he observed under the microscope. He first described the _____ based on fixed cells as "a concentration of protoplasm of conical form, endowed with amoeboid movements". _____ s are situated on the tips of neurites, either dendrites or axons, of the nerve cell. The sensory, motor, integrative, and adaptive functions of growing axons and dendrites are all contained within this specialized structure.

Exam Probability: **Low**

46. *Answer choices:*

(see index for correct answer)

- a. brain development
- b. Sensory maps and brain development
- c. Growth cone
- d. Developmental cognitive neuroscience

Guidance: level 1

:: Antidepressants ::

_____ s are drugs used for the treatment of major depressive disorder and of other conditions, including some anxiety disorders, some chronic pain conditions, and to help manage some addictions. Typical side-effects of _____ s include dry mouth, weight gain, lack of sex drive, anhedonia, emotional blunting, and in some cases erectile dysfunction. Most types of _____ s are typically safe to take, but may cause increased thoughts of suicide when taken by children, adolescents, and young adults. A discontinuation syndrome can occur after stopping any _____ which resembles recurrent depression. _____ s do not provide clinically significant reduction in depressive symptoms. Debate in the medical community centers around whether or not the observed results in patients can be attributed to the placebo effect.

Exam Probability: **Low**

47. *Answer choices:*
(see index for correct answer)

- a. Rhodiola rosea
- b. Safranal
- c. Tiazesim
- d. Antidepressant

Guidance: level 1

:: Agnosia ::

_____, also known as color vision deficiency, is the decreased ability to see color or differences in color. Simple tasks such as selecting ripe fruit, choosing clothing, and reading traffic lights can be more challenging. _____ may also make some educational activities more difficult. However, problems are generally minor, and most people find that they can adapt. People with total _____ may also have decreased visual acuity and be uncomfortable in bright environments.

Exam Probability: **Medium**

48. *Answer choices:*

(see index for correct answer)

- a. Color blindness
- b. Achromatopsia
- c. Finger agnosia
- d. Pure alexia

Guidance: level 1

:: Signal transduction ::

_____s, also known as guanine nucleotide-bindin _____s, are a family of proteins that act as molecular switches inside cells, and are involved in transmitting signals from a variety of stimuli outside a cell to its interior. Their activity is regulated by factors that control their ability to bind to and hydrolyze guanosine triphosphate to guanosine diphosphate. When they are bound to GTP, they are `on`, and, when they are bound to GDP, they are `off`. _____s belong to the larger group of enzymes called GTPases.

Exam Probability: **Low**

49. *Answer choices:*

(see index for correct answer)

- a. RAB27
- b. PHLPP
- c. Aurora B kinase
- d. G protein

Guidance: level 1

:: Embryology of nervous system ::

The _____ is a key developmental structure that serves as the basis for the nervous system. Opposite the primitive streak in the embryo, ectodermal tissue thickens and flattens to become the _____ . The region anterior to the primitive knot can be generally referred to as the _____ . Cells take on a columnar appearance in the process as they continue to lengthen and narrow. The ends of the _____ , known as the neural folds, push the ends of the plate up and together, folding into the neural tube, a structure critical to brain and spinal cord development. This process as a whole is termed primary neurulation.

Exam Probability: **Low**

50. *Answer choices:*

(see index for correct answer)

- a. Alar plate
- b. Optic stalk
- c. Otic pit
- d. Pontine flexure

Guidance: level 1

:: Animal intelligence ::

_____ , encephalization level or just encephalization is a relative brain size measure that is defined as the ratio between observed to predicted brain mass for an animal of a given size, based on nonlinear regression on a range of reference species.. It has been used as a proxy for intelligence and thus as a possible way of comparing the intelligences of different species. For this purpose it is a more refined measurement than the raw brain-to-body mass ratio, as it takes into account allometric effects. The relationship, expressed as a formula, has been developed for mammals, and may not yield relevant results when applied outside this group.

Exam Probability: **Medium**

51. *Answer choices:*

(see index for correct answer)

- a. Betsy
- b. Cephalopod intelligence
- c. Encephalization quotient
- d. Rolf

Guidance: level 1

:: Cerebrum ::

The _____ also known as paleostriatum or dorsal pallidum, is a subcortical structure of the brain. It consists of two adjacent segments, one external, known in rodents simply as the _____ , and one internal, known in rodents as the entopeduncular nucleus. It is part of the telencephalon, but retains close functional ties with the subthalamus in the diencephalon – both of which are part of the extrapyramidal motor system. The _____ is a major component of the basal ganglia, with principal inputs from the striatum, and principal direct outputs to the thalamus and the substantia nigra. The latter is made up of similar neuronal elements, has similar afferents from the striatum, similar projections to the thalamus, and has a similar synaptology. Neither receives direct cortical afferents, and both receive substantial additional inputs from the intralaminar thalamus.

Exam Probability: **Medium**

52. *Answer choices:*

(see index for correct answer)

- a. Optic tract
- b. Recurrent artery of Heubner
- c. Globus pallidus
- d. Genu of internal capsule

Guidance: level 1

:: Midbrain ::

The _____ or mesencephalon is a portion of the central nervous system associated with vision, hearing, motor control, sleep/wake, arousal, and temperature regulation.

Exam Probability: **Medium**

53. *Answer choices:*

(see index for correct answer)

- a. Substantia nigra
- b. Pedunculopontine nucleus
- c. Midbrain
- d. Ventral tegmental area

Guidance: level 1

:: Limbic system ::

The _____, also called the lateral hypothalamic area, contains the primary orexinergic nucleus within the hypothalamus that widely projects throughout the nervous system; this system of neurons mediates an array of cognitive and physical processes, such as promoting feeding behavior and arousal, reducing pain perception, and regulating body temperature, digestive functions, and blood pressure, among many others. Clinically significant disorders that involve dysfunctions of the orexinergic projection system include narcolepsy, motility disorders or functional gastrointestinal disorders involving visceral hypersensitivity, and eating disorders.

Exam Probability: **Medium**

54. *Answer choices:*

(see index for correct answer)

- a. Hippocampus
- b. Mammillothalamic fasciculus
- c. Olfaction
- d. Lateral hypothalamus

Guidance: level 1

:: Computing input devices ::

A _____, plural mice, is a small rodent characteristically having a pointed snout, small rounded ears, a body-length scaly tail and a high breeding rate. The best known _____ species is the common house _____. It is also a popular pet. In some places, certain kinds of field mice are locally common. They are known to invade homes for food and shelter.

Exam Probability: **Low**

55. *Answer choices:*

(see index for correct answer)

- a. Smart Board
- b. Leap Motion

- c. Mouse
- d. Robotic book scanner

Guidance: level 1

:: Neuroanatomy ::

The _____ is the principal midbrain nucleus of the auditory pathway and receives input from several peripheral brainstem nuclei in the auditory pathway, as well as inputs from the auditory cortex. The _____ has three subdivisions: the central nucleus, a dorsal cortex by which it is surrounded, and an external cortex which is located laterally. Its bimodal neurons are implicated in auditory-somatosensory interaction, receiving projections from somatosensory nuclei. This multisensory integration may underlie a filtering of self-effected sounds from vocalization, chewing, or respiration activities.

Exam Probability: **High**

56. *Answer choices:*
(see index for correct answer)

- a. Region II of hippocampus proper
- b. Inferior colliculus
- c. Locus coeruleus
- d. Grey matter

Guidance: level 1

:: Mental health ::

_____ is the use of psychological methods, particularly when based on regular personal interaction, to help a person change behavior and overcome problems in desired ways. _____ aims to improve an individual's well-being and mental health, to resolve or mitigate troublesome behaviors, beliefs, compulsions, thoughts, or emotions, and to improve relationships and social skills. Certain psychotherapies are considered evidence-based for treating some diagnosed mental disorders. Others have been criticized as pseudoscience.

Exam Probability: **Medium**

57. *Answer choices:*

(see index for correct answer)

- a. Psychotherapy
- b. Psychological trauma
- c. Care programme approach
- d. Psychotherapeutic Postural Integration

Guidance: level 1

:: Aphrodisiacs ::

_____ is the primary male sex hormone and an anabolic steroid. In male humans, _____ plays a key role in the development of male reproductive tissues such as testes and prostate, as well as promoting secondary sexual characteristics such as increased muscle and bone mass, and the growth of body hair. In addition, _____ is involved in health and well-being, and the prevention of osteoporosis. Insufficient levels of _____ in men may lead to abnormalities including frailty and bone loss.

Exam Probability: **Medium**

58. *Answer choices:*

(see index for correct answer)

- a. Yxaiio
- b. Crocin
- c. Bremelanotide
- d. UK-414,495

Guidance: level 1

:: Sleep ::

_____ is a long-term neurological disorder that involves a decreased ability to regulate sleep-wake cycles. Symptoms include periods of excessive daytime sleepiness that usually last from seconds to minutes and may occur at any time. About 70% of those affected also experience episodes of sudden loss of muscle strength, known as cataplexy. These experiences can be brought on by strong emotions. Less commonly, there may be inability to move or vivid hallucinations while falling asleep or waking up. People with _____ tend to sleep about the same number of hours per day as people without, but the quality of sleep tends to be worse.

Exam Probability: **Low**

59. *Answer choices:*
(see index for correct answer)

- a. Sleep diary
- b. World Sleep Day
- c. Circadian rhythm
- d. Narcolepsy

Guidance: level 1

Developmental Psychology

    Developmental psychology is the scientific study of how and why human beings change over the course of their life. Originally concerned with infants and children, the field has expanded to include adolescence, adult development, aging, and the entire lifespan. Developmental psychologists aim to explain how thinking, feeling, and behaviors change throughout life. This field examines change across three major dimensions: physical development, cognitive development, and socioemotional development. Within these three dimensions are a broad range of topics including motor skills, executive functions, moral understanding, language acquisition, social change, personality, emotional development, self-concept, and identity formation.

:: Psychoanalytic theory ::

_____ is the theory of personality organization and the dynamics of personality development that guides psychoanalysis, a clinical method for treating psychopathology. First laid out by Sigmund Freud in the late 19th century, _____ has undergone many refinements since his work. _____ came to full prominence in the last third of the twentieth century as part of the flow of critical discourse regarding psychological treatments after the 1960s, long after Freud's death in 1939, and its validity is now widely disputed or rejected. Freud had ceased his analysis of the brain and his physiological studies and shifted his focus to the study of the mind and the related psychological attributes making up the mind, and on treatment using free association and the phenomena of transference. His study emphasized the recognition of childhood events that could influence the mental functioning of adults. His examination of the genetic and then the developmental aspects gave the _____ its characteristics. Starting with his publication of The Interpretation of Dreams in 1899, his theories began to gain prominence.

Exam Probability: **Medium**

1. *Answer choices:*
(see index for correct answer)

- a. Anthony Wilden
- b. Lene Auestad
- c. Id, ego and super-ego
- d. Psychoanalytic theory

Guidance: level 1

:: Mood disorders ::

_____ , also called postnatal depression, is a type of mood disorder associated with childbirth, which can affect both sexes. Symptoms may include extreme sadness, low energy, anxiety, crying episodes, irritability, and changes in sleeping or eating patterns. Onset is typically between one week and one month following childbirth. PPD can also negatively affect the newborn child.

Exam Probability: **Medium**

2. *Answer choices:*

(see index for correct answer)

- a. Journal of Affective Disorders
- b. Mental breakdown
- c. Antenatal depression
- d. Inositol monophosphatase

Guidance: level 1

:: Cerebrum ::

In mammalian brain anatomy, the _____ is the cerebral cortex which covers the front part of the frontal lobe. The PFC contains the Brodmann areas BA8, BA9, BA10, BA11, BA12, BA13, BA14, BA24, BA25, BA32, BA44, BA45, BA46, a BA47.

Exam Probability: **High**

3. Answer choices:

(see index for correct answer)

- a. Prefrontal cortex
- b. Genu of internal capsule
- c. Posterior parahippocampal gyrus
- d. Cerebral peduncle

Guidance: level 1

:: Positive psychology ::

_____, sapience, or sagacity is the ability to think and act using knowledge, experience, understanding, common sense and insight. _____ is associated with attributes such as unbiased judgment, compassion, experiential self-knowledge, self-transcendence and non-attachment, and virtues such as ethics and benevolence.

Exam Probability: **Low**

4. Answer choices:

(see index for correct answer)

- a. Wisdom
- b. The Happiness Hypothesis
- c. World Kindness Movement
- d. The Centre of New Enlightenment

Guidance: level 1

:: Developmental psychology ::

_____ is the understanding that objects continue to exist even when they cannot be perceived . This is a fundamental concept studied in the field of developmental psychology, the subfield of psychology that addresses the development of young children's social and mental capacities. There is not yet scientific consensus on when the understanding of _____ emerges in human development.

Exam Probability: **Medium**

5. *Answer choices:*
(see index for correct answer)

- a. Behavior Rating Inventory of Executive Function
- b. Display rules
- c. Constructive Developmental Framework
- d. Object permanence

Guidance: level 1

:: Congenital disorders ::

_____ is a genetic disorder that affects mostly the lungs, but also the pancreas, liver, kidneys, and intestine. Long-term issues include difficulty breathing and coughing up mucus as a result of frequent lung infections. Other signs and symptoms may include sinus infections, poor growth, fatty stool, clubbing of the fingers and toes, and infertility in most males. Different people may have different degrees of symptoms.

Exam Probability: **Medium**

6. *Answer choices:*

(see index for correct answer)

- a. Cystic hygroma
- b. Cyclopia
- c. Vici syndrome
- d. Arachnoid cyst

Guidance: level 1

:: Globalization-related theories ::

_____ evolution, _____ evolutionism or cultural evolution are theories of cultural and social evolution that describe how cultures and societies change over time. Whereas _____ development traces processes that tend to increase the complexity of a society or culture, _____ evolution also considers process that can lead to decreases in complexity or that can produce variation or proliferation without any seemingly significant changes in complexity. _____ evolution is "the process by which structural reorganization is affected through time, eventually producing a form or structure which is qualitatively different from the ancestral form".

Exam Probability: **High**

7. *Answer choices:*

(see index for correct answer)

- a. cultural evolution
- b. Sociocultural
- c. Postmodernism

Guidance: level 1

:: Human pregnancy ::

_____ includes the development of the embryo and of the fetus during a viviparous animal's gestation. _____ starts with fertilization, in the germinal stage of embryonic development, and continues in fetal development until birth.

Exam Probability: **Low**

8. *Answer choices:*

(see index for correct answer)

- a. Forced pregnancy
- b. Amniotic sac
- c. Interspecific pregnancy
- d. Prenatal development

Guidance: level 1

:: Neuroanatomy ::

An _____ , or nerve fiber, is a long, slender projection of a nerve cell, or neuron, in vertebrates, that typically conducts electrical impulses known as action potentials away from the nerve cell body. The function of the _____ is to transmit information to different neurons, muscles, and glands. In certain sensory neurons , such as those for touch and warmth, the _____ s are called afferent nerve fibers and the electrical impulse travels along these from the periphery to the cell body, and from the cell body to the spinal cord along another branch of the same _____ . _____ dysfunction has caused many inherited and acquired neurological disorders which can affect both the peripheral and central neurons. Nerve fibers are classed into three types – group A nerve fibers, group B nerve fibers, and group C nerve fibers. Groups A and B are myelinated, and group C are unmyelinated. These groups include both sensory fibers and motor fibers. Another classification groups only the sensory fibers as Type I, Type II, Type III, and Type IV.

Exam Probability: **Medium**

9. *Answer choices:*

(see index for correct answer)

- a. All-or-none law
- b. Axon
- c. Stellate ganglion
- d. Nerve root

Guidance: level 1

:: Corporal punishments ::

_____ or physical punishment is a punishment intended to cause physical pain on a person. It is most often practised on minors, especially in home and school settings. Common methods include spanking or paddling. It has also historically been used on adults, particularly on prisoners and enslaved people. Other common methods include flagellation and caning.

Exam Probability: **Low**

10. *Answer choices:*

(see index for correct answer)

- a. Corporal punishment
- b. Batog

- c. Running the gauntlet
- d. Judicial corporal punishment

Guidance: level 1

:: Discrimination ::

In human social behavior, _____ is treatment or consideration of, or making a distinction towards, a person based on the group, class, or category to which the person is perceived to belong. These include age, colour, criminal record, height, disability, ethnicity, family status, gender identity, generation, genetic characteristics, marital status, nationality, race, religion, sex, and sexual orientation. _____ consists of treatment of an individual or group, based on their actual or perceived membership in a certain group or social category, "in a way that is worse than the way people are usually treated". It involves the group's initial reaction or interaction going on to influence the individual's actual behavior towards the group leader or the group, restricting members of one group from opportunities or privileges that are available to another group, leading to the exclusion of the individual or entities based on illogical or irrational decision making.

Exam Probability: **Medium**

11. *Answer choices:*
(see index for correct answer)

- a. Multiculturalism
- b. Homophobic propaganda
- c. Anti-Filipino sentiment
- d. Discrimination

Guidance: level 1

:: Motor control ::

_____ s are the abilities usually acquired during childhood as part of a child's motor learning. By the time they reach two years of age, almost all children are able to stand up, walk and run, walk up stairs, etc. These skills are built upon, improved and better controlled throughout early childhood, and continue in refinement throughout most of the individual's years of development into adulthood. These gross movements come from large muscle groups and whole body movement. These skills develop in a head-to-toe order. The children will typically learn head control, trunk stability, and then standing up and walking. It is shown that children exposed to outdoor play time activities will develop better _____ s.

Exam Probability: **High**

12. *Answer choices:*
(see index for correct answer)

- a. Saccadic suppression of image displacement
- b. Sensory-motor coupling
- c. Psychomotor retardation
- d. Premovement neuronal activity

Guidance: level 1

:: Developmental psychology ::

_____ is a concept related to intelligence. It looks at how a specific individual, at a specific age, performs intellectually, compared to average intellectual performance for that individual's actual chronological age. The intellectual performance is based on performance in tests and live assessments by a psychologist. The score achieved by the individual is compared to the median average scores at various ages, and the _____ is derived such that the individual's score equates to the average score at age x.

Exam Probability: **Low**

13. *Answer choices:*

(see index for correct answer)

- a. Cognitive development
- b. Child development
- c. Adult development
- d. Barrel children

Guidance: level 1

:: Reasoning ::

_____ s are steps in reasoning, moving from premises to logical consequences; etymologically, the word infer means to "carry forward". _____ is theoretically traditionally divided into deduction and induction, a distinction that in Europe dates at least to Aristotle. Deduction is _____ deriving logical conclusions from premises known or assumed to be true, with the laws of valid _____ being studied in logic. Induction is _____ from particular premises to a universal conclusion. A third type of _____ is sometimes distinguished, notably by Charles Sanders Peirce, distinguishing abduction from induction, where abduction is _____ to the best explanation.

Exam Probability: **Medium**

14. *Answer choices:*

(see index for correct answer)

- a. Akrasia
- b. Verbal reasoning
- c. Inference
- d. Toulmin method

Guidance: level 1

:: Learning ::

_____ is a method for teaching reading and writing of the English language by developing learners' phonemic awareness—the ability to hear, identify, and manipulate phonemes—in order to teach the correspondence between these sounds and the spelling patterns that represent them.

Exam Probability: **High**

15. *Answer choices:*

(see index for correct answer)

- a. Office of Distance Education
- b. Pavlovian
- c. Adaptive hypermedia
- d. Phonics

Guidance: level 1

:: Pediatrics ::

_____ is the first menstrual cycle, or first menstrual bleeding, in female humans. From both social and medical perspectives, it is often considered the central event of female puberty, as it signals the possibility of fertility.

Exam Probability: **Medium**

16. *Answer choices:*

(see index for correct answer)

- a. Rotavirus
- b. Orthoptics
- c. Menarche

- d. Reflex epilepsy

Guidance: level 1

:: Human development ::

_____ is the process of physical changes through which a child's body matures into an adult body capable of sexual reproduction. It is initiated by hormonal signals from the brain to the gonads: the ovaries in a girl, the testes in a boy. In response to the signals, the gonads produce hormones that stimulate libido and the growth, function, and transformation of the brain, bones, muscle, blood, skin, hair, breasts, and sex organs. Physical growth—height and weight—accelerates in the first half of _____ and is completed when an adult body has been developed. Until the maturation of their reproductive capabilities, the pre-pubertal physical differences between boys and girls are the external sex organs.

Exam Probability: **High**

17. *Answer choices:*
(see index for correct answer)

- a. Middle age
- b. Androgenic hair
- c. Young adult
- d. Puberty

Guidance: level 1

:: Death ::

_____ is the complete loss of brain function. It differs from persistent vegetative state, in which the person is alive and some autonomic functions remain. It is also distinct from an ordinary coma, whether induced medically or caused by injury and/or illness, even if it is very deep, as long as some brain and bodily activity and function remains; and it is also not the same as the condition known as locked-in syndrome. A differential diagnosis can medically distinguish these differing conditions.

Exam Probability: **Medium**

18. *Answer choices:*

(see index for correct answer)

- a. Ataxic respiration
- b. Coagulative necrosis
- c. Brain death
- d. Sasha and Zamani

Guidance: level 1

:: Youth ::

_____ is the direct influence on people by peers, or the effect on an individual who gets encouraged to follow their peers by changing their attitudes, values or behaviors to conform to those of the influencing group or individual. This can result in either a positive or negative effect, or both. Social groups affected include both membership groups, in which individuals are "formally" members, and cliques, in which membership is not clearly defined. However, a person does not need to be a member or be seeking membership of a group to be affected by _____. _____ can decrease one's confidence. It can affect the lives of the students drastically.

Exam Probability: **High**

19. *Answer choices:*

(see index for correct answer)

- a. National Youth Leadership Training
- b. Youth philanthropy
- c. Anti-oppressive education
- d. Peer pressure

Guidance: level 1

:: Philosophical arguments ::

_____ is a cognitive process of transferring information or meaning from a particular subject to another , or a linguistic expression corresponding to such a process. In a narrower sense, _____ is an inference or an argument from one particular to another particular, as opposed to deduction, induction, and abduction, in which at least one of the premises, or the conclusion, is general rather than particular in nature. The term _____ can also refer to the relation between the source and the target themselves, which is often a similarity, as in the biological notion of _____ .

Exam Probability: **Medium**

20. *Answer choices:*

(see index for correct answer)

- a. Analogy
- b. Myth of Er
- c. Private language argument
- d. Arguments for eternity

Guidance: level 1

:: Reflexes ::

A _____ , or _____ action, is an involuntary and nearly instantaneous movement in response to a stimulus. A _____ is made possible by neural pathways called _____ arcs which can act on an impulse before that impulse reaches the brain. The _____ is then an automatic response to a stimulus that does not receive or need conscious thought.

Exam Probability: **Medium**

21. *Answer choices:*

(see index for correct answer)

- a. Reflex
- b. Autogenic inhibition reflex
- c. Oculocardiac reflex
- d. Extensor digitorum reflex

Guidance: level 1

:: Shunning ::

_____ is a state of complete or near-complete lack of contact between an individual and society. It differs from loneliness, which reflects temporary and involuntary lack of contact with other humans in the world. _____ can be an issue for individuals of any age, though symptoms may differ by age group.

Exam Probability: **High**

22. *Answer choices:*

(see index for correct answer)

- a. Marginalisation
- b. Social isolation

- c. Disownment
- d. Cold shoulder

Guidance: level 1

:: Underwater diving physiology ::

_____ is the set of life-sustaining chemical reactions in organisms. The three main purposes of _____ are: the conversion of food to energy to run cellular processes; the conversion of food/fuel to building blocks for proteins, lipids, nucleic acids, and some carbohydrates; and the elimination of nitrogenous wastes. These enzyme-catalyzed reactions allow organisms to grow and reproduce, maintain their structures, and respond to their environments. .

Exam Probability: **High**

23. *Answer choices:*

(see index for correct answer)

- a. Metabolism
- b. Systemic circulation
- c. Respiratory quotient
- d. Perfusion

Guidance: level 1

:: Attachment theory ::

The _____ is a procedure devised by Mary Ainsworth in the 1970s to observe attachment relationships between a caregiver and child. It applies to children between the age of nine and 18 months. Broadly speaking, the attachment styles were secure, insecure. Later Mary Main and her husband Erik Hesse introduce the 3rd category, disorganized.

Exam Probability: **High**

24. *Answer choices:*
(see index for correct answer)

- a. Emotionally focused therapy
- b. Jointness
- c. Strange situation
- d. caregiving

Guidance: level 1

:: Prenatal sex discernment ::

_____ is a medical procedure used in prenatal diagnosis of chromosomal abnormalities and fetal infections, and also for sex determination, in which a small amount of amniotic fluid, which contains fetal tissues, is sampled from the amniotic sac surrounding a developing fetus, and then the fetal DNA is examined for genetic abnormalities. The most common reason to have an "amnio" is to determine whether a fetus has certain genetic disorders or a chromosomal abnormality, such as Down syndrome. _____ can diagnose these problems in the womb. _____ is performed when a woman is between 14 and 16 weeks gestation. Women who choose to have this test are primarily those at increased risk for genetic and chromosomal problems, in part because the test is invasive and carries a small risk of miscarriage. This process can be used for prenatal sex discernment and hence this procedure has legal restrictions in some countries.

Exam Probability: **Medium**

25. *Answer choices:*

(see index for correct answer)

- a. Amniocentesis
- b. Chorionic villus sampling
- c. Baby Gender Mentor
- d. Pre-Conception and Pre-Natal Diagnostic Techniques Act, 1994

Guidance: level 1

:: Developmental psychology ::

In developmental psychology and developmental biology, a _____ is a maturational stage in the lifespan of an organism during which the nervous system is especially sensitive to certain environmental stimuli. If, for some reason, the organism does not receive the appropriate stimulus during this " _____ " to learn a given skill or trait, it may be difficult, ultimately less successful, or even impossible, to develop some functions later in life. Functions that are indispensable to an organism's survival, such as vision, are particularly likely to develop during _____ s. " _____ " also relates to the ability to acquire one's first language. Researchers found that people who passed the " _____ " would not acquire their first language fluently.

Exam Probability: **High**

26. *Answer choices:*

(see index for correct answer)

- a. Human development
- b. Mental age
- c. Critical period
- d. Adult development

Guidance: level 1

:: Stage theories ::

Erikson's stages of _____, as articulated in the second half of the 20th century by Erik Erikson in collaboration with Joan Erikson, is a comprehensive psychoanalytic theory that identifies a series of eight stages that a healthy developing individual should pass through from infancy to late adulthood.

Exam Probability: **Medium**

27. *Answer choices:*

(see index for correct answer)

- a. stages of change
- b. Erikson's stages of psychosocial development
- c. Psychosocial development
- d. Piaget's theory of cognitive development

Guidance: level 1

:: Interpersonal relationships ::

An intimate relationship is an interpersonal relationship that involves physical or emotional _____. Although an intimate relationship is commonly a sexual relationship, it may also be a non-sexual relationship involving family, friends, or acquaintances.

Exam Probability: **High**

28. Answer choices:

(see index for correct answer)

- a. Joking relationship
- b. Bad boy
- c. Intimacy
- d. Khilwa

Guidance: level 1

:: Personality theories ::

In psychology, _____ is an approach to the study of human personality. Trait theorists are primarily interested in the measurement of traits, which can be defined as habitual patterns of behavior, thought, and emotion. According to this perspective, traits are aspects of personality that are relatively stable over time, differ across individuals, are relatively consistent over situations, and influence behavior. Traits are in contrast to states, which are more transitory dispositions.

Exam Probability: **Low**

29. Answer choices:

(see index for correct answer)

- a. Dispositionist
- b. Ego psychology
- c. Phenomenal field theory

- d. Trait theory

Guidance: level 1

:: Scientific method ::

_____ is a branch of mathematics working with data collection, organization, analysis, interpretation and presentation. In applying _____ to, for example, a scientific, industrial, or social problem, it is conventional to begin with a statistical population or a statistical model process to be studied. Populations can be diverse topics such as "all people living in a country" or "every atom composing a crystal". _____ deals with every aspect of data, including the planning of data collection in terms of the design of surveys and experiments.See glossary of probability and _____ .

Exam Probability: **Medium**

30. *Answer choices:*
(see index for correct answer)

- a. Evidence-based practice
- b. Statistics
- c. Inverse-square law
- d. Translational science

Guidance: level 1

:: Infancy ::

_____ or kangaroo mother care, sometimes called skin-to-skin contact, is a technique of newborn care where babies are kept chest-to-chest and skin-to-skin with a parent, typically their mother. It is most commonly used for low birth-weight preterm babies, who are more likely to suffer from hypothermia, while admitted to a neonatal unit to keep the baby warm and support early breastfeeding.

Exam Probability: **High**

31. *Answer choices:*

(see index for correct answer)

- a. Bassinet
- b. Kangaroo care
- c. Little Laureate
- d. Frederick Leboyer

Guidance: level 1

:: Developmental neuroscience ::

The development of the nervous system, or neural development, refers to the processes that generate, shape, and reshape the nervous system of animals, from the earliest stages of embryonic development to adulthood. The field of neural development draws on both neuroscience and developmental biology to describe and provide insight into the cellular and molecular mechanisms by which complex nervous systems develop, from the nematode and fruit fly to mammals. Defects in neural development can lead to malformations and a wide variety of sensory, motor, and cognitive impairments, including holoprosencephaly and other neurological disorders in the human such as Rett syndrome, Down syndrome and intellectual disability.

Exam Probability: **Medium**

32. *Answer choices:*

(see index for correct answer)

- a. Brain development
- b. Slit
- c. Reflective abstraction
- d. Integrative neuroscience

Guidance: level 1

:: Neurons ::

_____ is a lipid-rich substance formed in the central nervous system by glial cells called oligodendrocytes, and in the peripheral nervous system by Schwann cells. _____ insulates nerve cell axons to increase the speed at which information travels from one nerve cell body to another or, for example, from a nerve cell body to a muscle. The _____ ated axon can be likened to an electrical wire with insulating material around it. However, unlike the plastic covering on an electrical wire, _____ does not form a single long sheath over the entire length of the axon. Rather, each _____ sheath insulates the axon over a single section and, in general, each axon comprises multiple long _____ ated sections separated from each other by short gaps called Nodes of Ranvier. Each _____ sheath is formed by the concentric wrapping of an oligodendrocyte or Schwann cell process around the axon.

Exam Probability: **Medium**

33. *Answer choices:*

(see index for correct answer)

- a. Myelin
- b. Arcuate nucleus
- c. Rohon-Beard cell
- d. Head direction cells

Guidance: level 1

:: Developmental psychology ::

In Freudian psychology, _____ is a central element of the psychoanalytic sexual drive theory, that human beings, from birth, possess an instinctual libido that develops in five stages. Each stage the oral, the anal, the phallic, the latent, and the genital is characterized by the erogenous zone that is the source of the libidinal drive. Sigmund Freud proposed that if the child experienced sexual frustration in relation to any _____ al stage, they would experience anxiety that would persist into adulthood as a neurosis, a functional mental disorder.

Exam Probability: **High**

34. *Answer choices:*

(see index for correct answer)

- a. Keeper of the Meaning
- b. Mentalization
- c. Developmental disorder
- d. Developmental psychobiology

Guidance: level 1

:: Educational psychology ::

_____ is a phenomenon whereby something new and somehow valuable is formed. The created item may be intangible or a physical object.

Exam Probability: **High**

35. *Answer choices:*

(see index for correct answer)

- a. Strozzi Institute
- b. Formal education
- c. Distributed scaffolding
- d. Creativity

Guidance: level 1

:: Menopause ::

_____, also known as the climacteric, is the time in most women's lives when menstrual periods stop permanently, and they are no longer able to bear children. _____ typically occurs between 49 and 52 years of age. Medical professionals often define _____ as having occurred when a woman has not had any vaginal bleeding for a year. It may also be defined by a decrease in hormone production by the ovaries. In those who have had surgery to remove their uterus but still have ovaries, _____ may be considered to have occurred at the time of the surgery or when their hormone levels fell. Following the removal of the uterus, symptoms typically occur earlier, at an average of 45 years of age.

Exam Probability: **Medium**

36. *Answer choices:*

(see index for correct answer)

- a. Menopause

- b. Bioidentical hormone replacement therapy
- c. Greene Menopause Index
- d. Phytoserm

Guidance: level 1

:: Gastrulation ::

In all bilaterian animals, the _____ is one of the three primary germ layers in the very early embryo. The other two layers are the ectoderm and endoderm, with the _____ as the middle layer between them.

Exam Probability: **Medium**

37. *Answer choices:*
(see index for correct answer)

- a. Ectoderm
- b. Mesoderm

Guidance: level 1

:: Units of morphological analysis ::

In biology, a _____ is a sequence of nucleotides in DNA or RNA that codes for a molecule that has a function. During _____ expression, the DNA is first copied into RNA. The RNA can be directly functional or be the intermediate template for a protein that performs a function. The transmission of _____ s to an organism's offspring is the basis of the inheritance of phenotypic trait. These _____ s make up different DNA sequences called genotypes. Genotypes along with environmental and developmental factors determine what the phenotypes will be. Most biological traits are under the influence of poly _____ s as well as _____ –environment interactions. Some _____ tic traits are instantly visible, such as eye color or number of limbs, and some are not, such as blood type, risk for specific diseases, or the thousands of basic biochemical processes that constitute life.

Exam Probability: **High**

38. *Answer choices:*
(see index for correct answer)

- a. Mytheme
- b. Grapheme

Guidance: level 1

:: Psychiatry ::

A _____ is a physician who specializes in psychiatry, the branch of medicine devoted to the diagnosis, prevention, study, and treatment of mental disorders. _____ s are medical doctors, unlike psychologists, and must evaluate patients to determine whether their symptoms are the result of a physical illness, a combination of physical and mental ailments, or strictly psychiatric. A _____ usually works as the clinical leader of the multi-disciplinary team, which may comprise psychologists, social workers, occupational therapists and nursing staff. _____ s have broad training in a bio-psycho-social approach to assessment and management of mental illness.

Exam Probability: **High**

39. *Answer choices:*

(see index for correct answer)

- a. Psychopathology
- b. Psychiatrist
- c. Psychosis
- d. A Stranger in The Family: Culture, Families, and Therapy

Guidance: level 1

:: Human development ::

A _____ is a caregiver of the offspring in their own species. In humans, a _____ is the caretaker of a child. A biological _____ is a person whose gamete resulted in a child, a male through the sperm, and a female through the ovum. Biological _____ s are first-degree relatives and have 50% genetic meet. A female can also become a _____ through surrogacy. Some _____ s may be adoptive _____ s, who nurture and raise an offspring, but are not biologically related to the child. Orphans without adoptive _____ s can be raised by their grand _____ s or other family members.

Exam Probability: **Medium**

40. *Answer choices:*

(see index for correct answer)

- a. Parent
- b. Father
- c. Birth order
- d. Ephebos

Guidance: level 1

:: Scientific method ::

In the social sciences and life sciences, a _____ is a research method involving an up-close, in-depth, and detailed examination of a subject of study, as well as its related contextual conditions.

Exam Probability: **High**

41. *Answer choices:*

(see index for correct answer)

- a. Expert elicitation
- b. Case study
- c. Question-focused dataset
- d. The Logic of Modern Physics

Guidance: level 1

:: Stereotypes ::

In social psychology, a _____ is an over-generalized belief about a particular category of people. _____ s are generalized because one assumes that the _____ is true for each individual person in the category. While such generalizations may be useful when making quick decisions, they may be erroneous when applied to particular individuals. _____ s encourage prejudice and may arise for a number of reasons.

Exam Probability: **Low**

42. *Answer choices:*

(see index for correct answer)

- a. Jewish guilt
- b. Stereotype

- c. Boy racer
- d. Redneck joke

Guidance: level 1

:: Self ::

_____ is how one thinks of oneself in terms of to whom one is romantically or sexually attracted. _____ may also refer to sexual orientation identity, which is when people identify or dis-identify with a sexual orientation or choose not to identify with a sexual orientation. _____ and sexual behavior are closely related to sexual orientation, but they are distinguished, with identity referring to an individual's conception of themselves, behavior referring to actual sexual acts performed by the individual, and sexual orientation referring to romantic or sexual attractions toward persons of the opposite sex or gender, the same sex or gender, to both sexes or more than one gender, or to no one.

Exam Probability: **Medium**

43. *Answer choices:*
(see index for correct answer)

- a. Self-perception theory
- b. Sexual identity
- c. Mirror test
- d. Self-affirmation

Guidance: level 1

:: Friendship ::

_____ is a relationship of mutual affection between people. _____ is a stronger form of interpersonal bond than an association. _____ has been studied in academic fields such as communication, sociology, social psychology, anthropology, and philosophy. Various academic theories of _____ have been proposed, including social exchange theory, equity theory, relational dialectics, and attachment styles.

Exam Probability: **Medium**

44. *Answer choices:*

(see index for correct answer)

- a. Friendship
- b. Friendship bracelet
- c. Showmance
- d. Man date

Guidance: level 1

:: Attachment theory ::

A caregiver or carer is an unpaid or paid member of a person's social network who helps them with activities of daily living. _____ is most commonly used to address impairments related to old age, disability, a disease, or a mental disorder.

Exam Probability: **Low**

45. *Answer choices:*

(see index for correct answer)

- a. Attachment therapy
- b. Michael Rutter
- c. Dyadic Developmental Psychotherapy
- d. Caregiving

Guidance: level 1

:: Intellectual disability ::

Fetal alcohol spectrum disorders are a group of conditions that can occur in a person whose mother drank alcohol during pregnancy. Problems may include an abnormal appearance, short height, low body weight, small head size, poor coordination, low intelligence, behavior problems, and problems with hearing or seeing. Those affected are more likely to have trouble in school, legal problems, participate in high-risk behaviors, and have trouble with alcohol or other drugs. The most severe form of the condition is known as _____ . Other types include partial _____ , alcohol-related neurodevelopmental disorder and alcohol-related birth defects . Some accept only FAS as a diagnosis, seeing the evidence as inconclusive with respect to other types.

Exam Probability: **High**

46. *Answer choices:*

(see index for correct answer)

- a. Lead poisoning
- b. Fetal alcohol syndrome
- c. Noonan syndrome
- d. Congenital hypothyroidism

Guidance: level 1

:: HIV/AIDS ::

Human immunodeficiency virus infection and acquired immune deficiency syndrome is a spectrum of conditions caused by infection with the human immunodeficiency virus . Following initial infection, a person may not notice any symptoms or may experience a brief period of influenza-like illness. Typically, this is followed by a prolonged period with no symptoms. As the infection progresses, it interferes more with the immune system, increasing the risk of developing common infections such as tuberculosis, as well as other opportunistic infections, and tumors that rarely affect people who have uncompromised immune systems. These late symptoms of infection are referred to as acquired immunodeficiency syndrome . This stage is often also associated with unintended weight loss.

Exam Probability: **Medium**

47. *Answer choices:*

(see index for correct answer)

- a. 2F5 antibody
- b. AIDS
- c. Emtricitabine/rilpivirine/tenofovir
- d. Hairy leukoplakia

Guidance: level 1

:: Psychometrics ::

Mental chronometry is the study of _____ in perceptual-motor tasks to infer the content, duration, and temporal sequencing of mental operations. Mental chronometry is one of the core methodological paradigms of human experimental and cognitive psychology, but is also commonly analyzed in psychophysiology, cognitive neuroscience, and behavioral neuroscience to help elucidate the biological mechanisms underlying perception, attention, and decision-making across species.

Exam Probability: **High**

48. *Answer choices:*

(see index for correct answer)

- a. Fuzzy concept
- b. Repeatability
- c. Missing completely at random
- d. Reaction time

Guidance: level 1

:: Social status ::

_____ is an economic and sociological combined total measure of a person's work experience and of an individual's or family's economic and social position in relation to others, based on household income, earners' education, and occupation are examined, as well as combined income, whereas for an individual's SES only their own attributes are assessed. However, SES is more commonly used to depict an economic difference in society as a whole.

Exam Probability: **Low**

49. *Answer choices:*
(see index for correct answer)

- a. social distance
- b. Exploitation
- c. Social exchange

Guidance: level 1

:: Emotion ::

_____ is a mental state associated with the nervous system brought on by chemical changes variously associated with thoughts, feelings, behavioural responses, and a degree of pleasure or displeasure. There is currently no scientific consensus on a definition. _____ is often intertwined with mood, temperament, personality, disposition, and motivation.

Exam Probability: **Medium**

50. *Answer choices:*
(see index for correct answer)

- a. Emotion
- b. Voodoo death
- c. Interpersonal emotion regulation
- d. Emotional Freedom Techniques

Guidance: level 1

:: Cognitive neuroscience ::

_____ is the capacity to understand or feel what another person is experiencing from within their frame of reference, that is, the capacity to place oneself in another's position. Definitions of _____ encompass a broad range of emotional states. Types of _____ include cognitive _____ , emotional _____ , and somatic _____ .

Exam Probability: **Low**

51. Answer choices:

(see index for correct answer)

- a. Mind and Life Institute
- b. Mind Hacks
- c. Empathy
- d. Default mode network

Guidance: level 1

:: Religion ::

_____ is a cultural system of designated behaviors and practices, morals, worldviews, texts, sanctified places, prophecies, ethics, or organizations, that relates humanity to supernatural, transcendental, or spiritual elements. However, there is no scholarly consensus over what precisely constitutes a _____ .

Exam Probability: **Medium**

52. Answer choices:

(see index for correct answer)

- a. Calathumpian
- b. Natural religion
- c. Religious citizenship
- d. Spiritual but not religious

Guidance: level 1

:: Analytical psychology ::

In Neo-Freudian psychology, the _____ , as proposed by Carl Jung in his Theory of Psychoanalysis, is a girl's psychosexual competition with her mother for possession of her father. In the course of her psychosexual development, the complex is the girl's phallic stage; a boy's analogous experience is the Oedipus complex. The _____ occurs in the third—phallic stage—of five psychosexual development stages: the Oral, the Anal, the Phallic, the Latent, and the Genital—in which the source of libido pleasure is in a different erogenous zone of the infant's body.

Exam Probability: **High**

53. *Answer choices:*

(see index for correct answer)

- a. Self in Jungian psychology
- b. Don Juanism
- c. Electra complex
- d. Ego functions

Guidance: level 1

:: Thought ::

_____ is the analysis of facts to form a judgment. The subject is complex, and several different definitions exist, which generally include the rational, skeptical, unbiased analysis, or evaluation of factual evidence. _____ is self-directed, self-disciplined, self-monitored, and self-corrective thinking. It presupposes assent to rigorous standards of excellence and mindful command of their use. It entails effective communication and problem-solving abilities as well as a commitment to overcome native egocentrism and sociocentrism.

Exam Probability: **Low**

54. *Answer choices:*

(see index for correct answer)

- a. Idea
- b. Abstraction
- c. Po
- d. Systematic inventive thinking

Guidance: level 1

:: Behaviorism ::

_____ is a learning process through which the strength of a behavior is modified by reinforcement or punishment. It is also a procedure that is used to bring about such learning.

Exam Probability: **High**

55. Answer choices:

(see index for correct answer)

- a. Tootling
- b. Behavior management
- c. Mand
- d. Operant conditioning

Guidance: level 1

:: Moral psychology ::

_____ , also known as moral development, is a study in psychology that overlaps with moral philosophy. Children can make moral decisions about what is right and wrong from a young age; this makes morality fundamental to the human condition. _____ , however, is a part of morality that occurs both within and between individuals. Prominent contributors to this theory include Lawrence Kohlberg and Elliot Turiel. The term is sometimes used in a different sense: reasoning under conditions of uncertainty, such as those commonly obtained in a court of law. It is this sense that gave rise to the phrase, "To a moral certainty;" however, this idea is now seldom used outside of charges to juries.

Exam Probability: **High**

56. Answer choices:

(see index for correct answer)

- a. Defining Issues Test

- b. Moral reasoning
- c. Brian Leiter
- d. David Wong

Guidance: level 1

:: Imagination ::

A _____ is a proposed explanation for a phenomenon. For a _____ to be a scientific _____ , the scientific method requires that one can test it. Scientists generally base scientific hypotheses on previous observations that cannot satisfactorily be explained with the available scientific theories. Even though the words " _____ " and "theory" are often used synonymously, a scientific _____ is not the same as a scientific theory. A working _____ is a provisionally accepted _____ proposed for further research, in a process beginning with an educated guess or thought.

Exam Probability: **Low**

57. *Answer choices:*

(see index for correct answer)

- a. Hypothesis
- b. Escapism
- c. Guided imagery
- d. Imagination

Guidance: level 1

:: Visual perception ::

_____ commonly refers to the clarity of vision. _____ is dependent on optical and neural factors, i.e., the sharpness of the retinal focus within the eye, the health and functioning of the retina, and the sensitivity of the interpretative faculty of the brain.

Exam Probability: **High**

58. *Answer choices:*
(see index for correct answer)

- a. Oculesics
- b. Perceptual adaptation
- c. Visual acuity
- d. Persistence of vision

Guidance: level 1

:: Behaviorism ::

A _____ is a routine of behavior that is repeated regularly and tends to occur subconsciously.

Exam Probability: **High**

59. *Answer choices:*
(see index for correct answer)

- a. Counterconditioning
- b. Behavioral engineering
- c. Behavior management
- d. Habit

Guidance: level 1

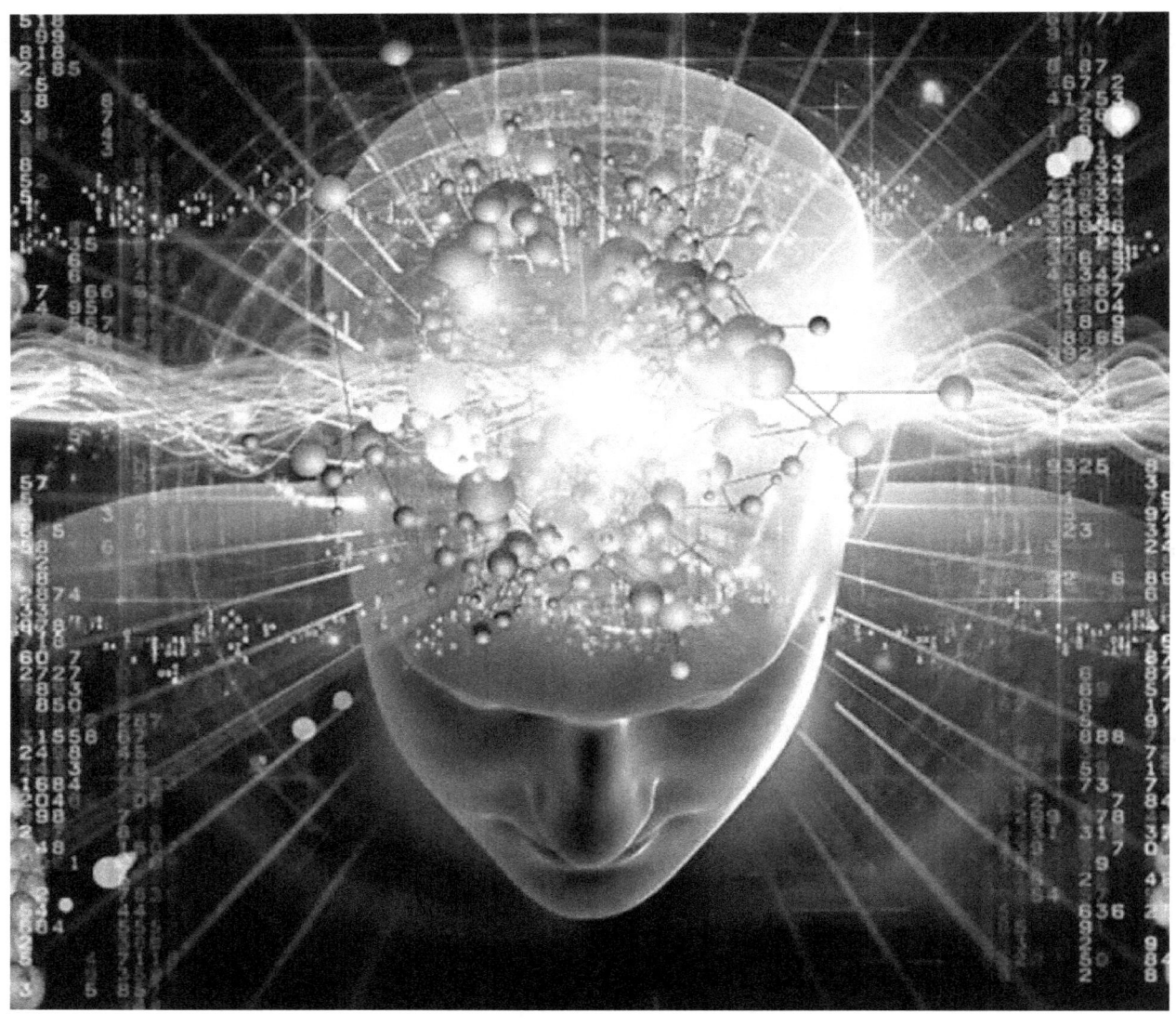

Cognitive Psychology

Cognitive psychology is the study of mental processes such as "attention, language use, memory, perception, problem solving, creativity, and thinking". Much of the work derived from cognitive psychology has been integrated into various other modern disciplines such as Cognitive Science and of psychological study, including educational psychology, social psychology, personality psychology, abnormal psychology, developmental psychology, and economics.

:: Educational psychology ::

_____ is the complex cognitive process of decoding symbols to derive meaning. It is a form of language processing.

Exam Probability: **Low**

1. *Answer choices:*

(see index for correct answer)

- a. Life-wide Learning
- b. Worked-example effect
- c. Reading
- d. Psychopedagogy

Guidance: level 1

:: Concepts ::

In linguistics, a _____ is the smallest element that can be uttered in isolation with objective or practical meaning.

Exam Probability: **Low**

2. *Answer choices:*

(see index for correct answer)

- a. Word
- b. Policy switch
- c. Definitionism
- d. Organizing principle

Guidance: level 1

:: Family ::

In the context of human society, a _____ is a group of people related either by consanguinity, affinity, or co-residence or some combination of these. Members of the immediate _____ may include spouses, parents, brothers, sisters, sons, and daughters. Members of the extended _____ may include grandparents, aunts, uncles, cousins, nephews, nieces, and siblings-in-law. Sometimes these are also considered members of the immediate _____ , depending on an individual's specific relationship with them.

Exam Probability: **Low**

3. *Answer choices:*

(see index for correct answer)

- a. Family Home Evening
- b. Association of Family Case Workers
- c. Family
- d. Triangulation

Guidance: level 1

:: Cognitive neuroscience ::

The _____ - FFA is a part of the human visual system that is specialized for facial recognition. It is located in the Inferior temporal cortex, in the fusiform gyrus.

Exam Probability: **High**

4. *Answer choices:*

(see index for correct answer)

- a. Bayesian approaches to brain function
- b. Crossmodal
- c. Associative Sequence Learning
- d. Frontal lobe disorder

Guidance: level 1

:: Memory biases ::

The _____ happens when a person's recall of episodic memories becomes less accurate because of post-event information. For example, in a study published in 1994, subjects were initially shown one of two different series of slides that depicted a college student at the university bookstore, with different objects of the same type changed in some slides. One version of the slides would, for example, show a screwdriver while the other would show a wrench, and the audio narrative accompanying the slides would only refer to the object as a "tool". In the second phase, subjects would read a narrative description of the events in the slides, except this time a specific tool was named, which would be the incorrect tool half the time. Finally, in the third phase, subjects had to list five examples of specific types of objects, such as tools, but were told to only list examples which they had not seen in the slides. Subjects who had read an incorrect narrative were far less likely to list the written object than the control subjects, and were far more likely to incorrectly list the item which they had actually seen.

Exam Probability: **Low**

5. *Answer choices:*

(see index for correct answer)

- a. Selective memory loss
- b. Gender differences in eyewitness memory
- c. Google effect
- d. Levels-of-processing effect

Guidance: level 1

:: Cognitive biases ::

The _____ is a tendency for people to encode information differently depending on the level on which they are implicated in the information. When people are asked to remember information when it is related in some way to themselves, the recall rate can be improved.

Exam Probability: **Medium**

6. *Answer choices:*

(see index for correct answer)

- a. Self-reference effect
- b. Attitude polarization
- c. Attribution bias
- d. Selective omission

Guidance: level 1

:: Developmental psychology ::

In developmental psychology and developmental biology, a _____ is a maturational stage in the lifespan of an organism during which the nervous system is especially sensitive to certain environmental stimuli. If, for some reason, the organism does not receive the appropriate stimulus during this " _____ " to learn a given skill or trait, it may be difficult, ultimately less successful, or even impossible, to develop some functions later in life. Functions that are indispensable to an organism's survival, such as vision, are particularly likely to develop during _____ s. " _____ " also relates to the ability to acquire one's first language. Researchers found that people who passed the " _____ " would not acquire their first language fluently.

Exam Probability: **Medium**

7. *Answer choices:*

(see index for correct answer)

- a. Behavior Rating Inventory of Executive Function
- b. object permanence
- c. Developmental psychobiology
- d. Constructive Developmental Framework

Guidance: level 1

:: Cerebrum ::

The _____ is one of the four major lobes of the cerebral cortex in the brain of mammals. The _____ is the visual processing center of the mammalian brain containing most of the anatomical region of the visual cortex. The primary visual cortex is Brodmann area 17, commonly called V1. Human V1 is located on the medial side of the _____ within the calcarine sulcus; the full extent of V1 often continues onto the posterior pole of the _____ . V1 is often also called striate cortex because it can be identified by a large stripe of myelin, the Stria of Gennari. Visually driven regions outside V1 are called extrastriate cortex. There are many extrastriate regions, and these are specialized for different visual tasks, such as visuospatial processing, color differentiation, and motion perception. The name derives from the overlying occipital bone, which is named from the Latin ob, behind, and caput, the head. Bilateral lesions of the _____ can lead to cortical blindness .

Exam Probability: **Medium**

8. *Answer choices:*

(see index for correct answer)

- a. Paleopallium
- b. Superior parietal lobule
- c. Metathalamus
- d. Occipital lobe

Guidance: level 1

:: Critical thinking ::

_____ , broadly construed, is anything presented in support of an assertion. This support may be strong or weak. The strongest type of _____ is that which provides direct proof of the truth of an assertion. At the other extreme is _____ that is merely consistent with an assertion but does not rule out other, contradictory assertions, as in circumstantial _____ .

Exam Probability: **Low**

9. *Answer choices:*

(see index for correct answer)

- a. Project Reason
- b. Interpretive discussion
- c. Foundation for Critical Thinking
- d. Precising definition

Guidance: level 1

:: Cognition ::

_____ is a psychological process related to an abstract or physical object, such as a person, situation, or message whereby one is able to think about it and use concepts to deal adequately with that object. _____ is a relation between the knower and an object of _____ . _____ implies abilities and dispositions with respect to an object of knowledge that are sufficient to support intelligent behaviour.

Exam Probability: **Low**

10. *Answer choices:*

(see index for correct answer)

- a. Understanding
- b. Volition
- c. Computational cognition
- d. Molecular cellular cognition

Guidance: level 1

:: Memory ::

The _____ , also known as the paleomammalian cortex, is a set of brain structures located on both sides of the thalamus, immediately beneath the medial temporal lobe of the cerebrum primarily in the midbrain.

Exam Probability: **Medium**

11. *Answer choices:*

(see index for correct answer)

- a. Personal-event memory
- b. Limbic system
- c. Metamemory
- d. Lethologica

Guidance: level 1

:: Second-language acquisition ::

An _____ is an action which is inaccurate or incorrect. In some usages, an _____ is synonymous with a mistake. In statistics, "_____" refers to the difference between the value which has been computed and the correct value. An _____ could result in failure or in a deviation from the intended performance or behaviour.

Exam Probability: **Low**

12. *Answer choices:*

(see index for correct answer)

- a. Error treatment
- b. Second-language phonology
- c. Error
- d. Paderborn method

Guidance: level 1

:: Memory ::

_____ is a category of processes that stabilize a memory trace after its initial acquisition. Consolidation is distinguished into two specific processes, synaptic consolidation, which is synonymous with late-phase long-term potentiation and occurs within the first few hours after learning, and systems consolidation, where hippocampus-dependent memories become independent of the hippocampus over a period of weeks to years. Recently, a third process has become the focus of research, reconsolidation, in which previously-consolidated memories can be made labile again through reactivation of the memory trace.

Exam Probability: **High**

13. *Answer choices:*

(see index for correct answer)

- a. Spaced repetition
- b. Tetris effect
- c. Muscle memory

- d. Recovered-memory therapy

Guidance: level 1

:: Deafness ::

_____ s are languages that use the visual-manual modality to convey meaning. Language is expressed via the manual signstream in combination with non-manual elements. _____ s are full-fledged natural languages with their own grammar and lexicon. This means that _____ s are not universal and they are not mutually intelligible, although there are also striking similarities among _____ s.

Exam Probability: **High**

14. *Answer choices:*

(see index for correct answer)

- a. Wolfram syndrome
- b. Ear trumpet
- c. Spatial hearing loss
- d. Sign language

Guidance: level 1

:: Optical illusions ::

The _____ or Titchener circles is an optical illusion of relative size perception. Named for its discoverer, the German psychologist Hermann Ebbinghaus , the illusion was popularized in the English-speaking world by Edward B. Titchener in a 1901 textbook of experimental psychology, hence its alternative name. In the best-known version of the illusion, two circles of identical size are placed near to each other, and one is surrounded by large circles while the other is surrounded by small circles. As a result of the juxtaposition of circles, the central circle surrounded by large circles appears smaller than the central circle surrounded by small circles.

Exam Probability: **High**

15. *Answer choices:*

(see index for correct answer)

- a. Hollow-Face illusion
- b. Jastrow illusion
- c. Ternus illusion
- d. Flash lag illusion

Guidance: level 1

:: Motivation ::

_____ is an individual's subjective evaluation of their own worth. _____ encompasses beliefs about oneself as well as emotional states, such as triumph, despair, pride, and shame. Smith and Mackie defined it by saying "The self-concept is what we think about the self; _____ , is the positive or negative evaluations of the self, as in how we feel about it."

Exam Probability: **High**

16. *Answer choices:*

(see index for correct answer)

- a. Reinforcing success
- b. Self-esteem
- c. Cooling Out
- d. Will to power

Guidance: level 1

:: Neuropsychology ::

_____ is the study and characterization of the behavioral modifications that follow a neurological trauma or condition. It is both an experimental and clinical field of psychology that aims to understand how behavior and cognition are influenced by brain functioning and is concerned with the diagnosis and treatment of behavioral and cognitive effects of neurological disorders. Whereas classical neurology focuses on the pathology of the nervous system and classical psychology is largely divorced from it, _____ seeks to discover how the brain correlates with the mind through the study of neurological patients. It thus shares concepts and concerns with neuropsychiatry and with behavioral neurology in general. The term _____ has been applied to lesion studies in humans and animals. It has also been applied in efforts to record electrical activity from individual cells in higher primates.

Exam Probability: **High**

17. *Answer choices:*

(see index for correct answer)

- a. Psychological refractory period
- b. Neural clique
- c. Brain fitness
- d. Neuropsychology

Guidance: level 1

:: Learning ::

_____ is a method for teaching reading and writing of the English language by developing learners' phonemic awareness—the ability to hear, identify, and manipulate phonemes—in order to teach the correspondence between these sounds and the spelling patterns that represent them.

Exam Probability: **Medium**

18. *Answer choices:*

(see index for correct answer)

- a. Phonics
- b. Digital teaching platform
- c. Berliner Modell
- d. Vocal learning

Guidance: level 1

:: Neuropsychology ::

_____ is the physiological and psychological state of being awoken or of sense organs stimulated to a point of perception. It involves activation of the ascending reticular activating system in the brain, which mediates wakefulness, the autonomic nervous system, and the endocrine system, leading to increased heart rate and blood pressure and a condition of sensory alertness, mobility, and readiness to respond.

Exam Probability: **Medium**

19. *Answer choices:*

(see index for correct answer)

- a. Athymhormia
- b. Cognitive rehabilitation therapy
- c. Adaptive resonance theory
- d. Arousal

Guidance: level 1

:: Memory biases ::

The _____ is the tendency for older adults to have increased recollection for events that occurred during their adolescence and early adulthood. It was identified through the study of autobiographical memory and the subsequent plotting of the age of encoding of memories to form the lifespan retrieval curve.

Exam Probability: **Low**

20. *Answer choices:*

(see index for correct answer)

- a. Childhood amnesia
- b. Reminiscence bump
- c. Cue-dependent forgetting
- d. Zeigarnik effect

Guidance: level 1

:: Heuristics ::

_____ or focalism is a cognitive bias where an individual relies too heavily on an initial piece of information offered when making decisions.

Exam Probability: **Medium**

21. *Answer choices:*

(see index for correct answer)

- a. Duck test
- b. Killer heuristic
- c. Guided Local Search
- d. Anchoring

Guidance: level 1

:: Branches of psychology ::

_____ refers to work done by those who apply experimental methods to psychological study and the processes that underlie it. Experimental psychologists employ human participants and animal subjects to study a great many topics, including sensation & perception, memory, cognition, learning, motivation, emotion; developmental processes, social psychology, and the neural substrates of all of these.

Exam Probability: **Medium**

22. *Answer choices:*

(see index for correct answer)

- a. Experimental psychology
- b. Ecopsychology
- c. Differential psychology
- d. Medical psychology

Guidance: level 1

:: Anxiety ::

_____ s are sudden periods of intense fear that may include palpitations, sweating, shaking, shortness of breath, numbness, or a feeling that something bad is going to happen. The maximum degree of symptoms occurs within minutes. Typically they last for about 30 minutes but the duration can vary from seconds to hours. There may be a fear of losing control or chest pain. _____ s themselves are not typically dangerous physically.

Exam Probability: **Medium**

23. *Answer choices:*
(see index for correct answer)

- a. The Worry Trap
- b. Anxiety threshold
- c. Panic attack
- d. schizotypal

Guidance: level 1

:: Cognitive science ::

A _____ is an explanation of someone's thought process about how something works in the real world. It is a representation of the surrounding world, the relationships between its various parts and a person's intuitive perception about his or her own acts and their consequences. _____s can help shape behaviour and set an approach to solving problems and doing tasks.

Exam Probability: **High**

24. *Answer choices:*

(see index for correct answer)

- a. Spatial relation
- b. Simplicity theory
- c. Cue validity
- d. Mental process

Guidance: level 1

:: Educational psychology ::

_____ , also known as reading disorder, is characterized by trouble with reading despite normal intelligence. Different people are affected to varying degrees. Problems may include difficulties in spelling words, reading quickly, writing words, "sounding out" words in the head, pronouncing words when reading aloud and understanding what one reads. Often these difficulties are first noticed at school. When someone who previously could read loses their ability, it is known as alexia. The difficulties are involuntary and people with this disorder have a normal desire to learn.

Exam Probability: **Medium**

25. *Answer choices:*

(see index for correct answer)

- a. Inquiry education
- b. Situated learning
- c. Legitimate peripheral participation
- d. Need for cognition

Guidance: level 1

:: Memory processes ::

_____ is the sensory memory register specific to auditory information. The sensory memory for sounds that people have just perceived is the form of _____ . Unlike visual memory, in which our eyes can scan the stimuli over and over, the auditory stimuli cannot be scanned over and over. Overall, echoic memories are stored for slightly longer periods of time than iconic memories. Auditory stimuli are received by the ear one at a time before they can be processed and understood. For instance, hearing the radio is very different from reading a magazine. A person can only hear the radio once at a given time, while the magazine can be read over and over again. It can be said that the _____ is like a "holding tank" concept, because a sound is unprocessed until the following sound is heard, and only then can it be made meaningful. This particular sensory store is capable of storing large amounts of auditory information that is only retained for a short period of time. This echoic sound resonates in the mind and is replayed for this brief amount of time shortly after the presentation of auditory stimuli. _____ encodes only moderately primitive aspects of the stimuli, for example pitch, which specifies localization to the non-association brain regions.

Exam Probability: **Medium**

26. *Answer choices:*

(see index for correct answer)

- a. Leveling and Sharpening
- b. Forgetting curve
- c. Echoic memory
- d. Intermediate-term memory

Guidance: level 1

:: Perception ::

An _____ is a distortion of the senses, which can reveal how the human brain normally organizes and interprets sensory stimulation. Though _____ s distort our perception of reality, they are generally shared by most people.

Exam Probability: **Medium**

27. *Answer choices:*

(see index for correct answer)

- a. Sensory threshold
- b. Disjunctivism
- c. Set
- d. Illusion

Guidance: level 1

:: Synesthesia ::

_____ is a perceptual phenomenon in which stimulation of one sensory or cognitive pathway leads to automatic, involuntary experiences in a second sensory or cognitive pathway. People who report a lifelong history of such experiences are known as synesthetes.

Exam Probability: **High**

28. *Answer choices:*

(see index for correct answer)

- a. Synesthesia
- b. The Man Who Tasted Shapes
- c. A Mango-Shaped Space
- d. Aromachologist

Guidance: level 1

:: Neuropsychology ::

_____ is a type of perceptual task requiring attention that typically involves an active scan of the visual environment for a particular object or feature among other objects or features. _____ can take place with or without eye movements. The ability to consciously locate an object or target amongst a complex array of stimuli has been extensively studied over the past 40 years. Practical examples of using _____ can be seen in everyday life, such as when one is picking out a product on a supermarket shelf, when animals are searching for food amongst piles of leaves, when trying to find your friend in a large crowd of people, or simply when playing _____ games such as Where's Wally Much previous literature on _____ used reaction time in order to measure the time it takes to detect the target amongst its distractors. An example of this could be a green square amongst a set of red circles. However, reaction time measurements do not always distinguish between the role of attention and other factors: a long reaction time might be the result of difficulty directing attention to the target, or slowed decision-making processes or slowed motor responses after attention is already directed to the target and the target has already been detected. Many _____ paradigms have therefore used eye movement as a means to measure the degree of attention given to stimuli. However, vast research to date suggests that eye movements can move independently of attention, and therefore eye movement measures do not completely capture the role of attention.

Exam Probability: **Medium**

29. *Answer choices:*

(see index for correct answer)

- a. Central nucleus of the amygdala
- b. Affectiva
- c. Neuropsychological assessment
- d. Psychological refractory period

Guidance: level 1

:: Substance abuse ::

_____ , also known as drug abuse, is a patterned use of a drug in which the user consumes the substance in amounts or with methods which are harmful to themselves or others, and is a form of substance-related disorder. Widely differing definitions of drug abuse are used in public health, medical and criminal justice contexts. In some cases criminal or anti-social behaviour occurs when the person is under the influence of a drug, and long term personality changes in individuals may occur as well. In addition to possible physical, social, and psychological harm, use of some drugs may also lead to criminal penalties, although these vary widely depending on the local jurisdiction.

Exam Probability: **Medium**

30. *Answer choices:*
(see index for correct answer)

- a. Residential Drug Abuse Program
- b. Substance abuse prevention
- c. Substance abuse
- d. Benzodiazepine misuse

Guidance: level 1

:: Optical illusions ::

The _____ is a geometrical-optical illusion that was first demonstrated by the Italian psychologist Mario Ponzo in 1911. He suggested that the human mind judges an object's size based on its background. He showed this by drawing two identical lines across a pair of converging lines, similar to railway tracks. The upper line looks longer because we interpret the converging sides according to linear perspective as parallel lines receding into the distance. In this context, we interpret the upper line as though it were farther away, so we see it as longer – a farther object would have to be longer than a nearer one for both to produce retinal images of the same size.

Exam Probability: **Low**

31. *Answer choices:*

(see index for correct answer)

- a. Watercolor illusion
- b. Impossible cube
- c. U.S.A.
- d. Motion aftereffect

Guidance: level 1

:: Cognitive science ::

_____ is an approach in the fields of cognitive science, that hopes to explain mental phenomena using artificial neural networks.

Exam Probability: **High**

32. *Answer choices:*

(see index for correct answer)

- a. Psychological effects of Internet use
- b. Mental model
- c. Dual-coding theory
- d. Concept

Guidance: level 1

:: Psycholinguistics ::

_____ is the property of a person or of a system that delivers information quickly and with expertise.

Exam Probability: **Medium**

33. *Answer choices:*

(see index for correct answer)

- a. Auditory moving-window
- b. Fluency
- c. Accents
- d. Maledictology

Guidance: level 1

:: Neuroanatomy ::

A _____ is an enclosed, cable-like bundle of _____ fibres called axons, in the peripheral nervous system. A _____ provides a common pathway for the electrochemical _____ impulses called action potentials that are transmitted along each of the axons to peripheral organs or, in the case of sensory _____ s, from the periphery back to the central nervous system. Each axon within the _____ is an extension of an individual neuron, along with other supportive cells such as Schwann cells that coat the axons in myelin.

Exam Probability: **Medium**

34. *Answer choices:*

(see index for correct answer)

- a. Olfactory tract
- b. Nerve
- c. Corpora arenacea
- d. Trochlear nucleus

Guidance: level 1

:: Emotions ::

_____ or attraction is a quality that causes an interest, desire in, or gravitation to something or someone. Attraction may also refer to the object of the attraction itself, as in tourist attraction.

Exam Probability: **Medium**

35. *Answer choices:*

(see index for correct answer)

- a. Shame
- b. Attractiveness
- c. Enthusiasm
- d. Schadenfreude

Guidance: level 1

:: Language acquisition ::

_____ is a process starting early in human life. Infants start without knowing a language, yet by 10 months, babies can distinguish speech sounds and engage in babbling. Some research has shown that the earliest learning begins in utero when the fetus starts to recognize the sounds and speech patterns of its mother's voice and differentiate them from other sounds after birth.

Exam Probability: **Medium**

36. *Answer choices:*

(see index for correct answer)

- a. Extensive reading
- b. Individual variation in second-language acquisition
- c. Bootstrapping
- d. Metalinguistic awareness

Guidance: level 1

:: Learning ::

_____ is a phenomenon of learning and memory that was first named and described by Ivan Pavlov in his studies of classical conditioning. In that context, it refers to the re-emergence of a previously extinguished conditioned response after a delay. Such a recovery of "lost" behaviors can be observed within a variety of domains, and the recovery of lost human memories is often of particular interest. For a mathematical model for _____ see Further Reading.

Exam Probability: **High**

37. *Answer choices:*

(see index for correct answer)

- a. Proactive learning
- b. Spontaneous recovery
- c. Youth work
- d. Summer learning loss

Guidance: level 1

:: Behaviorism ::

_____ , also known as graduated exposure therapy, is a type of behavior therapy developed by South African psychiatrist, Joseph Wolpe. It is used in the field of clinical psychology to help many people effectively overcome phobias and other anxiety disorders that are based on classical conditioning, and shares the same elements of both cognitive-behavioral therapy and applied behavior analysis. When used by the behavior analysts, it is based on radical behaviorism and functional analysis, as it incorporates counterconditioning principles, such as meditation and breathing. From the cognitive psychology perspective, however, cognitions and feelings trigger motor actions.

Exam Probability: **Low**

38. *Answer choices:*

(see index for correct answer)

- a. Rate of response
- b. Counterconditioning
- c. Systematic desensitization
- d. Behavioral engineering

Guidance: level 1

:: Intelligence by type ::

An intelligence quotient is a total score derived from several standardized tests designed to assess human intelligence. The abbreviation "IQ" was coined by the psychologist William Stern for the German term Intelligenzquotient, his term for a scoring method for _____ s at University of Breslau he advocated in a 1912 book. Historically, IQ is a score obtained by dividing a person's mental age score, obtained by administering an _____ , by the person's chronological age, both expressed in terms of years and months. The resulting fraction is multiplied by 100 to obtain the IQ score.

Exam Probability: **High**

39. *Answer choices:*

(see index for correct answer)

- a. Theory of multiple intelligences
- b. Intelligence test
- c. Intelligence quotient
- d. linguistic intelligence

Guidance: level 1

:: Educational psychology ::

An _____ is a component of a competence to do a certain kind of work at a certain level. Outstanding _____ can be considered "talent". An _____ may be physical or mental. _____ is inborn potential to do certain kinds of work whether developed or undeveloped. Ability is developed knowledge, understanding, learned or acquired abilities or attitude. The innate nature of _____ is in contrast to skills and achievement, which represent knowledge or ability that is gained through learning.

Exam Probability: **Medium**

40. *Answer choices:*
(see index for correct answer)

- a. Validity
- b. Psychopedagogy
- c. Aptitude
- d. Montessori education

Guidance: level 1

:: Behavioral concepts ::

_____ is a sub-topic of various branches of psychology that focuses on how people process, store, and apply information about other people and social situations. It focuses on the role that cognitive processes play in social interactions.

Exam Probability: **Low**

41. *Answer choices:*

(see index for correct answer)

- a. Attention
- b. Perceptual learning
- c. Relational frame theory
- d. Social cognition

Guidance: level 1

:: Self ::

An _____ is that which exists as a distinct entity. _____ ity is the state or quality of being an _____ ; particularly of being a person separate from other people and possessing their own needs or goals, rights and responsibilities. The exact definition of an _____ is important in the fields of biology, law, and philosophy.

Exam Probability: **Medium**

42. *Answer choices:*

(see index for correct answer)

- a. Sociometer
- b. Individual
- c. Gender-identity/role
- d. Self-abasement

Guidance: level 1

:: Developmental psychology ::

_____ is the process by which the sounds of language are heard, interpreted and understood. The study of _____ is closely linked to the fields of phonology and phonetics in linguistics and cognitive psychology and perception in psychology. Research in _____ seeks to understand how human listeners recognize speech sounds and use this information to understand spoken language. _____ research has applications in building computer systems that can recognize speech, in improving speech recognition for hearing- and language-impaired listeners, and in foreign-language teaching.

Exam Probability: **High**

43. *Answer choices:*

(see index for correct answer)

- a. Speech perception
- b. Evolutionary developmental psychology
- c. Critical period
- d. Cognitive development

Guidance: level 1

:: Sleep ::

_____ is a naturally recurring state of mind and body, characterized by altered consciousness, relatively inhibited sensory activity, inhibition of nearly all voluntary muscles, and reduced interactions with surroundings. It is distinguished from wakefulness by a decreased ability to react to stimuli, but more reactive than coma or disorders of consciousness, _____ displaying very different and active brain patterns.

Exam Probability: **High**

44. *Answer choices:*

(see index for correct answer)

- a. Sleep diary
- b. Sandman
- c. Microsleep
- d. Sleep

Guidance: level 1

:: Stroke ::

A _____ is a medical condition in which poor blood flow to the brain results in cell death. There are two main types of _____ : ischemic, due to lack of blood flow, and hemorrhagic, due to bleeding. Both result in parts of the brain not functioning properly. Signs and symptoms of a _____ may include an inability to move or feel on one side of the body, problems understanding or speaking, dizziness, or loss of vision to one side. Signs and symptoms often appear soon after the _____ has occurred. If symptoms last less than one or two hours it is known as a transient ischemic attack or mini-_____. A hemorrhagic _____ may also be associated with a severe headache. The symptoms of a _____ can be permanent. Long-term complications may include pneumonia or loss of bladder control.

Exam Probability: **High**

45. *Answer choices:*

(see index for correct answer)

- a. Middle cerebral artery syndrome
- b. Stroke
- c. Conduction aphasia
- d. Lateral pontine syndrome

Guidance: level 1

:: Speech error ::

A _____, also called parapraxis, is an error in speech, memory, or physical action that occurs due to the interference of an unconscious subdued wish or internal train of thought. The concept is part of classical psychoanalysis. Classical examples involve slips of the tongue, but psychoanalytic theory also embraces misreadings, mishearings, temporary forgettings, and the mislaying and losing of objects.

Exam Probability: **Low**

46. *Answer choices:*

(see index for correct answer)

- a. Eggcorn
- b. Freudian slip
- c. Hypercorrection
- d. Barbarism

Guidance: level 1

:: Brain ::

The _____ is an organ that serves as the center of the nervous system in all vertebrate and most invertebrate animals. The _____ is located in the head, usually close to the sensory organs for senses such as vision. The _____ is the most complex organ in a vertebrate's body. In a human, the cerebral cortex contains approximately 14–16 billion neurons, and the estimated number of neurons in the cerebellum is 55–70 billion. Each neuron is connected by synapses to several thousand other neurons. These neurons communicate with one another by means of long protoplasmic fibers called axons, which carry trains of signal pulses called action potentials to distant parts of the _____ or body targeting specific recipient cells.

Exam Probability: **Medium**

47. *Answer choices:*

(see index for correct answer)

- a. Neuromodulation
- b. Postcentral gyrus
- c. Artery of Percheron
- d. Yakovlevian torque

Guidance: level 1

:: Perception ::

In research, the _____ of a study means that the methods, materials and setting of the study must approximate the real-world that is being examined. Unlike internal and external validity, _____ is not necessary to the overall validity of a study.

Exam Probability: **Medium**

48. *Answer choices:*

(see index for correct answer)

- a. Sensual play
- b. Tone variator
- c. Lip reading
- d. Nous

Guidance: level 1

:: Signal transduction ::

A _____ is any member of a class of signaling molecules produced by glands in multicellular organisms that are transported by the circulatory system to target distant organs to regulate physiology and behavior. _____ s have diverse chemical structures, mainly of three classes: eicosanoids, steroids, and amino acid/protein derivatives . The glands that secrete _____ s comprise the endocrine signaling system. The term _____ is sometimes extended to include chemicals produced by cells that affect the same cell or nearby cells .

Exam Probability: **Low**

49. *Answer choices:*

(see index for correct answer)

- a. PRKAB2
- b. PRKCQ
- c. BCKDHA
- d. Phosphatidylinositol 4-phosphate

Guidance: level 1

:: Educational psychology ::

_____ , learning disorder or learning difficulty is a condition in the brain that causes difficulties comprehending or processing information and can be caused by several different factors. Given the "difficulty learning in a typical manner", this does not exclude the ability to learn in a different manner. Therefore, some people can be more accurately described as having a "learning difference", thus avoiding any misconception of being disabled with a lack of ability to learn and possible negative stereotyping. In the United Kingdom, the term " _____ " generally refers to an intellectual disability, while difficulties such as dyslexia and dyspraxia are usually referred to as "learning difficulties".

Exam Probability: **Low**

50. *Answer choices:*

(see index for correct answer)

- a. Marte Meo
- b. Learning disability
- c. Test score
- d. Integrative learning

Guidance: level 1

:: Human development ::

In psychology, _____ is a common emotional response to opposition, related to anger, annoyance and disappointment, _____ arises from the perceived resistance to the fulfillment of an individual's will or goal and is likely to increase when a will or goal is denied or blocked. There are two types of _____ ; internal and external. Internal _____ may arise from challenges in fulfilling personal goals, desires, instinctual drives and needs, or dealing with perceived deficiencies, such as a lack of confidence or fear of social situations. Conflict, such as when one has competing goals that interfere with one another, can also be an internal source of _____ and can create cognitive dissonance. External causes of _____ involve conditions outside an individual's control, such as a physical roadblock, a difficult task, or the perception of wasting time. There are multiple ways individuals cope with _____ such as passive-aggressive behavior, anger, or violence, although _____ may also propel positive processes via enhanced effort and strive. This broad range of potential outcomes makes it difficult to identify the original cause of _____ , as the responses may be indirect. However, a more direct and common response is a propensity towards aggression.

Exam Probability: **High**

51. *Answer choices:*

(see index for correct answer)

- a. Pubarche
- b. Zone of proximal development
- c. Mother

- d. Frustration

Guidance: level 1

:: Educational psychology ::

_____ is a statistical method used to describe variability among observed, correlated variables in terms of a potentially lower number of unobserved variables called factors. For example, it is possible that variations in six observed variables mainly reflect the variations in two unobserved variables. _____ searches for such joint variations in response to unobserved latent variables. The observed variables are modelled as linear combinations of the potential factors, plus "error" terms. _____ aims to find independent latent variables.

Exam Probability: **High**

52. *Answer choices:*
(see index for correct answer)

- a. Psychopedagogy
- b. Factor analysis
- c. Graphic organizer
- d. Shuhari

Guidance: level 1

:: Behaviorism ::

_____ is a non-associative learning process in which repeated administration of a stimulus results in the progressive amplification of a response. _____ often is characterized by an enhancement of response to a whole class of stimuli in addition to the one that is repeated. For example, repetition of a painful stimulus may make one more responsive to a loud noise.

Exam Probability: **High**

53. *Answer choices:*

(see index for correct answer)

- a. Applied behavior analysis
- b. Behavioral psychotherapy
- c. Motivating operation
- d. Sensitization

Guidance: level 1

:: Memory ::

Memory gaps and errors refer to the incorrect recall, or complete loss, of information in the memory system for a specific detail and/or event. _____ may include remembering events that never occurred, or remembering them differently from the way they actually happened. These errors or gaps can occur due to a number of different reasons, including the emotional involvement in the situation, expectations and environmental changes. As the retention interval between encoding and retrieval of the memory lengthens, there is an increase in both the amount that is forgotten, and the likelihood of a memory error occurring.

Exam Probability: **Medium**

54. *Answer choices:*

(see index for correct answer)

- a. Memory errors
- b. Memory implantation
- c. Collective memory
- d. Neuroanatomy of memory

Guidance: level 1

:: Memory processes ::

A _____ is a highly detailed, exceptionally vivid `snapshot` of the moment and circumstances in which a piece of surprising and consequential news was heard. The term "_____" suggests the surprise, indiscriminate illumination, detail, and brevity of a photograph; however flashbulb memories are only somewhat indiscriminate and are far from complete. Evidence has shown that although people are highly confident in their memories, the details of the memories can be forgotten.

Exam Probability: **Low**

55. *Answer choices:*

(see index for correct answer)

- a. Episodic memory
- b. Leveling and Sharpening
- c. Concurrent overlap
- d. Flashbulb memory

Guidance: level 1

:: Neuropeptides ::

_____s are endogenous opioid neuropeptides and peptide hormones in humans and other animals. They are produced by the central nervous system and the pituitary gland. The term "_____s" implies a pharmacological activity as opposed to a specific chemical formulation. It consists of two parts: endo- and -orphin; these are short forms of the words endogenous and morphine, intended to mean "a morphine-like substance originating from within the body". The class of _____s includes three compounds—a-_____, ß-_____, and -_____ —which preferentially bind to μ-opioid receptors. The principal function of _____s is to inhibit the communication of pain signals; they may also produce a feeling of euphoria very similar to that produced by other opioids.

Exam Probability: **Medium**

56. *Answer choices:*

(see index for correct answer)

- a. Agouti-related peptide
- b. Neuromedin U
- c. Relaxin-3
- d. Endorphin

Guidance: level 1

:: Neuropsychological assessment ::

_____ is the faculty of the brain by which information is encoded, stored, and retrieved when needed.

Exam Probability: **Low**

57. *Answer choices:*

(see index for correct answer)

- a. Natural language
- b. Adaptive memory
- c. forethought
- d. Problem solving

Guidance: level 1

:: Human behavior ::

In psychology, _____ is a lack of restraint manifested in disregard of social conventions, impulsivity, and poor risk assessment. _____ affects motor, instinctual, emotional, cognitive, and perceptual aspects with signs and symptoms similar to the diagnostic criteria for mania. Hypersexuality, hyperphagia, and aggressive outbursts are indicative of disinhibited instinctual drives.

Exam Probability: **Medium**

58. *Answer choices:*

(see index for correct answer)

- a. Disinhibition
- b. heredity and environment

- c. Nagging
- d. Relational disorder

Guidance: level 1

:: Artificial intelligence ::

_____ is a method for searching associative networks, biological and artificial neural networks, or semantic networks. The search process is initiated by labeling a set of source nodes with weights or "activation" and then iteratively propagating or "spreading" that activation out to other nodes linked to the source nodes. Most often these "weights" are real values that decay as activation propagates through the network. When the weights are discrete this process is often referred to as marker passing. Activation may originate from alternate paths, identified by distinct markers, and terminate when two alternate paths reach the same node. However brain studies show that several different brain areas play an important role in semantic processing.

Exam Probability: **Medium**

59. *Answer choices:*
(see index for correct answer)

- a. Agent systems reference model
- b. Spreading activation
- c. Blackbox planning system
- d. Mutual intelligence

Guidance: level 1

Abnormal Psychology

Abnormal psychology is the branch of psychology that studies unusual patterns of behavior, emotion and thought, which may or may not be understood as precipitating a mental disorder. Although many behaviors could be considered as abnormal, this branch of psychology generally deals with behavior in a clinical context. There is a long history of attempts to understand and control behavior deemed to be aberrant or deviant (statistically, functionally, morally or in some other sense), and there is often cultural variation in the approach taken. The field of abnormal psychology identifies multiple causes for different conditions, employing diverse theories from the general field of psychology and elsewhere, and much still hinges on what exactly is meant by "abnormal".

:: Psychopharmacology ::

The _____ s are a group of antipsychotic drugs used to treat psychiatric conditions. Some _____ s have received regulatory approval for schizophrenia, bipolar disorder, autism, and as an adjunct in major depressive disorder.

Exam Probability: **Medium**

1. *Answer choices:*
(see index for correct answer)

- a. Stimulant
- b. Dopamine receptor D2
- c. Reuptake enhancer
- d. Scandinavian College of Neuropsychopharmacology

Guidance: level 1

:: Multiracial affairs ::

An ethnic group, or an _____ , is a category of people who identify with each other based on similarities such as common ancestry, language, history, society, culture or nation. _____ is usually an inherited status based on the society in which one lives. Membership of an ethnic group tends to be defined by a shared cultural heritage, ancestry, origin myth, history, homeland, language or dialect, symbolic systems such as religion, mythology and ritual, cuisine, dressing style, art or physical appearance.

Exam Probability: **Medium**

2. Answer choices:

(see index for correct answer)

- a. Mulatto
- b. Quadroon
- c. Miss Saigon
- d. Tragic mulatto

Guidance: level 1

:: Antidepressants ::

_____ s are drugs used for the treatment of major depressive disorder and of other conditions, including some anxiety disorders, some chronic pain conditions , and to help manage some addictions. Typical side-effects of _____ s include dry mouth, weight gain, lack of sex drive, anhedonia, emotional blunting, and in some cases erectile dysfunction. Most types of _____ s are typically safe to take, but may cause increased thoughts of suicide when taken by children, adolescents, and young adults. A discontinuation syndrome can occur after stopping any _____ which resembles recurrent depression. _____ s do not provide clinically significant reduction in depressive symptoms. Debate in the medical community centers around whether or not the observed results in patients can be attributed to the placebo effect.

Exam Probability: **Low**

3. Answer choices:

(see index for correct answer)

- a. Trazium
- b. Antidepressant
- c. Fenmetozole
- d. Oleptro

Guidance: level 1

:: Sexual and gender identity disorders ::

_____ is a psychiatric diagnosis applied to those who are thought to have an excessive sexual or erotic interest in cross-dressing; this interest is often expressed in autoerotic behavior. It differs from cross-dressing for entertainment or other purposes that do not involve sexual arousal, and is categorized as a paraphilia in the Diagnostic and Statistical Manual of Mental Disorders. Sexual arousal in response to donning sex-typical clothing is homeovestism.

Exam Probability: **Low**

4. *Answer choices:*

(see index for correct answer)

- a. Female sexual arousal disorder
- b. SESAMO
- c. Skoptic syndrome
- d. Ego-dystonic sexual orientation

Guidance: level 1

:: Substance-related disorders ::

A _____, also known as a drug use disorder, is a medical condition in which the use of one or more substances leads to a clinically significant impairment or distress. _____s are characterized by an array of mental, physical, and behavioral symptoms that may cause problems related to loss of control, strain to one's interpersonal life, hazardous use, tolerance, and withdrawal. Drug classes that are involved in SUD include alcohol, phencyclidine, inhalants, stimulants, cannabis, "other hallucinogens", opioids, tobacco, and sedatives, hypnotics, and anxiolytics.

Exam Probability: **Low**

5. *Answer choices:*

(see index for correct answer)

- a. Goodenough Drug Strategy
- b. Bromism
- c. Substance use disorder
- d. Substance-related disorder

Guidance: level 1

:: Emotional and behavioral disorders in childhood and adolescence ::

_____ is listed in the DSM-5 under Disruptive, impulse-control, and conduct disorders and defined as "a pattern of angry/irritable mood, argumentative/defiant behavior, or vindictiveness" in children and adolescents. Unlike children with conduct disorder, children with _____ are not aggressive towards people or animals, do not destroy property, and do not show a pattern of theft or deceit.

Exam Probability: **Low**

6. *Answer choices:*

(see index for correct answer)

- a. Oppositional defiant disorder
- b. Stuttering
- c. Tourette syndrome
- d. Child pyromaniac

Guidance: level 1

:: Emotion ::

_____ is, e.g., the purification and purgation of emotions—particularly pity and fear—through art or any extreme change in emotion that results in renewal and restoration. It is a metaphor originally used by Aristotle in the Poetics, comparing the effects of tragedy on the mind of a spectator to the effect of a cathartic on the body. New work shows that metaphor is not allowed in definitions for Aristotle and thus, for a number of other reasons, too, Aristotle could not have written himself the word katharsis in that location, which helps explain why no one in 1000 years has been able to translate it to the satisfaction of the specialists in Aristotle.

Exam Probability: **Medium**

7. *Answer choices:*

(see index for correct answer)

- a. Affect consciousness
- b. Catharsis
- c. Emotional responsivity
- d. Emotional baggage

Guidance: level 1

:: Systems psychology ::

_____ , also referred to as couple and _____ , marriage and _____ , family systems therapy, and family counseling, is a branch of psychotherapy that works with families and couples in intimate relationships to nurture change and development. It tends to view change in terms of the systems of interaction between family members. It emphasizes family relationships as an important factor in psychological health.

Exam Probability: **Medium**

8. *Answer choices:*

(see index for correct answer)

- a. Human factors and ergonomics
- b. Human systems engineering
- c. Group-dynamic game
- d. Group behaviour

Guidance: level 1

:: Autonomic nervous system ::

The _____ , formerly the vegetative nervous system, is a division of the peripheral nervous system that supplies smooth muscle and glands, and thus influences the function of internal organs. The _____ is a control system that acts largely unconsciously and regulates bodily functions such as the heart rate, digestion, respiratory rate, pupillary response, urination, and sexual arousal. This system is the primary mechanism in control of the fight-or-flight response.

Exam Probability: **Low**

9. *Answer choices:*

(see index for correct answer)

- a. San Francisco Syncope Rule
- b. Autonomic nervous system
- c. preganglionic
- d. postganglionic

Guidance: level 1

:: Behavior ::

_____ is a concept introduced during the 1970s by Mark Snyder, that shows how much people monitor their self-presentations, expressive behavior, and nonverbal affective displays. Human beings generally differ in substantial ways in their abilities and desires to engage in expressive controls . It is defined as a personality trait that refers to an ability to regulate behavior to accommodate social situations. People concerned with their expressive self-presentation tend to closely monitor their audience in order to ensure appropriate or desired public appearances. Self-monitors try to understand how individuals and groups will perceive their actions. Some personality types commonly act spontaneously and others are more apt to purposely control and consciously adjust their behavior . Recent studies suggest that a distinction should be made between acquisitive and protective _____ due to their different interactions with metatraits. This differentiates the motive behind _____ behaviours: for the purpose of acquiring appraisal from others or protecting oneself from social disapproval .

Exam Probability: **Medium**

10. *Answer choices:*

(see index for correct answer)

- a. Challenging behaviour
- b. Cat intelligence
- c. Motion camouflage
- d. Self-monitoring

Guidance: level 1

:: Cognitive science ::

_____ is "the mental action or process of acquiring knowledge and understanding through thought, experience, and the senses". It encompasses many aspects of intellectual functions and processes such as attention, the formation of knowledge, memory and working memory, judgment and evaluation, reasoning and "computation", problem solving and decision making, comprehension and production of language. Cognitive processes use existing knowledge and generate new knowledge.

Exam Probability: **High**

11. *Answer choices:*

(see index for correct answer)

- a. Automatic and Controlled Processes

- b. Socio-cognitive
- c. Language and Communication Technologies
- d. Cognition

Guidance: level 1

:: Emotional issues ::

_____ is an anxiety disorder characterized by reoccurring unexpected panic attacks. Panic attacks are sudden periods of intense fear that may include palpitations, sweating, shaking, shortness of breath, numbness, or a feeling that something terrible is going to happen. The maximum degree of symptoms occurs within minutes. There may be ongoing worries about having further attacks and avoidance of places where attacks have occurred in the past.

Exam Probability: **High**

12. *Answer choices:*
(see index for correct answer)

- a. Affective forecasting
- b. Love-shyness
- c. Panic disorder
- d. Circle of Courage

Guidance: level 1

:: Personality disorders ::

_____ is traditionally a personality disorder characterized by persistent antisocial behavior, impaired empathy and remorse, and bold, disinhibited, and egotistical traits. It is sometimes considered synonymous with sociopathy. Different conceptions of _____ have been used throughout history that are only partly overlapping and may sometimes be contradictory.

Exam Probability: **Low**

13. *Answer choices:*

(see index for correct answer)

- a. Paranoid personality disorder
- b. Cluster B personality disorders
- c. Schizoid personality disorder
- d. Psychopathy

Guidance: level 1

:: Therapy ::

The therapeutic relationship refers to the relationship between a healthcare professional and a client. It is the means by which a therapist and a client hope to engage with each other, and effect beneficial change in the client.

Exam Probability: **Medium**

14. *Answer choices:*

(see index for correct answer)

- a. Reality testing
- b. regimen
- c. Therapeutic alliance

Guidance: level 1

:: Addiction ::

_____ is a brain disorder characterized by compulsive engagement in rewarding stimuli despite adverse consequences. Despite the involvement of a number of psychosocial factors, a biological process – one which is induced by repeated exposure to an addictive stimulus – is the core pathology that drives the development and maintenance of an _____ . The two properties that characterize all addictive stimuli are that they are reinforcing and intrinsically rewarding .

Exam Probability: **Medium**

15. *Answer choices:*

(see index for correct answer)

- a. Bottom line behaviour
- b. Addictive behavior
- c. Action on Addiction
- d. Top lines

Guidance: level 1

:: Sexual and gender identity disorders ::

_____ is painful sexual intercourse due to medical or psychological causes. The pain can primarily be on the external surface of the genitalia, or deeper in the pelvis upon deep pressure against the cervix. It can affect a small portion of the vulva or vagina or be felt all over the surface. Understanding the duration, location, and nature of the pain is important in identifying the causes of the pain.

Exam Probability: **Medium**

16. *Answer choices:*

(see index for correct answer)

- a. Vaginismus
- b. Female sexual arousal disorder
- c. Dyspareunia
- d. SESAMO

Guidance: level 1

:: Antipsychotics ::

_____s, also known as neuroleptics or major tranquilizers, are a class of medication primarily used to manage psychosis, principally in schizophrenia and bipolar disorder. _____s are usually effective in relieving symptoms of psychosis in the short term.

Exam Probability: **Medium**

17. *Answer choices:*

(see index for correct answer)

- a. F-15,063
- b. Pleurothotonus
- c. Biphenylindanone A
- d. Carfenazine

Guidance: level 1

:: Sleep disorders ::

_____, also known as sleeplessness, is a sleep disorder in which people have trouble sleeping. They may have difficulty falling asleep, or staying asleep as long as desired. _____ is typically followed by daytime sleepiness, low energy, irritability, and a depressed mood. It may result in an increased risk of motor vehicle collisions, as well as problems focusing and learning. _____ can be short term, lasting for days or weeks, or long term, lasting more than a month.

Exam Probability: **High**

18. *Answer choices:*

(see index for correct answer)

- a. Insomnia
- b. Canadian Sleep Society
- c. Stanford Protocol
- d. Cognitive behavioral therapy for insomnia

Guidance: level 1

:: Opioids ::

The term _____ originally referred medically to any psychoactive compound with sleep-inducing properties. In the United States, it has since become associated with opiates and opioids, commonly morphine and heroin, as well as derivatives of many of the compounds found within raw opium latex. The primary three are morphine, codeine, and thebaine.

Exam Probability: **High**

19. *Answer choices:*

(see index for correct answer)

- a. Ro4-1539
- b. Tonazocine
- c. Narcotic
- d. Prodilidine

Guidance: level 1

:: Cognitive neuroscience ::

_____ is the capacity to understand or feel what another person is experiencing from within their frame of reference, that is, the capacity to place oneself in another's position. Definitions of _____ encompass a broad range of emotional states. Types of _____ include cognitive _____, emotional _____, and somatic _____.

Exam Probability: **High**

20. *Answer choices:*

(see index for correct answer)

- a. Empathy
- b. Structural information theory
- c. Crossmodal
- d. Mind and Life Institute

Guidance: level 1

:: Philosophy of psychology ::

_____ is a set of theories and therapeutic techniques related to the study of the unconscious mind, which together form a method of treatment for mental-health disorders. The discipline was established in the early 1890s by Austrian neurologist Sigmund Freud and stemmed partly from the clinical work of Josef Breuer and others. _____ was later developed in different directions, mostly by students of Freud such as Alfred Adler and Carl Gustav Jung, and by neo-Freudians such as Erich Fromm, Karen Horney and Harry Stack Sullivan. Freud retained the term _____ for his own school of thought.

Exam Probability: **Low**

21. *Answer choices:*

(see index for correct answer)

- a. Introspection
- b. Psychoanalysis
- c. Cognitivism
- d. Mentalism

Guidance: level 1

:: Clinical psychology ::

_____ is the administration of psychological tests, which are designed to be "an objective and standardized measure of a sample of behavior". The term sample of behavior refers to an individual's performance on tasks that have usually been prescribed beforehand. The samples of behavior that make up a paper-and-pencil test, the most common type of test, are a series of items. Performance on these items produce a test score. A score on a well-constructed test is believed to reflect a psychological construct such as achievement in a school subject, cognitive ability, aptitude, emotional functioning, personality, etc. Differences in test scores are thought to reflect individual differences in the construct the test is supposed to measure. The science behind _____ is psychometrics.

Exam Probability: **High**

22. *Answer choices:*

(see index for correct answer)

- a. Prescriptive authority for psychologists movement
- b. Idiographic image
- c. Interoceptive exposure
- d. Doctor of Clinical Psychology

Guidance: level 1

:: Personality disorders ::

_____ is a personality disorder characterized by a lack of interest in social relationships, a tendency towards a solitary or sheltered lifestyle, secretiveness, emotional coldness, detachment, and apathy. Affected individuals may be unable to form intimate attachments to others and simultaneously demonstrate a rich, elaborate, and exclusively internal fantasy world.

Exam Probability: **Low**

23. *Answer choices:*

(see index for correct answer)

- a. Haltlose personality disorder
- b. Antisocial personality
- c. Narcissistic personality disorder
- d. Avoidant personality disorder

Guidance: level 1

:: Psychiatric diagnosis ::

_____ nervosa, also known as simply _____ , is an eating disorder characterized by binge eating followed by purging. Binge eating refers to eating a large amount of food in a short amount of time. Purging refers to the attempts to get rid of the food consumed. This may be done by vomiting or taking laxatives. Other efforts to lose weight may include the use of diuretics, stimulants, water fasting, or excessive exercise. Most people with _____ are at a normal weight. The forcing of vomiting may result in thickened skin on the knuckles and breakdown of the teeth. _____ is frequently associated with other mental disorders such as depression, anxiety, and problems with drugs or alcohol. There is also a higher risk of suicide and self-harm.

Exam Probability: **High**

24. *Answer choices:*

(see index for correct answer)

- a. dysmorphia
- b. schizophreniform
- c. Bulimia
- d. separation anxiety

Guidance: level 1

:: Sexual fetishism ::

_____ is the act of exposing in a public or semi-public context those parts of one's body that are not normally exposed for example, the breasts, genitals or buttocks. The practice may arise from a desire or compulsion to expose themselves in such a manner to groups of friends or acquaintances, or to strangers for their amusement or sexual satisfaction or to shock the bystander. Exposing oneself only to an intimate partner is normally not regarded as _____ . In law, the act of _____ may be called indecent exposure, "exposing one's person", or other expressions.

Exam Probability: **Medium**

25. *Answer choices:*

(see index for correct answer)

- a. Salirophilia
- b. Head shaving
- c. Homosexual fetishism
- d. Footjob

Guidance: level 1

:: Twelve-step programs ::

_____ is a self-enforced restraint from indulging in bodily activities that are widely experienced as giving pleasure. Most frequently, the term refers to sexual _____ , or _____ from alcohol, drugs, or food.

Exam Probability: **High**

26. *Answer choices:*

(see index for correct answer)

- a. Heroin Anonymous
- b. Serenity Prayer
- c. Workaholics Anonymous
- d. Abstinence

Guidance: level 1

:: Schizophrenia ::

_____ is a disused psychiatric diagnosis that originally designated a chronic, deteriorating psychotic disorder characterized by rapid cognitive disintegration, usually beginning in the late teens or early adulthood. Over the years, the term "_____" was gradually replaced by "schizophrenia", which remains in current diagnostic use.

Exam Probability: **Low**

27. *Answer choices:*

(see index for correct answer)

- a. Diagnosis of schizophrenia
- b. Dementia praecox
- c. Alogia
- d. Colorado v. Connelly

Guidance: level 1

:: Freudian psychology ::

In Freudian psychoanalysis, the _____ is the third stage of psychosexual development, spanning the ages of three to six years, wherein the infant's libido centers upon his or her genitalia as the erogenous zone. When children become aware of their bodies, the bodies of other children, and the bodies of their parents, they gratify physical curiosity by undressing and exploring each other and their genitals, the center of the _____ , in course of which they learn the physical differences between "male" and "female", and the gender differences between "boy" and "girl", experiences which alter the psychologic dynamics of the parent and child relationship. The _____ is the third of five Freudian psychosexual development stages: the oral, the anal, the phallic, the latent, and the genital.

Exam Probability: **Low**

28. *Answer choices:*

(see index for correct answer)

- a. Polycrates complex
- b. Narcissistic neurosis
- c. Anal expulsiveness
- d. Ego reduction

Guidance: level 1

:: Smoking ::

_____ is a practice in which a substance is burned and the resulting smoke breathed in to be tasted and absorbed into the bloodstream. Most commonly the substance is the dried leaves of the tobacco plant which have been rolled into a small square of rice paper to create a small, round cylinder called a "cigarette". _____ is primarily practiced as a route of administration for recreational drug use because the combustion of the dried plant leaves vaporizes and delivers active substances into the lungs where they are rapidly absorbed into the bloodstream and reach bodily tissue. In the case of cigarette _____ these substances are contained in a mixture of aerosol particles and gasses and include the pharmacologically active alkaloid nicotine; the vaporization creates heated aerosol and gas into a form that allows inhalation and deep penetration into the lungs where absorption into the bloodstream of the active substances occurs. In some cultures, _____ is also carried out as a part of various rituals, where participants use it to help induce trance-like states that, they believe, can lead them to spiritual enlightenment.

Exam Probability: **High**

29. *Answer choices:*
(see index for correct answer)

- a. Youth smoking
- b. Chipper
- c. Smoking
- d. History of smoking

Guidance: level 1

:: Mood disorders ::

_____ , also known simply as depression, is a mental disorder characterized by at least two weeks of low mood that is present across most situations. It is often accompanied by low self-esteem, loss of interest in normally enjoyable activities, low energy, and pain without a clear cause. People may also occasionally have false beliefs or see or hear things that others cannot. Some people have periods of depression separated by years in which they are normal, while others nearly always have symptoms present. _____ can negatively affect a person's personal life, work life, or education, as well as sleeping, eating habits, and general health. Between 2–8% of adults with major depression die by suicide, and about 50% of people who die by suicide had depression or another mood disorder.

Exam Probability: **Medium**

30. *Answer choices:*
(see index for correct answer)

- a. Melancholic depression
- b. Episodic dyscontrol syndrome
- c. Hospital Anxiety and Depression Scale
- d. Mood swing

Guidance: level 1

:: Childhood psychiatric disorders ::

_____ is an anxiety disorder in which a person who is normally capable of speech cannot speak in specific situations or to specific people. _____ usually co-exists with shyness or social anxiety. People with _____ stay silent even when the consequences of their silence include shame, social ostracism, or punishment.

Exam Probability: **Medium**

31. *Answer choices:*

(see index for correct answer)

- a. Adjustment disorder
- b. PANDAS
- c. Asperger syndrome
- d. Pediatric acute-onset neuropsychiatric syndrome

Guidance: level 1

:: Psychoanalysis ::

_____ is a class of functional mental disorders involving chronic distress but neither delusions nor hallucinations. The term is no longer used by the professional psychiatric community in the United States, having been eliminated from the Diagnostic and Statistical Manual of Mental Disorders in 1980 with the publication of DSM III. It is still used in the ICD-10 Chapter V F40–48.

Exam Probability: **Medium**

32. *Answer choices:*

(see index for correct answer)

- a. San Francisco Psychoanalytic Society and Institute
- b. Neurosis
- c. Psychoanalytic conceptions of language
- d. Controversial discussions

Guidance: level 1

:: Counseling ::

_____ is an immediate and short-term psychological care aimed at assisting individuals in a crisis situation in order to restore equilibrium to their bio-psycho-social functioning and to minimize the potential of long-term psychological trauma.

Exam Probability: **High**

33. *Answer choices:*

(see index for correct answer)

- a. Healing Through Creativity
- b. Crisis intervention
- c. American Association for Marriage and Family Therapy
- d. Direct therapeutic exposure

Guidance: level 1

:: Personality disorders ::

_____ is defined by the American Psychiatric Association as a personality disorder characterized by a pattern of excessive attention-seeking emotions, usually beginning in early adulthood, including inappropriately seductive behavior and an excessive need for approval. Histrionic people are lively, dramatic, vivacious, enthusiastic, and flirtatious. HPD is diagnosed four times as frequently in women as men. It affects 2–3% of the general population and 10–15% in inpatient and outpatient mental health institutions.

Exam Probability: **Medium**

34. *Answer choices:*
(see index for correct answer)

- a. Addictive personality
- b. Joan Lachkar
- c. Sadistic personality disorder
- d. Histrionic personality disorder

Guidance: level 1

:: Self ::

_____ is the personal sense of one's own gender. _____ can correlate with assigned sex at birth or can differ from it. All societies have a set of gender categories that can serve as the basis of the formation of a person's social identity in relation to other members of society.

Exam Probability: **Medium**

35. *Answer choices:*

(see index for correct answer)

- a. Selfishness
- b. Omnipotence
- c. Genealogical bewilderment
- d. Deidentification

Guidance: level 1

:: Devices to alter consciousness ::

_____ is the process of gaining greater awareness of many physiological functions primarily using instruments that provide information on the activity of those same systems, with a goal of being able to manipulate them at will. Some of the processes that can be controlled include brainwaves, muscle tone, skin conductance, heart rate and pain perception. In _____ , you are connected to electrical sensors that help you receive information about your body.

Exam Probability: **Low**

36. *Answer choices:*

(see index for correct answer)

- a. Association for Applied Psychophysiology and Biofeedback
- b. Biofeedback
- c. God helmet
- d. Project MKUltra

Guidance: level 1

:: Pharmacology ::

_____ is therapy using pharmaceutical drugs, as distinguished from therapy using surgery, radiation, movement, or other modes. Among physicians, sometimes the term medical therapy refers specifically to _____ as opposed to surgical or other therapy; for example, in oncology, medical oncology is thus distinguished from surgical oncology.

Exam Probability: **Medium**

37. *Answer choices:*

(see index for correct answer)

- a. Pharmacotherapy
- b. cross-tolerance

Guidance: level 1

:: Domestic violence ::

_____ is violence or other abuse by one person against another in a domestic setting, such as in marriage or cohabitation. It may be termed intimate partner violence when committed by a spouse or partner in an intimate relationship against the other spouse or partner, and can take place in heterosexual or same-sex relationships, or between former spouses or partners. _____ can also involve violence against children, parents, or the elderly. It takes a number of forms, including physical, verbal, emotional, economic, religious, reproductive, and sexual abuse, which can range from subtle, coercive forms to marital rape and to violent physical abuse such as choking, beating, female genital mutilation, and acid throwing that results in disfigurement or death. Domestic murders include stoning, bride burning, honor killings, and dowry deaths.

Exam Probability: **High**

38. *Answer choices:*
(see index for correct answer)

- a. Family Violence Prevention and Services Act
- b. Godelina
- c. International Violence Against Women Act
- d. Pimp stick

Guidance: level 1

:: Somatic psychology ::

A placebo is an inert substance or treatment which is not designed to have a therapeutic value. Common placebos include inert tablets, inert injections, sham surgery, and other procedures.

Exam Probability: **Low**

39. *Answer choices:*

(see index for correct answer)

- a. psychosomatic
- b. Placebo effect

Guidance: level 1

:: Mental health ::

_____ is the use of psychological methods, particularly when based on regular personal interaction, to help a person change behavior and overcome problems in desired ways. _____ aims to improve an individual's well-being and mental health, to resolve or mitigate troublesome behaviors, beliefs, compulsions, thoughts, or emotions, and to improve relationships and social skills. Certain psychotherapies are considered evidence-based for treating some diagnosed mental disorders. Others have been criticized as pseudoscience.

Exam Probability: **Medium**

40. *Answer choices:*

(see index for correct answer)

- a. Biological psychopathology
- b. Person-centered counseling
- c. Mental health consumer
- d. Psychotherapy

Guidance: level 1

:: Psychedelics, dissociatives and deliriants ::

A _____ is a perception in the absence of external stimulus that has qualities of real perception. _____ s are vivid, substantial, and are perceived to be located in external objective space. They are distinguishable from several related phenomena, such as dreaming, which does not involve wakefulness; pseudo _____ , which does not mimic real perception, and is accurately perceived as unreal; illusion, which involves distorted or misinterpreted real perception; and imagery, which does not mimic real perception and is under voluntary control. _____ s also differ from "delusional perceptions", in which a correctly sensed and interpreted stimulus is given some additional significance.

Exam Probability: **Low**

41. *Answer choices:*
(see index for correct answer)

- a. Hallucination
- b. Turn on, tune in, drop out

- c. Designer drug
- d. Convention on Psychotropic Substances

Guidance: level 1

:: Substance abuse ::

_____ , also known as drug abuse, is a patterned use of a drug in which the user consumes the substance in amounts or with methods which are harmful to themselves or others, and is a form of substance-related disorder. Widely differing definitions of drug abuse are used in public health, medical and criminal justice contexts. In some cases criminal or anti-social behaviour occurs when the person is under the influence of a drug, and long term personality changes in individuals may occur as well. In addition to possible physical, social, and psychological harm, use of some drugs may also lead to criminal penalties, although these vary widely depending on the local jurisdiction.

Exam Probability: **Low**

42. *Answer choices:*

(see index for correct answer)

- a. Inhalant
- b. Substance abuse
- c. National Drug Evidence Centre
- d. Alcohol abuse

Guidance: level 1

:: Twelve-step programs ::

_____ describes itself as a "nonprofit fellowship or society of men and women for whom drugs had become a major problem". _____ uses a traditional 12-step model that has been expanded and developed for people with varied substance abuse issues and is the second-largest 12-step organization.

Exam Probability: **High**

43. *Answer choices:*

(see index for correct answer)

- a. Pills Anonymous
- b. Celebrate Recovery
- c. Sex Addicts Anonymous
- d. Narcotics Anonymous

Guidance: level 1

:: Human development ::

_____ is the process of physical changes through which a child's body matures into an adult body capable of sexual reproduction. It is initiated by hormonal signals from the brain to the gonads: the ovaries in a girl, the testes in a boy. In response to the signals, the gonads produce hormones that stimulate libido and the growth, function, and transformation of the brain, bones, muscle, blood, skin, hair, breasts, and sex organs. Physical growth—height and weight—accelerates in the first half of _____ and is completed when an adult body has been developed. Until the maturation of their reproductive capabilities, the pre-pubertal physical differences between boys and girls are the external sex organs.

Exam Probability: **High**

44. *Answer choices:*

(see index for correct answer)

- a. Continuum concept
- b. Social orphan
- c. Puberty
- d. Fraternal birth order and male sexual orientation

Guidance: level 1

:: Defence mechanisms ::

A _____ is an exaggerated or irrational thought pattern involved in the onset and perpetuation of psychopathological states, especially those more influenced by psychosocial factors, such as depression and anxiety. Psychiatrist Aaron T. Beck laid the groundwork for the study of these distortions, and his student David D. Burns continued research on the topic. Burns, in The Feeling Good Handbook, described personal and professional anecdotes related to _____ s and their elimination.

Exam Probability: **Low**

45. *Answer choices:*
(see index for correct answer)

- a. Introjection
- b. Motivated forgetting
- c. Defensive pessimism
- d. Cognitive distortion

Guidance: level 1

:: Statistical terminology ::

In the design of experiments, treatments are applied to experimental units in the treatment group. In comparative experiments, members of the complementary group, the _____ , receive either no treatment or a standard treatment.

Exam Probability: **Low**

46. *Answer choices:*

(see index for correct answer)

- a. uncorrelated
- b. Likelihood
- c. Dependent variable
- d. Control group

Guidance: level 1

:: Sleep ::

A _____ is a natural, internal process that regulates the sleep-wake cycle and repeats roughly every 24 hours. It can refer to any biological process that displays an endogenous, entrainable oscillation of about 24 hours. These 24-hour rhythms are driven by a circadian clock, and they have been widely observed in plants, animals, fungi, and cyanobacteria.

Exam Probability: **Low**

47. *Answer choices:*

(see index for correct answer)

- a. Nocturnal penile tumescence
- b. Ferber method
- c. Seven Sleepers
- d. Sleepover

Guidance: level 1

:: Schizophrenia ::

In psychology, _____, or poverty of speech, is a general lack of additional, unprompted content seen in normal speech. As a symptom, it is commonly seen in patients suffering from schizophrenia, and is considered a negative symptom. It can complicate psychotherapy severely because of the considerable difficulty in holding a fluent conversation.

Exam Probability: **Medium**

48. *Answer choices:*
(see index for correct answer)

- a. Alogia
- b. Social construction of schizophrenia
- c. Schizoaffective
- d. Sluggish schizophrenia

Guidance: level 1

:: Neuroanatomy ::

A _____ is an enclosed, cable-like bundle of _____ fibres called axons, in the peripheral nervous system. A _____ provides a common pathway for the electrochemical _____ impulses called action potentials that are transmitted along each of the axons to peripheral organs or, in the case of sensory _____ s, from the periphery back to the central nervous system. Each axon within the _____ is an extension of an individual neuron, along with other supportive cells such as Schwann cells that coat the axons in myelin.

Exam Probability: **Low**

49. *Answer choices:*
(see index for correct answer)

- a. Lenticular fasciculus
- b. Superior colliculus
- c. Lorenzo Tenchini
- d. Pleasure center

Guidance: level 1

:: Catecholamines ::

_____, also called noradrenaline or noradrenalin, is an organic chemical in the catecholamine family that functions in the brain and body as a hormone and neurotransmitter. The name "noradrenaline", derived from Latin roots meaning "at/alongside the kidneys", is more commonly used in the United Kingdom; in the United States, "_____", derived from Greek roots having that same meaning, is usually preferred. "_____" is also the international nonproprietary name given to the drug. Regardless of which name is used for the substance itself, parts of the body that produce or are affected by it are referred to as noradrenergic.

Exam Probability: **High**

50. *Answer choices:*

(see index for correct answer)

- a. Rimiterol
- b. Oxidopamine
- c. Deoxyepinephrine
- d. Norepinephrine

Guidance: level 1

:: Behaviorism ::

A _____ is a system of contingency management based on the systematic reinforcement of target behavior. The reinforcers are symbols or tokens that can be exchanged for other reinforcers. A _____ is based on the principles of operant conditioning and behavioral economics and can be situated within applied behavior analysis. In applied settings token economies are used with children and adults; however, they have been successfully modeled with pigeons in lab settings.

Exam Probability: **Low**

51. *Answer choices:*

(see index for correct answer)

- a. Shaping
- b. Token economy
- c. The Analysis of Verbal Behavior
- d. Systematic desensitization

Guidance: level 1

:: Analytical psychology ::

In Neo-Freudian psychology, the _____ , as proposed by Carl Jung in his Theory of Psychoanalysis, is a girl's psychosexual competition with her mother for possession of her father. In the course of her psychosexual development, the complex is the girl's phallic stage; a boy's analogous experience is the Oedipus complex. The _____ occurs in the third—phallic stage —of five psychosexual development stages: the Oral, the Anal, the Phallic, the Latent, and the Genital—in which the source of libido pleasure is in a different erogenous zone of the infant's body.

Exam Probability: **High**

52. *Answer choices:*

(see index for correct answer)

- a. Metanoia
- b. Enantiodromia
- c. Self in Jungian psychology
- d. Ego functions

Guidance: level 1

:: Consciousness ::

_____ is the knowledge or mastery of an event or subject gained through involvement in or exposure to it. Terms in philosophy such as "empirical knowledge" or "a posteriori knowledge" are used to refer to knowledge based on _____ . A person with considerable _____ in a specific field can gain a reputation as an expert. The concept of _____ generally refers to know-how or procedural knowledge, rather than propositional knowledge: on-the-job training rather than book-learning.

Exam Probability: **Medium**

53. *Answer choices:*

(see index for correct answer)

- a. Choiceless awareness
- b. Experience
- c. Planetary consciousness
- d. Self-conscious

Guidance: level 1

:: Psychodynamics ::

_____ or psychoanalytic psychotherapy is a form of depth psychology, the primary focus of which is to reveal the unconscious content of a client's psyche in an effort to alleviate psychic tension.

Exam Probability: **Medium**

54. Answer choices:

(see index for correct answer)

- a. Mentalization-based treatment
- b. Psychodynamics
- c. Psychodynamic psychotherapy
- d. Ennio Foppiani

Guidance: level 1

:: Euphoriants ::

_____ , also known as coke, is a strong stimulant mostly used as a recreational drug. It is commonly snorted, inhaled as smoke, or dissolved and injected into a vein. Mental effects may include loss of contact with reality, an intense feeling of happiness, or agitation. Physical symptoms may include a fast heart rate, sweating, and large pupils. High doses can result in very high blood pressure or body temperature. Effects begin within seconds to minutes of use and last between five and ninety minutes. _____ has a small number of accepted medical uses such as numbing and decreasing bleeding during nasal surgery.

Exam Probability: **Medium**

55. Answer choices:

(see index for correct answer)

- a. Tianeptine
- b. Diacetyldihydromorphine

- c. Poppy tea
- d. Cocaine

Guidance: level 1

:: Psychoanalysis ::

_____ is a person's perception of the aesthetics or sexual attractiveness of their own body. It involves how a person sees themselves, compared to the standards that have been set by society. The Austrian neurologist and psychoanalyst Paul Schilder coined the phrase body-image in his book The Image and Appearance of the Human Body .Human society has at all times placed great value on beauty of the human body, but a person's perception of their own body may not correspond to society's standards.

Exam Probability: **Medium**

56. *Answer choices:*
(see index for correct answer)

- a. World Council for Psychotherapy
- b. Body image
- c. Basic anxiety
- d. Narcissistic leadership

Guidance: level 1

:: Behaviorism ::

In behavioral psychology, _____ is a consequence applied that will strengthen an organism's future behavior whenever that behavior is preceded by a specific antecedent stimulus. This strengthening effect may be measured as a higher frequency of behavior, longer duration, greater magnitude, or shorter latency. There are two types of _____, known as positive _____ and negative _____; positive is where by a reward is offered on expression of the wanted behaviour and negative is taking away an undesirable element in the persons environment whenever the desired behaviour is achieved.

Exam Probability: **Low**

57. *Answer choices:*

(see index for correct answer)

- a. Reinforcing
- b. Licensed behavior analyst
- c. Counterconditioning
- d. Beyond Freedom and Dignity

Guidance: level 1

:: Psychiatry ::

A _____ is a physician who specializes in psychiatry, the branch of medicine devoted to the diagnosis, prevention, study, and treatment of mental disorders. _____ s are medical doctors, unlike psychologists, and must evaluate patients to determine whether their symptoms are the result of a physical illness, a combination of physical and mental ailments, or strictly psychiatric. A _____ usually works as the clinical leader of the multi-disciplinary team, which may comprise psychologists, social workers, occupational therapists and nursing staff. _____ s have broad training in a bio-psycho-social approach to assessment and management of mental illness.

Exam Probability: **Medium**

58. *Answer choices:*

(see index for correct answer)

- a. Psychopathology
- b. Butler Committee
- c. Psychiatrist
- d. Clinical neuroscience

Guidance: level 1

:: Mass hysteria ::

_____ is a diagnostic category used in some psychiatric classification systems. It is sometimes applied to patients who present with neurological symptoms, such as numbness, blindness, paralysis, or fits, which are not consistent with a well-established organic cause, which cause significant distress, and can be traced back to a psychological trigger. It is thought that these symptoms arise in response to stressful situations affecting a patient's mental health or an ongoing mental health condition such as depression. _____ was retained in DSM-5, but given the subtitle functional neurological symptom disorder. The new criteria cover the same range of symptoms, but remove the requirements for a psychological stressor to be present and for feigning to be disproved.

Exam Probability: **Medium**

59. *Answer choices:*

(see index for correct answer)

- a. Mad Gasser of Mattoon
- b. Hollinwell incident
- c. Conversion disorder
- d. Dancing Plague of 1518

Guidance: level 1

Social Psychology

Social psychology is the scientific study of how people's thoughts, feelings, and behaviors are influenced by the actual, imagined, or implied presence of others. In this definition, scientific refers to the empirical investigation using the scientific method. The terms thoughts, feelings, and behavior refer to psychological variables that can be measured in humans. The statement that others' presence may be imagined or implied suggests that humans are malleable to social influences even when alone, such as when watching television or following internalized cultural norms. Social psychologists typically explain human behavior as a result of the interaction of mental states and social situations.

:: Motivation ::

_____ is an individual's subjective evaluation of their own worth. _____ encompasses beliefs about oneself as well as emotional states, such as triumph, despair, pride, and shame. Smith and Mackie defined it by saying "The self-concept is what we think about the self; _____, is the positive or negative evaluations of the self, as in how we feel about it."

Exam Probability: **Medium**

1. *Answer choices:*

(see index for correct answer)

- a. Online participation
- b. Self-efficacy
- c. Self-esteem
- d. Work motivation

Guidance: level 1

:: Training ::

_____ is teaching, or developing in oneself or others, any skills and knowledge that relate to specific useful competencies. _____ has specific goals of improving one's capability, capacity, productivity and performance. It forms the core of apprenticeships and provides the backbone of content at institutes of technology. In addition to the basic _____ required for a trade, occupation or profession, observers of the labor-market recognize as of 2008 the need to continue _____ beyond initial qualifications: to maintain, upgrade and update skills throughout working life. People within many professions and occupations may refer to this sort of _____ as professional development.

Exam Probability: **Medium**

2. *Answer choices:*

(see index for correct answer)

- a. Personal trainer
- b. Head coach
- c. Cyberoam Academy
- d. Hot potato

Guidance: level 1

:: Aggression ::

_____ is a 1963 book by the ethologist Konrad Lorenz; it was translated into English in 1966. As he writes in the prologue, "the subject of this book is aggression, that is to say the fighting instinct in beast and man which is directed against members of the same species."

Exam Probability: **Low**

3. *Answer choices:*

(see index for correct answer)

- a. Fight-or-flight response
- b. Snarl
- c. Verbal aggressiveness
- d. On Aggression

Guidance: level 1

:: Shunning ::

_____ is a state of complete or near-complete lack of contact between an individual and society. It differs from loneliness, which reflects temporary and involuntary lack of contact with other humans in the world. _____ can be an issue for individuals of any age, though symptoms may differ by age group.

Exam Probability: **Low**

4. *Answer choices:*

(see index for correct answer)

- a. Petalism
- b. Vitandus

- c. Marginalisation
- d. Herem

Guidance: level 1

:: Emotions ::

_____ can consist of one or more emotions such as anger, resentment, inadequacy, helplessness or disgust. In its original meaning, _____ is distinct from envy, though the two terms have popularly become synonymous in the English language, with _____ now also taking on the definition originally used for envy alone.

Exam Probability: **High**

5. *Answer choices:*
(see index for correct answer)

- a. Jealousy
- b. Panic
- c. Happiness
- d. Admiration

Guidance: level 1

:: Ethology ::

_____ or innate behavior is the inherent inclination of a living organism towards a particular complex behavior. The simplest example of an _____ive behavior is a fixed action pattern, in which a very short to medium length sequence of actions, without variation, are carried out in response to a corresponding clearly defined stimulus.

Exam Probability: **Low**

6. *Answer choices:*
(see index for correct answer)

- a. Animal Behavior Society
- b. Personal grooming
- c. Instinct
- d. Hibernation

Guidance: level 1

:: Social information processing ::

A _____ is a social structure made up of a set of social actors, sets of dyadic ties, and other social interactions between actors. The _____ perspective provides a set of methods for analyzing the structure of whole social entities as well as a variety of theories explaining the patterns observed in these structures. The study of these structures uses _____ analysis to identify local and global patterns, locate influential entities, and examine network dynamics.

Exam Probability: **Low**

7. *Answer choices:*

(see index for correct answer)

- a. On the Ground News Reports
- b. Diaspora
- c. Path
- d. Social network

Guidance: level 1

:: Human female reproductive system ::

The _____ is an organ found in the female reproductive system that produces an ovum. When released, this travels down the fallopian tube into the uterus, where it may become fertilized by a sperm. There is an _____ found on the left and right sides of the body. The ovaries also secrete hormones that play a role in the menstrual cycle and fertility. The _____ progresses through many stages beginning in the prenatal period through menopause. It is also an endocrine gland because of the various hormones that it secretes.

Exam Probability: **Medium**

8. *Answer choices:*

(see index for correct answer)

- a. Vulva
- b. Fallopian tube
- c. Uterus
- d. Ovary

Guidance: level 1

:: Behavioral concepts ::

_____ is the behavioral and cognitive process of selectively concentrating on a discrete aspect of information, whether deemed subjective or objective, while ignoring other perceivable information. It is a state of arousal. It is the taking possession by the mind in clear and vivid form of one out of what seem several simultaneous objects or trains of thought. Focalization, the concentration of consciousness, is of its essence. _____ has also been described as the allocation of limited cognitive processing resources.

Exam Probability: **Medium**

9. *Answer choices:*

(see index for correct answer)

- a. Modelling
- b. Behavioral contrast
- c. Social cognition
- d. Role taking theory

Guidance: level 1

:: Personality ::

The first personality assessment measures were developed in the 1920s and were intended to ease the process of personnel selection, particularly in the armed forces. Since these early efforts, a wide variety of personality scales and questionnaires have been developed, including the Minnesota Multiphasic Personality Inventory, the Sixteen Personality Factor Questionnaire, the Comrey Personality Scales, among many others. Although popular especially among personnel consultants, the Myers–Briggs Type Indicator has numerous psychometric deficiencies. More recently, a number of instruments based on the Five Factor Model of personality have been constructed such as the Revised NEO Personality Inventory. However, the Big Five and related Five Factor Model have been challenged for accounting for less than two-thirds of the known trait variance in the normal personality sphere alone.

Exam Probability: **Low**

10. *Answer choices:*
(see index for correct answer)

- a. Behavioral epigenetics
- b. Bicultural identity
- c. Personality test
- d. Adjective Check List

Guidance: level 1

:: Imagination ::

A _____ is a proposed explanation for a phenomenon. For a _____ to be a scientific _____, the scientific method requires that one can test it. Scientists generally base scientific hypotheses on previous observations that cannot satisfactorily be explained with the available scientific theories. Even though the words "_____" and "theory" are often used synonymously, a scientific _____ is not the same as a scientific theory. A working _____ is a provisionally accepted _____ proposed for further research, in a process beginning with an educated guess or thought.

Exam Probability: **Low**

11. *Answer choices:*

(see index for correct answer)

- a. erotic fantasy
- b. Hypothesis
- c. Worldbuilding
- d. Creative visualization

Guidance: level 1

:: Fertility ::

_____ is the inability of a person, animal or plant to reproduce by natural means. It is usually not the natural state of a healthy adult, except notably among certain eusocial species.

Exam Probability: **Low**

12. *Answer choices:*

(see index for correct answer)

- a. Chi Nei Tsang
- b. Medical abortion
- c. Fertility
- d. Spermatogenesis arrest

Guidance: level 1

:: Attitude change ::

In the psychology of motivation, _____ is a theory of attitude change, proposed by Fritz Heider. It conceptualizes the cognitive consistency motive as a drive toward psychological balance. The consistency motive is the urge to maintain one's values and beliefs over time. Heider proposed that "sentiment" or liking relationships are balanced if the affect valence in a system multiplies out to a positive result.

Exam Probability: **Low**

13. *Answer choices:*

(see index for correct answer)

- a. Attitudinal fix
- b. Behavior change methods
- c. social comparison
- d. Balance theory

Guidance: level 1

:: Abnormal psychology ::

A _____ is a type of anxiety disorder, defined by a persistent and excessive fear of an object or situation. The _____ typically results in a rapid onset of fear and is present for more than six months. The affected person goes to great lengths to avoid the situation or object, to a degree greater than the actual danger posed. If the feared object or situation cannot be avoided, the affected person experiences significant distress. With blood or injury _____ , fainting may occur. Agora _____ is often associated with panic attacks. Usually a person has _____ s to a number of objects or situations.

Exam Probability: **Low**

14. *Answer choices:*

(see index for correct answer)

- a. Boanthropy
- b. Self-neglect

- c. Somatoform disorder
- d. Zero stroke

Guidance: level 1

:: Racism ::

_____ is the belief in the superiority of one race over another, which often results in discrimination and prejudice towards people based on their race or ethnicity. The use of the term " _____ " does not easily fall under a single definition.

Exam Probability: **Medium**

15. *Answer choices:*
(see index for correct answer)

- a. Expert Committee on Questions of Population and Racial Policy
- b. Save the Pearls: Revealing Eden
- c. Persecution of people with albinism
- d. Keling

Guidance: level 1

:: Reasoning ::

_____s are steps in reasoning, moving from premises to logical consequences; etymologically, the word infer means to "carry forward". _____ is theoretically traditionally divided into deduction and induction, a distinction that in Europe dates at least to Aristotle . Deduction is _____ deriving logical conclusions from premises known or assumed to be true, with the laws of valid _____ being studied in logic. Induction is _____ from particular premises to a universal conclusion. A third type of _____ is sometimes distinguished, notably by Charles Sanders Peirce, distinguishing abduction from induction, where abduction is _____ to the best explanation.

Exam Probability: **High**

16. *Answer choices:*

(see index for correct answer)

- a. Journal of Formalized Reasoning
- b. Inference
- c. Toulmin method
- d. Logical reasoning

Guidance: level 1

:: Human rights abuses ::

_____ are moral principles or norms that describe certain standards of human behaviour and are regularly protected as natural and legal rights in municipal and international law. They are commonly understood as inalienable, fundamental rights "to which a person is inherently entitled simply because she or he is a human being" and which are "inherent in all human beings", regardless of their nation, location, language, religion, ethnic origin or any other status. They are applicable everywhere and at every time in the sense of being universal, and they are egalitarian in the sense of being the same for everyone. They are regarded as requiring empathy and the rule of law and imposing an obligation on persons to respect the _____ of others, and it is generally considered that they should not be taken away except as a result of due process based on specific circumstances; for example, _____ may include freedom from unlawful imprisonment, torture and execution.

Exam Probability: **High**

17. *Answer choices:*

(see index for correct answer)

- a. Kidnapping
- b. Human rights
- c. Faeq al-Mir arrest controversy
- d. Bad Nenndorf interrogation centre

Guidance: level 1

:: Emotions ::

Frank D. Cox, Educational Psychology PhD, says that _____ can be distinguished from romantic love only when looking back on a particular interest. _____ may also develop into a mature love. Goldstein and Brandon describe _____ as the first stage of a relationship before developing into a mature intimacy. Phillips describes how the illusions of _____ s inevitably lead to disappointment when learning the truth about a lover. It is an object of extravagant, short-lived passion or the temporary love of an adolescent.

Exam Probability: **Low**

18. *Answer choices:*

(see index for correct answer)

- a. Acedia
- b. Sadness
- c. Infatuation
- d. Comfort

Guidance: level 1

:: Kinship and descent ::

_____, also called matrimony or wedlock, is a socially or ritually recognised union between spouses that establishes rights and obligations between those spouses, as well as between them and any resulting biological or adopted children and affinity. The definition of _____ varies around the world not only between cultures and between religions, but also throughout the history of any given culture and religion, evolving to both expand and constrict in who and what is encompassed, but typically it is principally an institution in which interpersonal relationships, usually sexual, are acknowledged or sanctioned. In some cultures, _____ is recommended or considered to be compulsory before pursuing any sexual activity. When defined broadly, _____ is considered a cultural universal. A _____ ceremony is known as a wedding.

Exam Probability: **Low**

19. *Answer choices:*

(see index for correct answer)

- a. Phratry
- b. Cadet
- c. Chinese compound surname
- d. Marriage

Guidance: level 1

:: Developmental psychology ::

Biologically, a _____ is a human being between the stages of birth and puberty, or between the developmental period of infancy and puberty. The legal definition of _____ generally refers to a minor, otherwise known as a person younger than the age of majority.

Exam Probability: **Medium**

20. *Answer choices:*

(see index for correct answer)

- a. Ontogenetic parade
- b. Autism spectrum
- c. Child
- d. Infant Potty Training

Guidance: level 1

:: Second-language acquisition ::

An _____ is an action which is inaccurate or incorrect. In some usages, an _____ is synonymous with a mistake. In statistics, "_____" refers to the difference between the value which has been computed and the correct value. An _____ could result in failure or in a deviation from the intended performance or behaviour.

Exam Probability: **High**

21. *Answer choices:*

(see index for correct answer)

- a. Error
- b. Theories of second-language acquisition
- c. CANAL-F
- d. Second-language acquisition classroom research

Guidance: level 1

:: Consciousness ::

_____ is a heightened sense of self-awareness. It is a preoccupation with oneself, as opposed to the philosophical state of self-awareness, which is the awareness that one exists as an individual being, though the two terms are commonly used interchangeably or synonymously. An unpleasant feeling of _____ may occur when one realizes that one is being watched or observed, the feeling that "everyone is looking" at oneself. Some people are habitually more self-conscious than others. Unpleasant feelings of _____ are sometimes associated with shyness or paranoia.

Exam Probability: **Medium**

22. *Answer choices:*

(see index for correct answer)

- a. Animal consciousness
- b. Experience

- c. Self-consciousness
- d. Mental substance

Guidance: level 1

:: Casual sex ::

_____ , also known as sex addiction, is a state characterized by compulsive participation or engagement in sexual activity, particularly sexual intercourse, despite negative consequences.

Exam Probability: **High**

23. *Answer choices:*
(see index for correct answer)

- a. Trade
- b. 2010 Duke University faux sex thesis controversy
- c. Hookup culture
- d. One-night stand

Guidance: level 1

:: Social psychology ::

The _____ is the front of an animal's head that features three of the head's sense organs, the eyes, nose, and mouth, and through which animals express many of their emotions. The _____ is crucial for human identity, and damage such as scarring or developmental deformities affects the psyche adversely.

Exam Probability: **High**

24. *Answer choices:*

(see index for correct answer)

- a. Personal space
- b. Face
- c. Chinese social relations
- d. Mortality salience

Guidance: level 1

:: Cognitive biases ::

In social psychology, _____ , also known as correspondence bias or attribution effect, is the concept that, in contrast to interpretations of their own behavior, people tend to emphasize the agent's internal characteristics , rather than external factors, in explaining other people's behavior. This effect has been described as "the tendency to believe that what people do reflects who they are".

Exam Probability: **Medium**

25. Answer choices:

(see index for correct answer)

- a. Fundamental attribution error
- b. Illusion of external agency
- c. Zero-risk bias
- d. Recency principle

Guidance: level 1

:: Gender ::

_____ is a set of attributes, behaviors, and roles generally associated with girls and women. _____ is socially constructed, but made up of both socially-defined and biologically-created factors. This makes it distinct from the definition of the biological female sex, as both males and females can exhibit feminine traits.

Exam Probability: **Medium**

26. Answer choices:

(see index for correct answer)

- a. Female
- b. Malakia
- c. Gender neutrality
- d. Femininity

Guidance: level 1

:: Discrimination ::

A _____ is the application of different sets of principles for situations that are, in principle, the same, and is often used to describe freedom that is given to one party over another. A double-standard arises when two or more people, circumstances, or events are treated differently even though they should be treated the same way. Margaret Eichler, author of The _____ : A Feminist Critique of Feminist Social Science, explains that a _____ "implies that two things which are the same are measured by different standards".

Exam Probability: **Low**

27. *Answer choices:*

(see index for correct answer)

- a. Speciesism
- b. Communion and the developmentally disabled
- c. Anti-Hinduism
- d. Double standard

Guidance: level 1

:: Psychometrics ::

An _____ is the articulation of operationalization used in defining the terms of a process needed to determine the nature of an item or phenomenon and its properties such as duration, quantity, extension in space, chemical composition, etc. Since the degree of operationalization can vary itself, it can result in a more or less _____ . The procedures included in definitions should be repeatable by anyone or at least by peers.

Exam Probability: **High**

28. *Answer choices:*
(see index for correct answer)

- a. Figure rating scale
- b. Assessment Systems Corporation
- c. Multistage testing
- d. Normal curve equivalent

Guidance: level 1

:: Personality ::

_____ is a branch of psychology that studies personality and its variation among individuals. It is a scientific study which aims to show how people are individually different due to psychological forces. Its areas of focus include.

Exam Probability: **High**

29. Answer choices:

(see index for correct answer)

- a. Bicultural identity
- b. Taiheki
- c. Agreeableness
- d. Personality psychology

Guidance: level 1

:: Motivational theories ::

A _____ is something that is necessary for an organism to live a healthy life. _____ s are distinguished from wants in that, in the case of a _____, a deficiency causes a clear adverse outcome: a dysfunction or death. In other words, a _____ is something required for a safe, stable and healthy life while a want is a desire, wish or aspiration. When _____ s or wants are backed by purchasing power, they have the potential to become economic demands.

Exam Probability: **High**

30. Answer choices:

(see index for correct answer)

- a. Community recognition
- b. Need
- c. Aspiration Management

- d. Need for power

Guidance: level 1

:: LGBT-related legislation ::

_____ is the marriage of two persons of the same sex or gender, entered into in a civil or religious ceremony.

Exam Probability: **Low**

31. *Answer choices:*

(see index for correct answer)

- a. Article 200
- b. Section 213 of the Norwegian Penal Code
- c. Section 377A of the Penal Code
- d. Buggery

Guidance: level 1

:: BDSM terminology ::

_____ is the giving or receiving of pleasure from acts involving the receipt or infliction of pain or humiliation. Practitioners of _____ may seek sexual gratification from their acts. While the terms sadist and masochist refer respectively to one who enjoys giving and receiving pain, practitioners of _____ may switch between activity and passivity.

Exam Probability: **Low**

32. *Answer choices:*

(see index for correct answer)

- a. Impact play
- b. Risk-aware consensual kink
- c. Dominance and submission
- d. Sadomasochism

Guidance: level 1

:: Gender ::

_____ is the process of development of the differences between males and females from an undifferentiated zygote. As male and female individuals develop from zygotes into fetuses, into infants, children, adolescents, and eventually into adults, sex and gender differences at many levels develop: genes, chromosomes, gonads, hormones, anatomy, and psyche.

Exam Probability: **Low**

33. *Answer choices:*

(see index for correct answer)

- a. Victorian masculinity
- b. Postgenderism
- c. Cisgender
- d. Sexual differentiation

Guidance: level 1

:: Social psychology ::

_____ is a perspective in sociology and in social psychology that considers most of everyday activity to be the acting out of socially defined categories . Each role is a set of rights, duties, expectations, norms and behaviors that a person has to face and fulfill. The model is based on the observation that people behave in a predictable way, and that an individual's behavior is context specific, based on social position and other factors. The theatre is a metaphor often used to describe _____ .

Exam Probability: **High**

34. *Answer choices:*

(see index for correct answer)

- a. Body language
- b. Construals
- c. Role theory

- d. Chinese social relations

Guidance: level 1

:: Multiracial affairs ::

An ethnic group, or an _____ , is a category of people who identify with each other based on similarities such as common ancestry, language, history, society, culture or nation. _____ is usually an inherited status based on the society in which one lives. Membership of an ethnic group tends to be defined by a shared cultural heritage, ancestry, origin myth, history, homeland, language or dialect, symbolic systems such as religion, mythology and ritual, cuisine, dressing style, art or physical appearance.

Exam Probability: **High**

35. *Answer choices:*
(see index for correct answer)

- a. Mixed-blood
- b. Miss Saigon
- c. Afro-Arab
- d. Interracial marriage

Guidance: level 1

:: Psychology terminology ::

_____ is a situational predicament in which people are or feel themselves to be at risk of conforming to stereotypes about their social group. _____ is purportedly a contributing factor to long-standing racial and gender gaps in academic performance. It may occur whenever an individual's performance might confirm a negative stereotype because _____ is thought to arise from a particular situation, rather than from an individual's personality traits or characteristics. Since most people have at least one social identity which is negatively stereotyped, most people are vulnerable to _____ if they encounter a situation in which the stereotype is relevant. Situational factors that increase _____ can include the difficulty of the task, the belief that the task measures their abilities, and the relevance of the stereotype to the task. Individuals show higher degrees of _____ on tasks they wish to perform well on and when they identify strongly with the stereotyped group. These effects are also increased when they expect discrimination due to their identification with a negatively stereotyped group. Repeated experiences of _____ can lead to a vicious circle of diminished confidence, poor performance, and loss of interest in the relevant area of achievement.

Exam Probability: **High**

36. *Answer choices:*

(see index for correct answer)

- a. Folk psychology
- b. Tip of the tongue
- c. sociocultural perspective
- d. Mental toughness

Guidance: level 1

:: Fertility ::

A _____ or foetus is the unborn offspring of an animal that develops from an embryo. Following embryonic development the fetal stage of development takes place. In human prenatal development, fetal development begins from the ninth week after fertilisation and continues until birth. Prenatal development is a continuum, with no clear defining feature distinguishing an embryo from a _____ . However, a _____ is characterized by the presence of all the major body organs, though they will not yet be fully developed and functional and some not yet situated in their final anatomical location.

Exam Probability: **Low**

37. *Answer choices:*
(see index for correct answer)

- a. Human fertilization
- b. Estrogen
- c. Spermatogenesis arrest
- d. Careto

Guidance: level 1

:: Sexual abuse ::

_____, also referred to as molestation, is usually undesired sexual behavior by one person upon another. It is often perpetrated using force or by taking advantage of another. When force is immediate, of short duration, or infrequent, it is called sexual assault. The offender is referred to as a _____ r or molester. The term also covers any behavior by an adult or older adolescent towards a child to stimulate any of the involved sexually. The use of a child, or other individuals younger than the age of consent, for sexual stimulation is referred to as child _____ or statutory rape.

Exam Probability: **Medium**

38. *Answer choices:*

(see index for correct answer)

- a. Giving Victims a Voice
- b. Compliance
- c. Rind et al. controversy
- d. molestation

Guidance: level 1

:: Human sexuality ::

Sexually transmitted infections, also referred to as _____ s, are infections that are commonly spread by sexual activity, especially vaginal intercourse, anal sex and oral sex. Many times STIs initially do not cause symptoms. This results in a greater risk of passing the disease on to others. Symptoms and signs of disease may include vaginal discharge, penile discharge, ulcers on or around the genitals, and pelvic pain. STIs can be transmitted to an infant before or during childbirth and may result in poor outcomes for the baby. Some STIs may cause problems with the ability to get pregnant.

Exam Probability: **Medium**

39. *Answer choices:*

(see index for correct answer)

- a. Orgasm
- b. Walk of shame
- c. Sexually transmitted disease
- d. Zestra

Guidance: level 1

:: Statistical terminology ::

In mathematical modeling, statistical modeling and experimental sciences, the values of dependent variables depend on the values of _____ s. The dependent variables represent the output or outcome whose variation is being studied. The _____ s, also known in a statistical context as regressors, represent inputs or causes, that is, potential reasons for variation. In an experiment, any variable that the experimenter manipulates can be called an _____ . Models and experiments test the effects that the _____ s have on the dependent variables. Sometimes, even if their influence is not of direct interest, _____ s may be included for other reasons, such as to account for their potential confounding effect.

Exam Probability: **Medium**

40. *Answer choices:*

(see index for correct answer)

- a. Dependent variable
- b. Independent variable
- c. Likelihood
- d. Control group

Guidance: level 1

:: Marriage ::

_____ occurs when a married person engages in sexual activity with someone other than his or her spouse. From a different perspective, it also applies to a single person having sex with a married person. From a religious perspective, it could also have a third interpretation as referring to sex between people who are not in a conjugal relationship.

Exam Probability: **Low**

41. *Answer choices:*

(see index for correct answer)

- a. Extramarital sex
- b. Late Bloomer Bride
- c. Vena amoris
- d. Catherinette

Guidance: level 1

:: Affirmative action ::

_____ , also known as reservation in India and Nepal, positive discrimination / action in the United Kingdom, and employment equity in Canada and South Africa, is the policy of promoting the education and employment of members of groups that are known to have previously suffered from discrimination. Historically and internationally, support for _____ has sought to achieve goals such as bridging inequalities in employment and pay, increasing access to education, promoting diversity, and redressing apparent past wrongs, harms, or hindrances.

Exam Probability: **Medium**

42. *Answer choices:*

(see index for correct answer)

- a. Universal access to education
- b. Affirmative action
- c. Special rights
- d. Principle-policy puzzle

Guidance: level 1

:: Mental health ::

_____ is the use of psychological methods, particularly when based on regular personal interaction, to help a person change behavior and overcome problems in desired ways. _____ aims to improve an individual's well-being and mental health, to resolve or mitigate troublesome behaviors, beliefs, compulsions, thoughts, or emotions, and to improve relationships and social skills. Certain psychotherapies are considered evidence-based for treating some diagnosed mental disorders. Others have been criticized as pseudoscience.

Exam Probability: **Medium**

43. *Answer choices:*

(see index for correct answer)

- a. Naikan
- b. Postural Integration
- c. Brief Cognitive Assessment Tool
- d. Psychotherapy

Guidance: level 1

:: HIV/AIDS ::

Human immunodeficiency virus infection and acquired immune deficiency syndrome is a spectrum of conditions caused by infection with the human immunodeficiency virus . Following initial infection, a person may not notice any symptoms or may experience a brief period of influenza-like illness. Typically, this is followed by a prolonged period with no symptoms. As the infection progresses, it interferes more with the immune system, increasing the risk of developing common infections such as tuberculosis, as well as other opportunistic infections, and tumors that rarely affect people who have uncompromised immune systems. These late symptoms of infection are referred to as acquired immunodeficiency syndrome . This stage is often also associated with unintended weight loss.

Exam Probability: **High**

44. *Answer choices:*
(see index for correct answer)

- a. Diffuse infiltrative lymphocytosis syndrome
- b. Udaan Trust
- c. Michellamine

- d. Long-term nonprogressor

Guidance: level 1

:: Human female reproductive system ::

The _____ or _____ uteri is the lower part of the uterus in the human female reproductive system. The _____ is usually 2 to 3 cm long and roughly cylindrical in shape, which changes during pregnancy. The narrow, central cervical canal runs along its entire length, connecting the uterine cavity and the lumen of the vagina. The opening into the uterus is called the internal os, and the opening into the vagina is called the external os. The lower part of the _____ , known as the vaginal portion of the _____ , bulges into the top of the vagina. The _____ has been documented anatomically since at least the time of Hippocrates, over 2,000 years ago.

Exam Probability: **High**

45. *Answer choices:*
(see index for correct answer)

- a. Cervix
- b. Human female reproductive system
- c. G-Spot
- d. Perineal sponge

Guidance: level 1

:: Memory ::

The _____ , also known as the paleomammalian cortex, is a set of brain structures located on both sides of the thalamus, immediately beneath the medial temporal lobe of the cerebrum primarily in the midbrain.

Exam Probability: **High**

46. *Answer choices:*

(see index for correct answer)

- a. Tetris effect
- b. Memory play
- c. Limbic system
- d. Nutt v. National Institute Inc.

Guidance: level 1

:: Self ::

_____ is a type of motivation that works to make people feel good about themselves and to maintain self-esteem. This motive becomes especially prominent in situations of threat, failure or blows to one's self-esteem.
_____ involves a preference for positive over negative self-views. It is one of the four self-evaluation motives along with self-assessment, self-verification and self-improvement. Self-evaluation motives drive the process of self-regulation, that is, how people control and direct their own actions.

Exam Probability: **High**

47. *Answer choices:*

(see index for correct answer)

- a. Self-enhancement
- b. Self-handicapping
- c. Self-fulfillment
- d. Illusory superiority

Guidance: level 1

:: History of human sexuality ::

An _____ is any utterance or act that strongly offends the prevalent morality of the time. It is derived from the Latin obscaena a cognate of the Ancient Greek root skene, because some potentially offensive content, such as murder or sex, was depicted offstage in classical drama. The word can be used to indicate a strong moral repugnance, in expressions such as "obscene profits" or "the _____ of war". As a legal term, it usually refers to graphic depictions of people engaged in sexual and excretory activity.

Exam Probability: **Medium**

48. *Answer choices:*

(see index for correct answer)

- a. Sex at Dawn

- b. Droit du seigneur
- c. Rita Banerji
- d. Obscenity

Guidance: level 1

:: Abuse ::

A _____ is a prejudice-motivated crime which occurs when a perpetrator targets a victim because of their membership in a certain social group or race.

Exam Probability: **Low**

49. *Answer choices:*

(see index for correct answer)

- a. Abuse of process
- b. Strip search phone call scam
- c. Hate crime
- d. Hate mail

Guidance: level 1

:: Interpersonal relationships ::

An intimate relationship is an interpersonal relationship that involves physical or emotional _____ . Although an intimate relationship is commonly a sexual relationship, it may also be a non-sexual relationship involving family, friends, or acquaintances.

Exam Probability: **Low**

50. *Answer choices:*

(see index for correct answer)

- a. Reciprocal liking
- b. Sexual relationship
- c. Intimacy
- d. Belongingness

Guidance: level 1

:: Psychodynamics ::

_____ is a theoretical phenomenon characterized by unconscious redirection of the feelings a person has about their parents, as one example, on to the therapist. It usually concerns feelings from a primary relationship during childhood. At times, this projection can be considered inappropriate. _____ was first described by Sigmund Freud, the founder of psychoanalysis, who considered it an important part of psychoanalytic treatment.

Exam Probability: **Medium**

51. *Answer choices:*

(see index for correct answer)

- a. Paradoxical intention
- b. Transference
- c. Ennio Foppiani
- d. Interpassivity

Guidance: level 1

:: Sexual acts ::

_____ is an oral sex act performed by a person on the female genitalia. The clitoris is the most sexually sensitive part of the human female genitalia, and its stimulation may result in female sexual arousal or orgasm.

Exam Probability: **Medium**

52. *Answer choices:*

(see index for correct answer)

- a. Turkey slap
- b. Ass to mouth
- c. Sloppy seconds
- d. Cunnilingus

Guidance: level 1

:: Neuropsychological assessment ::

_____ consists of using generic or ad hoc methods in an orderly manner to find solutions to problems. Some of the problem-solving techniques developed and used in philosophy, artificial intelligence, computer science, engineering, mathematics, or medicine are related to mental problem-solving techniques studied in psychology.

Exam Probability: **High**

53. *Answer choices:*

(see index for correct answer)

- a. Natural language
- b. forethought
- c. Memory
- d. Adaptive memory

Guidance: level 1

:: Pediatrics ::

_____ is the first menstrual cycle, or first menstrual bleeding, in female humans. From both social and medical perspectives, it is often considered the central event of female puberty, as it signals the possibility of fertility.

Exam Probability: **Medium**

54. *Answer choices:*

(see index for correct answer)

- a. Apnea of prematurity
- b. Menarche
- c. Craniotabes
- d. Pediatric plastic surgery

Guidance: level 1

:: Cognitive science ::

_____ is "the mental action or process of acquiring knowledge and understanding through thought, experience, and the senses". It encompasses many aspects of intellectual functions and processes such as attention, the formation of knowledge, memory and working memory, judgment and evaluation, reasoning and "computation", problem solving and decision making, comprehension and production of language. Cognitive processes use existing knowledge and generate new knowledge.

Exam Probability: **Low**

55. *Answer choices:*

(see index for correct answer)

- a. Cognition

- b. Cognitive inhibition
- c. Behavioural sciences
- d. Spatial relation

Guidance: level 1

:: Dispositional beliefs ::

_____ es can be learned implicitly within cultural contexts. People may develop _____ es toward or against an individual, an ethnic group, a sexual or gender identity, a nation, a religion, a social class, a political party, theoretical paradigms and ideologies within academic domains, or a species. _____ ed means one-sided, lacking a neutral viewpoint, or not having an open mind. _____ can come in many forms and is related to prejudice and intuition.

Exam Probability: **High**

56. *Answer choices:*

(see index for correct answer)

- a. Commercialism
- b. Phonocentrism
- c. Graphocentrism
- d. Bias

Guidance: level 1

:: Cognition ::

In the field of psychology, _____ is the mental discomfort experienced by a person who holds two or more contradictory beliefs, ideas, or values. This discomfort is triggered by a situation in which a person's belief clashes with new evidence perceived by the person. When confronted with facts that contradict beliefs, ideals, and values, people will try to find a way to resolve the contradiction to reduce their discomfort.

Exam Probability: **High**

57. *Answer choices:*
(see index for correct answer)

- a. Reductionism
- b. Gnosology
- c. Language of thought hypothesis
- d. Negative priming

Guidance: level 1

:: Conformity ::

In sociology, _____ is the process of internalizing the norms and ideologies of society. _____ encompasses both learning and teaching and is thus "the means by which social and cultural continuity are attained".

Exam Probability: **High**

58. *Answer choices:*

(see index for correct answer)

- a. Sheeple
- b. Mindguard
- c. Deindividuation
- d. Socialization

Guidance: level 1

:: Sexual fetishism ::

_____ is the act of exposing in a public or semi-public context those parts of one`s body that are not normally exposed for example, the breasts, genitals or buttocks. The practice may arise from a desire or compulsion to expose themselves in such a manner to groups of friends or acquaintances, or to strangers for their amusement or sexual satisfaction or to shock the bystander. Exposing oneself only to an intimate partner is normally not regarded as _____ . In law, the act of _____ may be called indecent exposure, "exposing one`s person", or other expressions.

Exam Probability: **High**

59. *Answer choices:*

(see index for correct answer)

- a. Mixed boxing
- b. Medical fetishism
- c. Ethnic pornography
- d. Exhibitionism

Guidance: level 1

Applied Psychology

Applied psychology is the use of psychological methods and findings of scientific psychology to solve practical problems of human and animal behavior and experience. Mental health, organizational psychology, business management, education, health, product design, ergonomics, and law are just a few of the areas that have been influenced by the application of psychological principles and findings. Some of the areas of applied psychology include clinical psychology, counseling psychology, evolutionary psychology, industrial and organizational psychology, legal psychology, neuropsychology, occupational health psychology, human factors, forensic psychology, engineering psychology, school psychology, sports psychology, traffic psychology, community psychology, medical psychology.

:: Industrial and organizational psychology ::

_____ is an approach to leadership that emphasizes building the leader's legitimacy through honest relationships with followers which value their input and are built on an ethical foundation. Generally, authentic leaders are positive people with truthful self-concepts who promote openness. By building trust and generating enthusiastic support from their subordinates, authentic leaders are able to improve individual and team performance. This approach has been fully embraced by many leaders and leadership coaches who view _____ as an alternative to leaders who emphasize profit and share price over people and ethics. _____ is a growing area of study in academic research on leadership which has recently grown from obscurity to the beginnings of a fully mature concept.

Exam Probability: **Medium**

1. *Answer choices:*

(see index for correct answer)

- a. Adaptive performance
- b. Authentic leadership
- c. Trait leadership
- d. Job analysis

Guidance: level 1

:: Human resource management ::

Frederick Herzberg, an American psychologist, originally developed the concept of ` _____ ` in 1968, in an article that he published on pioneering studies at AT&T. The concept stemmed from Herzberg's motivator-hygiene theory, which is based on the premise that job attitude is a construct of two independent factors, namely job satisfaction and job dissatisfaction. Job satisfaction encompasses intrinsic factors that arise from the work itself, including achievement and advancement; whilst job dissatisfaction stems from factors external to the actual work, including company policy and the quality of supervision.

Exam Probability: **High**

2. *Answer choices:*

(see index for correct answer)

- a. Voluntary redundancy
- b. Cross-cultural capital
- c. Job enrichment
- d. Progressive discipline

Guidance: level 1

:: Validity (statistics) ::

_____ is the extent to which a test is subjectively viewed as covering the concept it purports to measure. It refers to the transparency or relevance of a test as it appears to test participants. In other words, a test can be said to have _____ if it "looks like" it is going to measure what it is supposed to measure. For instance, if a test is prepared to measure whether students can perform multiplication, and the people to whom it is shown all agree that it looks like a good test of multiplication ability, this demonstrates _____ of the test. _____ is often contrasted with content validity and construct validity.

Exam Probability: **High**

3. *Answer choices:*

(see index for correct answer)

- a. Face validity
- b. Statistical conclusion validity
- c. Content validity
- d. Construct validity

Guidance: level 1

:: Psychometrics ::

Art therapy is a creative method of expression used as a therapeutic technique. Art therapy, as a creative arts therapy modality, originated in the fields of art and psychotherapy and may vary in definition.

Exam Probability: **High**

4. *Answer choices:*

(see index for correct answer)

- a. Fuzzy concept
- b. Figure rating scale
- c. Congruence coefficient
- d. House-Tree-Person test

Guidance: level 1

:: Psychological schools ::

_____ pertains to the theory and practice of Alfred Adler, whose school of psychotherapy is called individual psychology.

Exam Probability: **Low**

5. *Answer choices:*

(see index for correct answer)

- a. Individual psychology
- b. Ecological systems theory
- c. Archetypal psychology
- d. Psychical school

Guidance: level 1

:: Collaboration ::

_____ is the process of groups of organisms working or acting together for common, mutual, or some underlying benefit, as opposed to working in competition for selfish benefit. Many animal and plant species cooperate both with other members of their own species and with members of other species.

Exam Probability: **Low**

6. *Answer choices:*

(see index for correct answer)

- a. Government Open Code Collaborative
- b. Zoho Office Suite
- c. Credit
- d. Cooperation

Guidance: level 1

:: Human behavior ::

_____ is the quality of being self-assured and confident without being aggressive. In the field of psychology and psychotherapy, it is a learnable skill and mode of communication. Dorland's Medical Dictionary defines _____ as.

Exam Probability: **Medium**

7. *Answer choices:*

(see index for correct answer)

- a. Distraction
- b. Breastfeeding
- c. National Survey of Sexual Health and Behavior
- d. Troll

Guidance: level 1

:: Aggression ::

_____ is overt or covert, often harmful, social interaction with the intention of inflicting damage or other unpleasantness upon another individual. It may occur either reactively or without provocation. In humans, frustration due to blocked goals can cause _____ . Human _____ can be classified into direct and indirect _____ ; whilst the former is characterized by physical or verbal behavior intended to cause harm to someone, the latter is characterized by behavior intended to harm the social relations of an individual or group.

Exam Probability: **High**

8. *Answer choices:*

(see index for correct answer)

- a. Aggression
- b. Workplace safety in healthcare settings
- c. Mobbing
- d. Relational aggression

Guidance: level 1

:: Motivation ::

A _____ is an idea of the future or desired result that a person or a group of people envisions, plans and commits to achieve. People endeavor to reach _____ s within a finite time by setting deadlines.

Exam Probability: **High**

9. *Answer choices:*

(see index for correct answer)

- a. Delayed gratification
- b. Incentivisation
- c. Generalized expected utility
- d. Goal

Guidance: level 1

:: Child abuse ::

_____ or child maltreatment is physical, sexual, and/or psychological maltreatment or neglect of a child or children, especially by a parent or a caregiver. _____ may include any act or failure to act by a parent or a caregiver that results in actual or potential harm to a child, and can occur in a child's home, or in the organizations, schools or communities the child interacts with.

Exam Probability: **Low**

10. *Answer choices:*

(see index for correct answer)

- a. Early infanticidal childrearing
- b. Child abuse
- c. Religious abuse
- d. Andrew John Yellowbear Jr.

Guidance: level 1

:: Defence mechanisms ::

In psychoanalytic theory, _____ is a defense mechanism in which emotions and impulses which are anxiety-producing or perceived to be unacceptable are mastered by exaggeration of the directly opposing tendency. The _____ s belong to Level III of neurotic defense mechanisms, which also include dissociation, displacement, intellectualization, and repression.

Exam Probability: **Low**

11. *Answer choices:*

(see index for correct answer)

- a. Reaction formation
- b. Exaggeration
- c. Altruism
- d. Psychological projection

Guidance: level 1

:: Analysands of Sigmund Freud ::

_____ was an Austrian psychoanalyst, writer, and teacher. Born in Vienna, he was one of Sigmund Freud's closest colleagues for 20 years, a prolific writer on psychoanalytic themes, the editor of two eminent analytic journals of the era, the managing director of Freud's publishing house, and a creative theorist and therapist. In 1926, Rank left Vienna for Paris, and for the remainder of his life, he led a successful career as a lecturer, writer, and therapist in France and the United States.

Exam Probability: **Low**

12. *Answer choices:*

(see index for correct answer)

- a. Louise Bryant
- b. Jakob Julius David
- c. Heinz Hartmann
- d. Otto Rank

Guidance: level 1

:: Motivation ::

In organizational behavior and industrial and organizational psychology, _____ is an individual's psychological attachment to the organization. The basis behind many of these studies was to find ways to improve how workers feel about their jobs so that these workers would become more committed to their organizations. _____ predicts work variables such as turnover, organizational citizenship behavior, and job performance. Some of the factors such as role stress, empowerment, job insecurity and employability, and distribution of leadership have been shown to be connected to a worker's sense of _____.

Exam Probability: **Low**

13. *Answer choices:*

(see index for correct answer)

- a. Organizational commitment
- b. Morale
- c. Burnout
- d. The best thing God gave us

Guidance: level 1

:: Psychotherapy ::

_____ is a technique that is used in counseling, training, and solving disputes or conflicts. It requires that the listener fully concentrate, understand, respond and then remember what is being said. This is opposed to reflective listening where the listener repeats back to the speaker what they have just heard to confirm understanding of both parties. Empathic listening is about giving people an outlet for their emotions before being able to be more open, which is sharing experiences and being able to accept new perspectives on the troubled topic that is the reason of emotional suffering. Listening skills may establish flow rather than closed mindedness, negative emotions include stress, anger and frustration.

Exam Probability: **Medium**

14. *Answer choices:*
(see index for correct answer)

- a. The Primal Scream
- b. Active listening
- c. Human Modelling
- d. Melodic intonation therapy

Guidance: level 1

:: Mental health ::

_____ is the use of psychological methods, particularly when based on regular personal interaction, to help a person change behavior and overcome problems in desired ways. _____ aims to improve an individual's well-being and mental health, to resolve or mitigate troublesome behaviors, beliefs, compulsions, thoughts, or emotions, and to improve relationships and social skills. Certain psychotherapies are considered evidence-based for treating some diagnosed mental disorders. Others have been criticized as pseudoscience.

Exam Probability: **Low**

15. *Answer choices:*

(see index for correct answer)

- a. Self-injury Awareness Day
- b. Retman
- c. Mental health consumer
- d. Symptom targeted intervention

Guidance: level 1

:: Psychoactive drugs ::

A _____ drug, psychopharmaceutical, or psychotropic drug is a chemical substance that changes brain function and results in alterations in perception, mood, consciousness, cognition, or behavior. These substances may be used medically; recreationally; to purposefully improve performance or alter one`s consciousness; as entheogens; for ritual, spiritual, or shamanic purposes; or for research. Some categories of _____ drugs, which have therapeutic value, are prescribed by physicians and other healthcare practitioners. Examples include anesthetics, analgesics, anticonvulsant and antiparkinsonian drugs as well as medications used to treat neuropsychiatric disorders, such as antidepressants, anxiolytics, antipsychotics, and stimulant medications. Some _____ substances may be used in the detoxification and rehabilitation programs for persons dependent on or addicted to other _____ drugs.

Exam Probability: **Low**

16. *Answer choices:*
(see index for correct answer)

- a. Cold-Food Powder
- b. Mitragyna speciosa
- c. Psychoactive
- d. Psychotropic

Guidance: level 1

:: Scientific method ::

In the social sciences and life sciences, a _____ is a research method involving an up-close, in-depth, and detailed examination of a subject of study, as well as its related contextual conditions.

Exam Probability: **Low**

17. *Answer choices:*

(see index for correct answer)

- a. Retrodiction
- b. Consilience
- c. Blind taste test
- d. Selection bias

Guidance: level 1

:: Psychological testing ::

The _____ is a psychological test that measures suggestibility. It was created in 1983 by Icelandic psychologist Gísli Hannes Guðjónsson and involves reading the subject a short story and testing their recall. It has been used in court cases in several jurisdictions but has been the subject of various criticisms.

Exam Probability: **High**

18. *Answer choices:*

(see index for correct answer)

- a. Problem Video Game Playing Questionnaire
- b. Gudjonsson suggestibility scale
- c. Psychological evaluation
- d. Trier social stress test

Guidance: level 1

:: Psychoanalysis ::

_____ is a class of functional mental disorders involving chronic distress but neither delusions nor hallucinations. The term is no longer used by the professional psychiatric community in the United States, having been eliminated from the Diagnostic and Statistical Manual of Mental Disorders in 1980 with the publication of DSM III. It is still used in the ICD-10 Chapter V F40–48.

Exam Probability: **Low**

19. *Answer choices:*

(see index for correct answer)

- a. Interobject
- b. British Psychoanalytic Council
- c. Unus mundus
- d. Neurosis

Guidance: level 1

:: Behaviorism ::

_____ is a third generation behavior therapy for treating depression. It is one of many functional analytic psychotherapies which are based on a Skinnerian psychological model of behavior change, generally referred to as applied behavior analysis. This area is also a part of what is called clinical behavior analysis and makes up one of the most effective practices in the professional practice of behavior analysis.

Exam Probability: **High**

20. *Answer choices:*

(see index for correct answer)

- a. Rate of response
- b. Flooding
- c. Autoclitic
- d. Behavioral activation

Guidance: level 1

:: Applied psychology ::

_____ is the study of the genetic basis of political behavior and attitudes. It combines behavior genetics, psychology, and political science and it is closely related to the emerging fields of neuropolitics and political physiology.

Exam Probability: **Low**

21. *Answer choices:*

(see index for correct answer)

- a. Steve Peters
- b. Audience segmentation
- c. Battlemind
- d. Genopolitics

Guidance: level 1

:: Psychometrics ::

A descriptive statistic is a summary statistic that quantitatively describes or summarizes features of a collection of information, while _____ in the mass noun sense is the process of using and analyzing those statistics. _____ is distinguished from inferential statistics, in that _____ aims to summarize a sample, rather than use the data to learn about the population that the sample of data is thought to represent. This generally means that _____, unlike inferential statistics, is not developed on the basis of probability theory, and are frequently nonparametric statistics. Even when a data analysis draws its main conclusions using inferential statistics, _____ are generally also presented. For example, in papers reporting on human subjects, typically a table is included giving the overall sample size, sample sizes in important subgroups, and demographic or clinical characteristics such as the average age, the proportion of subjects of each sex, the proportion of subjects with related comorbidities, etc.

Exam Probability: **Medium**

22. *Answer choices:*

(see index for correct answer)

- a. Congruence coefficient
- b. Multidimensional scaling
- c. Correction for attenuation
- d. Descriptive statistics

Guidance: level 1

:: Self ::

Altruistic suicide is sacrifice of one's life to save or benefit others, for the good of the group, or to preserve the traditions and honor of a society. It is always intentional. Benevolent suicide refers to the self sacrifice of one's own life for the sake of the greater good. Such sacrifice may be for the sake of executing a particular action, or for the sake of keeping a natural balance in the society. It is a theme or concept of a custom of sacrifice typically found within certain types of science fiction stories. However, real examples of these customs have been recorded to exist among some indigenous people, such as certain Inuit tribes. This was seen by Émile Durkheim in his study Suicide as the product of over-integration with society.

Exam Probability: **Medium**

23. *Answer choices:*

(see index for correct answer)

- a. Self-knowledge
- b. End-of-history illusion
- c. Self-denial
- d. Self-sacrifice

Guidance: level 1

:: Emotions ::

_____ is an emotion characterized by an unpleasant state of inner turmoil, often accompanied by nervous behaviour such as pacing back and forth, somatic complaints, and rumination. It is the subjectively unpleasant feelings of dread over anticipated events, such as the feeling of imminent death. _____ is not the same as fear, which is a response to a real or perceived immediate threat, whereas _____ involves the expectation of future threat. _____ is a feeling of uneasiness and worry, usually generalized and unfocused as an overreaction to a situation that is only subjectively seen as menacing. It is often accompanied by muscular tension, restlessness, fatigue and problems in concentration. _____ can be appropriate, but when experienced regularly the individual may suffer from an _____ disorder.

Exam Probability: **Medium**

24. *Answer choices:*

(see index for correct answer)

- a. Patience
- b. Nostalgia
- c. Emotions in virtual communication
- d. Forgiveness

Guidance: level 1

:: Systems psychology ::

_____ is a branch of both theoretical psychology and applied psychology that studies human behaviour and experience in complex systems. It is inspired by systems theory and systems thinking, and based on the theoretical work of Roger Barker, Gregory Bateson, Humberto Maturana and others. Groups and individuals are considered as systems in homeostasis. Alternative terms here are "systemic psychology", "systems behavior", and "systems-based psychology".

Exam Probability: **Medium**

25. *Answer choices:*

(see index for correct answer)

- a. Group-dynamic game
- b. Human relations movement
- c. Engineering psychology
- d. Systems psychology

Guidance: level 1

:: Psychological schools ::

_____ is a form of cognitive behavioral therapy developed by Aldo R. Pucci, Psy.D., DCBT the current president of the National Association of Cognitive-Behavioral Therapists and founder of the _____ Institute.

Exam Probability: **Medium**

26. Answer choices:

(see index for correct answer)

- a. Institute for International and Cross-Cultural Psychology
- b. Rational living therapy
- c. Cultural-historical psychology
- d. Cognitive therapy

Guidance: level 1

:: Motivation ::

_____ is an individual's subjective evaluation of their own worth. _____ encompasses beliefs about oneself as well as emotional states, such as triumph, despair, pride, and shame. Smith and Mackie defined it by saying "The self-concept is what we think about the self; _____ , is the positive or negative evaluations of the self, as in how we feel about it."

Exam Probability: **Low**

27. Answer choices:

(see index for correct answer)

- a. Motives for spying
- b. Locus of control
- c. Self-efficacy
- d. Self-esteem

Guidance: level 1

:: Organizational psychology ::

_____ is a theory of leadership where a leader works with teams to identify needed change, creating a vision to guide the change through inspiration, and executing the change in tandem with committed members of a group; it is an integral part of the Full Range Leadership Model. _____ serves to enhance the motivation, morale, and job performance of followers through a variety of mechanisms; these include connecting the follower's sense of identity and self to a project and to the collective identity of the organization; being a role model for followers in order to inspire them and to raise their interest in the project; challenging followers to take greater ownership for their work, and understanding the strengths and weaknesses of followers, allowing the leader to align followers with tasks that enhance their performance.

Exam Probability: **High**

28. *Answer choices:*

(see index for correct answer)

- a. Happiness at work
- b. Transformational leadership
- c. Gay-friendly
- d. Policy alienation

Guidance: level 1

:: Human behavior ::

_____ is the reason for people's actions, willingness and goals. _____ is derived from the word motive in the English language which is defined as a need that requires satisfaction. These needs could also be wants or desires that are acquired through influence of culture, society, lifestyle, etc. or generally innate. _____ is one's direction to behaviour, or what causes a person to want to repeat a behaviour, a set of force that acts behind the motives. An individual's _____ may be inspired by others or events or it may come from within the individual. _____ has been considered as one of the most important reasons that inspires a person to move forward in life. _____ results from the interaction of both conscious and unconscious factors. Mastering _____ to allow sustained and deliberate practice is central to high levels of achievement e.g. in the worlds of elite sport, medicine or music.

Exam Probability: **Medium**

29. *Answer choices:*

(see index for correct answer)

- a. Theories of political behavior
- b. Distraction
- c. Environmental enrichment
- d. Motivation

Guidance: level 1

:: Intelligence tests ::

The _____ is a psychological test. It is designed to measure psychological planning capacity and foresight. It is a nonverbal test of intelligence. It was developed by University of Hawaii psychology Professor Stanley Porteus.

Exam Probability: **Low**

30. *Answer choices:*

(see index for correct answer)

- a. G factor
- b. Kaufman Assessment Battery for Children
- c. Army alpha
- d. Porteus Maze Test

Guidance: level 1

:: Organizational behavior ::

_____ is a fundamental concept in the effort to understand and describe, both qualitatively and quantitatively, the nature of the relationship between an organization and its employees. An "engaged employee" is defined as one who is fully absorbed by and enthusiastic about their work and so takes positive action to further the organization`s reputation and interests. An engaged employee has a positive attitude towards the organization and its values. In contrast, a disengaged employee may range from someone doing the bare minimum at work , up to an employee who is actively damaging the company`s work output and reputation.

Exam Probability: **Medium**

31. *Answer choices:*

(see index for correct answer)

- a. Achievement Motivation Inventory
- b. Workplace bullying
- c. Organizational behavior
- d. Organizational justice

Guidance: level 1

:: Behaviorism ::

_____ refers to behavior-change procedures that were employed during the 1970s and early 1980s. Based on methodological behaviorism, overt behavior was modified with presumed consequences, including artificial positive and negative reinforcement contingencies to increase desirable behavior, or administering positive and negative punishment and/or extinction to reduce problematic behavior. For the treatment of phobias, habituation and punishment were the basic principles used in flooding, a subcategory of desensitization.

Exam Probability: **Low**

32. *Answer choices:*

(see index for correct answer)

- a. Behavior modification

- b. Reinforcing
- c. Association for Contextual Behavioral Science
- d. Licensed behavior analyst

Guidance: level 1

:: Educational psychology ::

_____ is the branch of psychology concerned with the scientific study of human learning. The study of learning processes, from both cognitive and behavioral perspectives, allows researchers to understand individual differences in intelligence, cognitive development, affect, motivation, self-regulation, and self-concept, as well as their role in learning. The field of _____ relies heavily on quantitative methods, including testing and measurement, to enhance educational activities related to instructional design, classroom management, and assessment, which serve to facilitate learning processes in various educational settings across the lifespan.

Exam Probability: **Low**

33. *Answer choices:*
(see index for correct answer)

- a. Collaborative learning
- b. Subvocalization
- c. Problem-based learning
- d. Educational psychology

Guidance: level 1

:: Personality tests ::

The _____ is a self-report inventory created by Harrison Gough and currently published by Consulting Psychologists Press. The test was first published in 1956, and the most recent revision was published in 1987. It was created in a similar manner to the Minnesota Multiphasic Personality Inventory —with which it shares 194 items. But unlike the MMPI, which focuses on maladjustment or clinical diagnosis, the CPI was created to assess the everyday "folk-concepts" that ordinary people use to describe the behavior of the people around them.

Exam Probability: **High**

34. *Answer choices:*

(see index for correct answer)

- a. Holland Codes
- b. California Psychological Inventory
- c. Robin Hood Morality Test
- d. Multidimensional Personality Questionnaire

Guidance: level 1

:: Personality tests ::

_____ s are flat faces on geometric shapes. The organization of naturally occurring _____ s was key to early developments in crystallography, since they reflect the underlying symmetry of the crystal structure. Gemstones commonly have _____ s cut into them in order to improve their appearance by allowing them to reflect light.

Exam Probability: **Medium**

35. *Answer choices:*

(see index for correct answer)

- a. Facet
- b. Test Construction Strategies
- c. Projective test
- d. Bartle Test

Guidance: level 1

:: Educational psychology ::

One's _____ is a collection of beliefs about oneself. Generally, _____ embodies the answer to "Who am I".

Exam Probability: **High**

36. *Answer choices:*

(see index for correct answer)

- a. Reading disability
- b. Self-concept
- c. Knowledge transfer
- d. Melodic learning

Guidance: level 1

:: Group processes ::

_____ or group therapy is a form of psychotherapy in which one or more therapists treat a small group of clients together as a group. The term can legitimately refer to any form of psychotherapy when delivered in a group format, including cognitive behavioural therapy or interpersonal therapy, but it is usually applied to psychodynamic group therapy where the group context and group process is explicitly utilised as a mechanism of change by developing, exploring and examining interpersonal relationships within the group.

Exam Probability: **High**

37. *Answer choices:*

(see index for correct answer)

- a. Struggle session
- b. Honor system
- c. Group psychotherapy
- d. Henri Tajfel

Guidance: level 1

:: Forensic psychology ::

_____ is the intersection between psychology and the justice system. It involves understanding fundamental legal principles, particularly with regard to expert witness testimony and the specific content area of concern, as well as relevant jurisdictional considerations in order to be able to interact appropriately with judges, attorneys, and other legal professionals. An important aspect of _____ is the ability to testify in court as an expert witness, reformulating psychological findings into the legal language of the courtroom, providing information to legal personnel in a way that can be understood. Further, in order to be a credible witness, the forensic psychologist must understand the philosophy, rules, and standards of the judicial system. Primarily, they must understand the adversarial system. There are also rules about hearsay evidence and most importantly, the exclusionary rule. Lack of a firm grasp of these procedures will result in the forensic psychologist losing credibility in the courtroom. A forensic psychologist can be trained in clinical, social, organizational, or any other branch of psychology.

Exam Probability: **Low**

38. *Answer choices:*

(see index for correct answer)

- a. Capital Jury Project
- b. Police psychology
- c. Forensic psychology
- d. Element

Guidance: level 1

:: Abnormal psychology ::

The _____ , also called the Hamilton Depression Rating Scale, abbreviated HAM-D, is a multiple item questionnaire used to provide an indication of depression, and as a guide to evaluate recovery. Max Hamilton originally published the scale in 1960 and revised it in 1966, 1967, 1969, and 1980. The questionnaire is designed for adults and is used to rate the severity of their depression by probing mood, feelings of guilt, suicide ideation, insomnia, agitation or retardation, anxiety, weight loss, and somatic symptoms.

Exam Probability: **High**

39. *Answer choices:*
(see index for correct answer)

- a. Models of abnormality
- b. Hamilton Rating Scale for Depression
- c. Amotivational syndrome
- d. Spectrum approach

Guidance: level 1

:: Survey methodology ::

A _____ study is a type of survey, questionnaire, or poll in which respondents read the question and select a response by themselves without researcher interference. A _____ is any method which involves asking a participant about their feelings, attitudes, beliefs and so on. Examples of _____ s are questionnaires and interviews; _____ s are often used as a way of gaining participants' responses in observational studies and experiments.

Exam Probability: **High**

40. *Answer choices:*

(see index for correct answer)

- a. Opinion poll
- b. Inverse probability weighting
- c. Self-report
- d. Census

Guidance: level 1

:: Human resource management ::

An _____ is a formal scheme used to promote or encourage specific actions or behavior by a specific group of people during a defined period of time. _____ s are particularly used in business management to motivate employees and in sales to attract and retain customers. Scientific literature also refers to this concept as pay for performance.

Exam Probability: **High**

41. *Answer choices:*

(see index for correct answer)

- a. Anaplan
- b. Incentive program
- c. Management by observation
- d. Appreciative inquiry

Guidance: level 1

:: Behavioural sciences ::

_____ , which is also known as occupational psychology, organizational psychology, and work and organizational psychology, is an applied discipline within psychology. I/O psychology is the science of human behaviour relating to work and applies psychological theories and principles to organizations and individuals in their places of work as well as the individual's work-life more generally. I/O psychologists are trained in the scientist–practitioner model. They contribute to an organization's success by improving the performance, motivation, job satisfaction, and occupational safety and health as well as the overall health and well-being of its employees. An I/O psychologist conducts research on employee behaviours and attitudes, and how these can be improved through hiring practices, training programs, feedback, and management systems.

Exam Probability: **Medium**

42. *Answer choices:*

(see index for correct answer)

- a. Industrial and organizational psychology
- b. Criminology
- c. Correlates of crime
- d. Personnel selection

Guidance: level 1

:: Intelligence by type ::

_____ is the capacity to know oneself and to know others. Social scientist Ross Honeywill believes _____ is an aggregated measure of self- and social-awareness, evolved social beliefs and attitudes, and a capacity and appetite to manage complex social change. Psychologist, Nicholas Humphrey believes that it is _____ , rather than quantitative intelligence, that defines who we are as humans.

Exam Probability: **Low**

43. *Answer choices:*
(see index for correct answer)

- a. Intelligence Test
- b. linguistic intelligence
- c. Communication quotient
- d. Social intelligence

Guidance: level 1

:: Personality traits ::

_____ is the personality trait of being careful, or diligent. _____ implies a desire to do a task well, and to take obligations to others seriously. Conscientious people tend to be efficient and organized as opposed to easy-going and disorderly. They exhibit a tendency to show self-discipline, act dutifully, and aim for achievement; they display planned rather than spontaneous behavior; and they are generally dependable. It is manifested in characteristic behaviors such as being neat, and systematic; also including such elements as carefulness, thoroughness, and deliberation _____ is one of the five traits of both the Five Factor Model and the HEXACO model of personality and is an aspect of what has traditionally been referred to as having character. Conscientious individuals are generally hard-working, and reliable. They are also likely to be conformists. When taken to an extreme, they may also be "workaholics", perfectionists, and compulsive in their behavior. People who score low on _____ tend to be laid back, less goal-oriented, and less driven by success; they also are more likely to engage in antisocial and criminal behavior.

Exam Probability: **Low**

44. *Answer choices:*
(see index for correct answer)

- a. Autotelic
- b. Consideration of future consequences
- c. Conscientiousness
- d. Psychoticism

Guidance: level 1

:: Group processes ::

_____ is the act of matching attitudes, beliefs, and behaviors to group norms or politics. Norms are implicit, specific rules, shared by a group of individuals, that guide their interactions with others. People often choose to conform to society rather than to pursue personal desires because it is often easier to follow the path others have made already, rather than creating a new one. This tendency to conform occurs in small groups and/or society as a whole, and may result from subtle unconscious influences, or direct and overt social pressure. _____ can occur in the presence of others, or when an individual is alone. For example, people tend to follow social norms when eating or watching television, even when alone.

Exam Probability: **Low**

45. *Answer choices:*

(see index for correct answer)

- a. Groupshift
- b. Group action
- c. Dancing in the Streets
- d. Learning circle

Guidance: level 1

:: Misogyny ::

_____ is a type of harassment technique that relates to a sexual nature and the unwelcome or inappropriate promise of rewards in exchange for sexual favors. _____ includes a range of actions from mild transgressions to sexual abuse or assault. Harassment can occur in many different social settings such as the workplace, the home, school, churches, etc. Harassers or victims may be of any gender.

Exam Probability: **Low**

46. *Answer choices:*

(see index for correct answer)

- a. Sexual harassment
- b. Misogyny in hip hop culture
- c. Male privilege
- d. Finkbeiner test

Guidance: level 1

:: Behaviorism ::

_____ is intended to identify issues associated with the interface of technology and the human operators in a system and to generate recommended design practices that consider the strengths and limitations of the human operators.

Exam Probability: **Medium**

47. Answer choices:

(see index for correct answer)

- a. Brainwave entrainment
- b. Logical behaviorism
- c. Task analysis
- d. Adolescent Community Reinforcement Approach

Guidance: level 1

:: Cognitive science ::

_____ is the process of acquiring new, or modifying existing, knowledge, behaviors, skills, values, or preferences. The ability to learn is possessed by humans, animals, and some machines; there is also evidence for some kind of _____ in some plants. Some _____ is immediate, induced by a single event, but much skill and knowledge accumulates from repeated experiences. The changes induced by _____ often last a lifetime, and it is hard to distinguish learned material that seems to be "lost" from that which cannot be retrieved.

Exam Probability: **High**

48. Answer choices:

(see index for correct answer)

- a. Mechanical philosophy
- b. Learning

- c. Psychological effects of Internet use
- d. Connectionism

Guidance: level 1

:: Alcohol abuse ::

_____ is a mental disorder that can develop after a person is exposed to a traumatic event, such as sexual assault, warfare, traffic collisions, or other threats on a person's life. Symptoms may include disturbing thoughts, feelings, or dreams related to the events, mental or physical distress to trauma-related cues, attempts to avoid trauma-related cues, alterations in how a person thinks and feels, and an increase in the fight-or-flight response. These symptoms last for more than a month after the event. Young children are less likely to show distress, but instead may express their memories through play. A person with PTSD is at a higher risk for suicide and intentional self-harm.

Exam Probability: **High**

49. *Answer choices:*

(see index for correct answer)

- a. Iomazenil
- b. Alcoholic liver disease
- c. Michigan Alcoholism Screening Test
- d. Posttraumatic stress disorder

Guidance: level 1

:: Emotional issues ::

_____ is a chronic state of physical and emotional depletion that results from excessive job and/or personal demands and continuous stress. It describes a feeling of being emotionally overextended and exhausted by one's work. It is manifested by both physical fatigue and a sense of feeling psychologically and emotionally "drained".

Exam Probability: **Low**

50. *Answer choices:*

(see index for correct answer)

- a. Emotional literacy
- b. Universalization
- c. The Emotional Intelligence Appraisal
- d. Emotional tyranny

Guidance: level 1

:: Neuropsychological tests ::

The _____ is a neuropsychological test of visual attention and task switching. It consists of two parts in which the subject is instructed to connect a set of 25 dots as quickly as possible while still maintaining accuracy. The test can provide information about visual search speed, scanning, speed of processing, mental flexibility, as well as executive functioning. It is sensitive to detecting cognitive impairment associated with dementia, for example, Alzheimer's disease.

Exam Probability: **High**

51. *Answer choices:*

(see index for correct answer)

- a. Thurstone Word Fluency Test
- b. Trail Making Test
- c. Stroop effect
- d. Ammons Quick Test

Guidance: level 1

:: Mood disorders ::

The _____ is a 10-item questionnaire that was developed to identify women who have postpartum depression. Items of the scale correspond to various clinical depression symptoms, such as guilt feeling, sleep disturbance, low energy, anhedonia, and suicidal ideation. Overall assessment is done by total score, which is determined by adding together the scores for each of the 10 items. Higher scores indicate more depressive symptoms. The EPDS may be used within 8 weeks postpartum and it also can be applied for depression screening during pregnancy.

Exam Probability: **Low**

52. *Answer choices:*
(see index for correct answer)

- a. Spring fever
- b. Psychoneuroendocrinology
- c. Hysteroid dysphoria
- d. Edinburgh Postnatal Depression Scale

Guidance: level 1

:: Neuropsychological tests ::

The _____ or BDAE is a neuropsychological battery used to evaluate adults suspected of having aphasia, and is currently in its third edition. It was created by Harold Goodglass and Edith Kaplan. The BDAE evaluates language skills based on perceptual modalities, processing functions, and response modalities. Administration time ranges from 20 to 45 minutes for the shortened version but it can last up to 120 minutes for the extended version of the assessment. There are five subtests which include: conversational & expository speech, auditory comprehension, oral expression, reading, and writing. In the extended version all questions are asked while in the shortened version only a few questions are asked within each subtest. Many other tests are sometimes used by neurologists and speech language pathologists on a case-by-case basis, and other comprehensive tests exist like the Western Aphasia Battery.

Exam Probability: **High**

53. *Answer choices:*

(see index for correct answer)

- a. Lexical decision task
- b. Test of Variables of Attention
- c. Bender-Gestalt Test
- d. Task switching

Guidance: level 1

:: Evaluation methods ::

_____ is a set of techniques and tools for process improvement. Though as a shortened form it may be found written as 6S, it should not be confused with the methodology known as 6S.

Exam Probability: **High**

54. *Answer choices:*

(see index for correct answer)

- a. Separation test
- b. Contingent valuation
- c. Student Achievement and School Accountability Programs
- d. Six Sigma

Guidance: level 1

:: Terrorism tactics ::

A _____ is a person who is held by one of two belligerent parties to the other or seized as security for the carrying out of an agreement, or as a preventive measure against war.

Exam Probability: **High**

55. *Answer choices:*

(see index for correct answer)

- a. Dry run
- b. Suitcase nuke
- c. Juramentado
- d. Hostage

Guidance: level 1

:: Industrial and organizational psychology ::

_____ is a family of procedures to identify the content of a job in terms of activities involved and attributes or job requirements needed to perform the activities. _____ provides information of organizations which helps to determine which employees are best fit for specific jobs. Through _____ , the analyst needs to understand what the important tasks of the job are, how they are carried out, and the necessary human qualities needed to complete the job successfully.

Exam Probability: **High**

56. *Answer choices:*
(see index for correct answer)

- a. Job analysis
- b. Perceived organizational support
- c. Adaptive performance
- d. Workforce productivity

Guidance: level 1

:: Social psychology ::

_____ is a term originated by the US military. The US Department of Defense gives this definition.

Exam Probability: **Medium**

57. *Answer choices:*
(see index for correct answer)

- a. Perception management
- b. Abnormality
- c. Breaching experiment
- d. Parasocial interaction

Guidance: level 1

:: Educational psychology ::

_____ is a statistical method used to describe variability among observed, correlated variables in terms of a potentially lower number of unobserved variables called factors. For example, it is possible that variations in six observed variables mainly reflect the variations in two unobserved variables. _____ searches for such joint variations in response to unobserved latent variables. The observed variables are modelled as linear combinations of the potential factors, plus "error" terms. _____ aims to find independent latent variables.

Exam Probability: **Medium**

58. *Answer choices:*
(see index for correct answer)

- a. Overlearning
- b. Melodic learning
- c. Learning disability
- d. Factor analysis

Guidance: level 1

:: Personality traits ::

_____ is one of the domains which are used to describe human personality in the Five Factor Model. Openness involves five facets, or dimensions, including active imagination, aesthetic sensitivity, attentiveness to inner feelings, preference for variety, and intellectual curiosity. A great deal of psychometric research has demonstrated that these facets or qualities are significantly correlated. Thus, openness can be viewed as a global personality trait consisting of a set of specific traits, habits, and tendencies that cluster together.

Exam Probability: **Medium**

59. *Answer choices:*

(see index for correct answer)

- a. Minnesota nice
- b. Type D personality
- c. HEXACO model of personality structure
- d. Openness to experience

Guidance: level 1

People

Psychologists can be seen as practicing within two general categories of psychology: applied psychology which includes "practitioners" or "professionals", and research-orientated psychology which includes "scientists", or "scholars". The training models endorsed by the American Psychological Association (APA) require that applied psychologists be trained as both researchers and practitioners,[3] and that they possess advanced degrees.

Psychologists typically have one of two degrees (PsyD or PhD). The PhD prepares a psychologist to conduct scientific research for a career in academia; whereas, the PsyD prepares for clinical practice (e.g. testing, psychotherapy). Both PsyD and PhD programs can prepare students to be licensed psychologists, and training in these types of programs prepares graduates to take state licensing exams.

Within the two main categories are many further types of psychologists as reflected by the 56 professional classifications recognized by the APA, including clinical, counseling, and educational psychologists. Such professionals work with persons in a variety of therapeutic contexts. People often think of the discipline as involving only such clinical or counseling psychologists. While counseling and psychotherapy are common activities for psychologists, these applied fields are just two branches in the larger domain of psychology. There are other classifications such as industrial, organizational and community psychologists, whose professionals mainly apply psychological research, theories, and techniques to "real-world" problems of business, industry, social benefit organizations, government, and academia.

:: Racism ::

_____ is any system in which principles of property law are applied to people, allowing individuals to own, buy and sell other individuals, as a de jure form of property. A slave is unable to withdraw unilaterally from such an arrangement and works without remuneration. Many scholars now use the term chattel _____ to refer to this specific sense of legalised, de jure _____. In a broader sense, however, the word _____ may also refer to any situation in which an individual is de facto forced to work against their own will. Scholars also use the more generic terms such as unfree labour or forced labour to refer to such situations. However, and especially under _____ in broader senses of the word, slaves may have some rights and protections according to laws or customs.

Exam Probability: **Low**

1. *Answer choices:*

(see index for correct answer)

- a. Angelfood McSpade
- b. White supremacy
- c. Prussian Settlement Commission
- d. Racial policy of Nazi Germany

Guidance: level 1

:: Slavery ::

_____, African Holocaust, Holocaust of Enslavement, or Black Holocaust are political neologisms popularized from 1998 onwards and used to describe the history and ongoing effects of atrocities inflicted on African people, particularly when committed by non-Africans and argued as "continued to the present day" through imperialism, colonialism and other forms of oppression. For example, Maulana Karenga puts slavery in the broader context of the _____, suggesting that its effects exceed mere physical persecution and legal disenfranchisement: the "destruction of human possibility involved redefining African humanity to the world, poisoning past, present and future relations with others who only know us through this stereotyping and thus damaging the truly human relations among peoples".

Exam Probability: **Low**

2. *Answer choices:*

(see index for correct answer)

- a. Helots
- b. Maafa
- c. R v Tang
- d. Manumission

Guidance: level 1

:: Blood diamonds ::

The National Union for the Total Independence of Angola is the second-largest political party in Angola. Founded in 1966, _____ fought alongside the Popular Movement for the Liberation of Angola in the Angolan War for Independence and then against the MPLA in the ensuing civil war. The war was one of the most prominent Cold War proxy wars, with _____ receiving military aid from the United States and South Africa while the MPLA received support from the Soviet Union and its allies.

Exam Probability: **Low**

3. *Answer choices:*

(see index for correct answer)

- a. Blood diamond
- b. Economy of Angola
- c. United Nations Security Council Resolution 864
- d. UNITA

Guidance: level 1

:: War in Darfur ::

The _____ is a Sudanese rebel group based in the region of Darfur. The group was formed when it broke away from the Justice and Equality Movement in 2004. The NMRD came into existence because its founding members felt that JEM focused too much on the political rather than the social and economic needs of the Fur people. JEM merged with the Alliance of Revolutionary Forces of West Sudan on January 20, 2006.

Exam Probability: **High**

4. *Answer choices:*

(see index for correct answer)

- a. International Criminal Court investigation in Darfur
- b. United Nations Security Council Resolution 1706
- c. National Movement for Reform and Development
- d. Sand and Sorrow

Guidance: level 1

INDEX: Correct Answers

Foundations of Psychology

1. d: Cognition

2. : Gestalt therapy

3. c: Communication

4. c: Sexual abuse

5. c: Prenatal development

6. c: Learning

7. d: Clinical psychology

8. a: Understanding

9. : Acculturation

10. c: Projective test

11. d: Brain damage

12. a: Encoding

13. d: Inference

14. : Language

15. d: Intelligence Test

16. b: Instinct

17. b: Stress management

18. b: Nerve

19. d: Mental health

20. : Humanistic psychology

21. c: Mind

22. c: Neuroimaging

23. : Case study

24. d: Aphasia

25. a: Axon

26. : Habit

27. a: Zygote

28. : Naturalistic observation

29. b: Knowledge

30. a: Child development

31. a: Conformity

32. d: Parietal lobe

33. : Psychiatrist

34. d: Psychoactive drug

35. c: Personality Assessment Inventory

36. a: Therapeutic alliance

37. b: Dementia

38. b: Absolute threshold

39. a: Self-efficacy

40. a: Friendship

41. c: Mood disorder

42. c: Estrogen

43. a: Agoraphobia

44. d: Biofeedback

45. d: Central nervous system

46. b: Interdependence

47. b: Operant conditioning

48. b: Autonomic nervous system

49. c: Alcoholics Anonymous

50. b: Family

51. : Cerebral cortex

52. d: Facial expression

53. : Functional MRI

54. d: Social psychology

55. : Color vision

56. b: Perception

57. d: Linguistics

58. d: Education

59. b: Discrimination

History of Psychology

1. a: Awareness

2. : Limen

3. : Being

4. : Interactionism

5. d: Generalization

6. : Personality

7. d: Zeigarnik effect

8. a: Explanation

9. b: Strong inference

10. d: Denial

11. : Subjectivity

12. b: Epiphenomenalism

13. : Institutional review board

14. a: Intentionality

15. c: Primary source

16. b: Outlier

17. a: Voluntary action

18. b: Behavior

19. b: Disinhibition

20. a: Mind

21. b: Mental disorder

22. c: Thrownness

23. : Associationism

24. : Existentialism

25. : Sleep

26. : Confounding

27. : Scientific method

28. b: Self

29. a: Reflexology

30. c: Psycholinguistics

31. d: Humor

32. : Libido

33. d: Goal

34. a: Statistical significance

35. c: Content validity

36. d: Problem

37. d: Civilization and Its Discontents

38. : Positive psychology

39. b: Aristotle

40. : Genius

41. a: Applied research

42. : Diagnostic and Statistical Manual of Mental Disorders

43. d: Logotherapy

44. : Information

45. d: Essentialism

46. d: Individual

47. a: Random assignment

48. : Archival research

49. d: Personalism

50. d: Functional analysis

51. a: Countertransference

52. : Sensitivity training

53. a: Concurrent validity

54. c: Variability hypothesis

55. a: External validity

56. a: Individual psychology

57. a: Canadian Psychological Association

58. c: Psychophysics

59. d: Humanism

Educational Psychology

1. d: E-learning

2. c: Personalization

3. a: Frequency distribution

4. d: Ecological fallacy

5. a: Socioeconomic Status

6. a: Trial and error

7. a: Symbol

8. d: Visual processing

9. a: Criterion validity

10. c: Memory

11. : Reflective practice

12. : Social cognitive theory

13. d: Effect size

14. d: Attention deficit hyperactivity disorder

15. a: Psychosocial development

16. b: Conceptualization

17. c: Self-esteem

18. a: Intelligence

19. : Pervasive developmental disorder

20. c: Interview

21. : Brain

22. : Logical consequence

23. d: TRACE

24. b: Aptitude

25. d: Learning disability

26. a: Response to intervention

27. a: Stratified sampling

28. a: Field research

29. a: Adaptive behavior

30. d: Bias

31. d: Placebo

32. c: Dependent variable

33. a: Wikipedia

34. c: Self-determination theory

35. : Augmentative and alternative communication

36. c: Dual-coding theory

37. d: Deafness

38. b: Self-concept

39. c: Representativeness heuristic

40. a: Serial position effect

41. c: Individualized Education Program

42. b: Test anxiety

43. a: Regression analysis

44. c: Ethics

45. c: Language development

46. a: Discovery learning

47. d: Grounded theory

48. d: Census

49. : Motivation

50. a: Bilingual education

51. b: Hormone

52. a: Sampling error

53. : Differentiated instruction

54. : Conceptual change

55. : Savant syndrome

56. d: Imagery

57. d: Inductive reasoning

58. b: Authentic assessment

59. a: Statistical inference

Biopsychology

1. d: Visual agnosia

2. a: Reflex

3. b: Dendritic spine

4. b: Vomiting

5. : Slow-wave sleep

6. : Motor cortex

7. c: Limbic system

8. b: Alertness

9. a: Circadian rhythm

10. d: Saccule

11. c: Insulin

12. c: Consciousness

13. a: Subarachnoid space

14. b: Semicircular canal

15. a: Peripheral nervous system

16. a: Striatum

17. : Endolymph

18. c: Interneuron

19. d: Putamen

20. : Depolarization

21. b: Inflammation

22. b: Drinking

23. a: Flumazenil

24. : Choroid plexus

25. d: Synapse

26. a: Alcohol abuse

27. : Clostridium botulinum

28. d: Substance P

29. a: MDMA

30. b: Sleep paralysis

31. b: Zeitgeber

32. c: Lateral geniculate nucleus

33. : Cingulate cortex

34. : Paralysis

35. c: Dura mater

36. : Scopolamine

37. c: Pia mater

38. b: Planning

39. a: Peripheral vision

40. b: Emotion

41. a: Declarative memory

42. c: Lateral inhibition

43. d: Orbitofrontal cortex

44. a: Medial lemniscus

45. c: Occipital lobe

46. c: Growth cone

47. d: Antidepressant

48. a: Color blindness

49. d: G protein

50. : Neural plate

51. c: Encephalization quotient

52. c: Globus pallidus

53. c: Midbrain

54. d: Lateral hypothalamus

55. c: Mouse

56. b: Inferior colliculus

57. a: Psychotherapy

58. : Testosterone

59. d: Narcolepsy

Developmental Psychology

1. d: Psychoanalytic theory

2. : Postpartum depression

3. a: Prefrontal cortex

4. a: Wisdom

5. d: Object permanence

6. : Cystic fibrosis

7. b: Sociocultural

8. d: Prenatal development

9. b: Axon

10. a: Corporal punishment

11. d: Discrimination

12. : Gross motor skill

13. : Mental age

14. c: Inference

15. d: Phonics

16. c: Menarche

17. d: Puberty

18. c: Brain death

19. d: Peer pressure

20. a: Analogy

21. a: Reflex

22. b: Social isolation

23. a: Metabolism

24. c: Strange situation

25. a: Amniocentesis

26. c: Critical period

27. c: Psychosocial development

28. c: Intimacy

29. d: Trait theory

30. b: Statistics

31. b: Kangaroo care

32. a: Brain development

33. a: Myelin

34. : Psychosexual development

35. d: Creativity

36. a: Menopause

37. b: Mesoderm

38. c: Gene

39. b: Psychiatrist

40. a: Parent

41. b: Case study

42. b: Stereotype

43. b: Sexual identity

44. a: Friendship

45. d: Caregiving

46. b: Fetal alcohol syndrome

47. b: AIDS

48. d: Reaction time

49. d: Socioeconomic status

50. a: Emotion

51. c: Empathy

52. : Religion

53. c: Electra complex

54. : Critical thinking

55. d: Operant conditioning

56. b: Moral reasoning

57. a: Hypothesis

58. c: Visual acuity

59. d: Habit

Cognitive Psychology

1. c: Reading

2. a: Word

3. c: Family

4. : Fusiform face area

5. : Misinformation effect

6. a: Self-reference effect

7. : Critical period

8. d: Occipital lobe

9. : Evidence

10. a: Understanding

11. b: Limbic system

12. c: Error

13. : Memory consolidation

14. d: Sign language

15. : Ebbinghaus illusion

16. b: Self-esteem

17. d: Neuropsychology

18. a: Phonics

19. d: Arousal

20. b: Reminiscence bump

21. d: Anchoring

22. a: Experimental psychology

23. c: Panic attack

24. : Mental model

25. : Dyslexia

26. c: Echoic memory

27. d: Illusion

28. a: Synesthesia

29. : Visual search

30. c: Substance abuse

31. : Ponzo illusion

32. : Connectionism

33. b: Fluency

34. b: Nerve

35. b: Attractiveness

36. : Language development

37. b: Spontaneous recovery

38. c: Systematic desensitization

39. b: Intelligence test

40. c: Aptitude

41. d: Social cognition

42. b: Individual

43. a: Speech perception

44. d: Sleep

45. b: Stroke

46. b: Freudian slip

47. : Brain

48. : Ecological validity

49. : Hormone

50. b: Learning disability

51. d: Frustration

52. b: Factor analysis

53. d: Sensitization

54. a: Memory errors

55. d: Flashbulb memory

56. d: Endorphin

57. : Memory

58. a: Disinhibition

59. b: Spreading activation

Abnormal Psychology

1. : Atypical antipsychotic

2. : Ethnicity

3. b: Antidepressant

4. : Transvestic fetishism

5. c: Substance use disorder

6. a: Oppositional defiant disorder

7. b: Catharsis

8. : Family therapy

9. b: Autonomic nervous system

10. d: Self-monitoring

11. d: Cognition

12. c: Panic disorder

13. d: Psychopathy

14. c: Therapeutic alliance

15. : Addiction

16. c: Dyspareunia

17. : Antipsychotic

18. a: Insomnia

19. c: Narcotic

20. a: Empathy

21. b: Psychoanalysis

22. : Psychological testing

23. : Schizoid personality disorder

24. c: Bulimia

25. : Exhibitionism

26. d: Abstinence

27. b: Dementia praecox

28. : Phallic stage

29. c: Smoking

30. : Major depressive disorder

31. : Selective mutism

32. b: Neurosis

33. b: Crisis intervention

34. d: Histrionic personality disorder

35. : Gender identity

36. b: Biofeedback

37. a: Pharmacotherapy

38. : Domestic violence

39. b: Placebo effect

40. d: Psychotherapy

41. a: Hallucination

42. b: Substance abuse

43. d: Narcotics Anonymous

44. c: Puberty

45. d: Cognitive distortion

46. d: Control group

47. : Circadian rhythm

48. a: Alogia

49. : Nerve

50. d: Norepinephrine

51. b: Token economy

52. : Electra complex

53. b: Experience

54. c: Psychodynamic psychotherapy

55. d: Cocaine

56. b: Body image

57. : Reinforcement

58. c: Psychiatrist

59. c: Conversion disorder

Social Psychology

1. c: Self-esteem

2. : Training

3. d: On Aggression

4. : Social isolation

5. a: Jealousy

6. c: Instinct

7. d: Social network

8. d: Ovary

9. : Attention

10. c: Personality test

11. b: Hypothesis

12. : Infertility

13. d: Balance theory

14. : Phobia

15. : Racism

16. b: Inference

17. b: Human rights

18. c: Infatuation

19. d: Marriage

20. c: Child

21. a: Error

22. c: Self-consciousness

23. : Sexual addiction

24. b: Face

25. a: Fundamental attribution error

26. d: Femininity

27. d: Double standard

28. : Operational definition

29. d: Personality psychology

30. b: Need

31. : Same-sex marriage

32. d: Sadomasochism

33. d: Sexual differentiation

34. c: Role theory

35. : Ethnicity

36. : Stereotype threat

37. : Fetus

38. : Sexual abuse

39. c: Sexually transmitted disease

40. b: Independent variable

41. a: Extramarital sex

42. b: Affirmative action

43. d: Psychotherapy

44. : AIDS

45. a: Cervix

46. c: Limbic system

47. a: Self-enhancement

48. d: Obscenity

49. c: Hate crime

50. c: Intimacy

51. b: Transference

52. d: Cunnilingus

53. : Problem solving

54. b: Menarche

55. a: Cognition

56. d: Bias

57. : Cognitive dissonance

58. d: Socialization

59. d: Exhibitionism

Applied Psychology

1. b: Authentic leadership

2. c: Job enrichment

3. a: Face validity

4. d: House-Tree-Person test

5. : Adlerian

6. d: Cooperation

7. : Assertiveness

8. a: Aggression

9. d: Goal

10. b: Child abuse

11. a: Reaction formation

12. d: Otto Rank

13. a: Organizational commitment

14. b: Active listening

15. : Psychotherapy

16. c: Psychoactive

17. : Case study

18. b: Gudjonsson suggestibility scale

19. d: Neurosis

20. d: Behavioral activation

21. d: Genopolitics

22. d: Descriptive statistics

23. d: Self-sacrifice

24. : Anxiety

25. d: Systems psychology

26. b: Rational living therapy

27. d: Self-esteem

28. b: Transformational leadership

29. d: Motivation

30. d: Porteus Maze Test

31. : Employee engagement

32. a: Behavior modification

33. d: Educational psychology

34. b: California Psychological Inventory

35. a: Facet

36. b: Self-concept

37. c: Group psychotherapy

38. c: Forensic psychology

39. b: Hamilton Rating Scale for Depression

40. c: Self-report

41. b: Incentive program

42. a: Industrial and organizational psychology

43. d: Social intelligence

44. c: Conscientiousness

45. : Conformity

46. a: Sexual harassment

47. : Behavioral engineering

48. b: Learning

49. d: Posttraumatic stress disorder

50. : Emotional exhaustion

51. b: Trail Making Test

52. d: Edinburgh Postnatal Depression Scale

53. : Boston Diagnostic Aphasia Examination

54. d: Six Sigma

55. d: Hostage

56. a: Job analysis

57. a: Perception management

58. d: Factor analysis

59. d: Openness to experience

People

1. : Slavery

2. b: Maafa

3. d: UNITA

4. c: National Movement for Reform and Development

CPSIA information can be obtained
at www.ICGtesting.com
Printed in the USA
LVHW011538301019
635718LV00004B/523/P